Praise for *Wheeling the Deal*

"FDR's body and Sammy Glick's brain? No, but close - and better. Mon Oncle d'Amerique has nothing on Chip Jacobs' Mon Oncle d'Hollywood, the picaresque, quadriplegic Gordon, who is at least as good a story as anything he helped to put on film: welfare case to Oscar-caliber movies, co-starring Ed Wood and Pope John XXIII, with snappy dialogue and auto crack-ups, lions and tiger rugs and TV bears, one Serene Highness and many spectacular lownesses. Gordon is a premiere citizen of Hollywood As She is Spoken -- unsentimental but believing utterly in the art of the possible."
— **Patt Morrison, award-winning columnist, commentator and author of *RIO L.A.***

"This amazing book is all heart. Chip Jacobs blends the skills of an investigative journalist, the glitz of Hollywood, and the smooth storytelling of fiction to weave a profile of his larger-than-life uncle that will leave you crying, laughing and gasping in wonder, often on the same page. Bravo!"
— **Denise Hamilton, author of *EVE DIAMOND* mystery series**

"Readers looking for a glamorous Hollywood story or a tale of gentle uplift should be warned: This is not that book. Instead, Chip Jacobs has written something far better -- a witty, clear-eyed account of a charming and utterly impossible man whose ferocious willpower transformed his personal nightmare into a lifelong Technicolor hallucination."
— **A. J. Langguth, author of *MY VIETNAM***

"Though not about a celebrity or newsmaker, this life being told by Chip Jacobs is an extraordinary one in the history of Hollywood. The raw courage and almost unbelievable stamina of Gordon Zahler – abetted by both love and luck – turns this irresistible biography into a page turner."
— **William Robert Faith, author of *BOB HOPE: A LIFE IN COMEDY***

Meet a 95-lb dynamo who rolled over Hollywood.

WHEELING THE DEAL:
The Outrageous Legend of Gordon Zahler, Hollywood's Flashiest Quadriplegic

by
Chip Jacobs

Behler™
PUBLICATIONS
California
USA

Behler Publications
California

Wheeling the Deal
A Behler Publications Book

Copyright © 2008 by Chip Jacobs
Cover design by Cathy Scott – www.mbcdesigns.com
Author photograph courtesy of Bain Photography
Chapter photos courtesy of Jacobs family

Library of Congress Cataloging-in-Publication Data

Jacobs, Chip.
  Wheeling the deal : the outrageous legend of Gordon Zahler, Hollywood's flashiest quadriplegic /
by Chip Jacobs.
    p. cm.
  ISBN 978-1-933016-47-4 (trade pbk. : alk. paper) 1. Quadriplegics--Biography. I. Title.
  RC406.Q33J3374 2008
  362.43092--dc22
  [B]
                        2007013569

FIRST PRINTING

ISBN 978-1-933016-47-4
Published by Behler Publications, LLC
Lake Forest, California
www.behlerpublications.com

Manufactured in the United States of America

To my grandmother, Rose Zahler, the strongest woman the family ever produced.

"Show me a hero and I will write you a tragedy."
-- F. Scott Fitzgerald.

"To one who has faith, no explanation is necessary. To one without faith, no explanation is possible."

-- Saint Thomas Aquinas

Acknowledgements

Exhuming the past to bring this book to life meant plenty of heavy lifting. Fortunately, I never had to shoulder the burden alone.

My mom, who often worried what she'd unleashed by asking me to write her brother's biography, bravely cut through, her own pain when it counted to reveal her family's tortured history. My dad and brother Paul never wavered in providing me with their memories, either, even when they weren't sure where all this would lead. My wife, Kate, and our children were my trustiest pillars. Not only did they put up with my obsessions in shaping this book: they made room in our house for a ghost named Gordon for the many years he lived with us. To all of them, I say thank you for believing.

Beyond my family, I owe everything to Gordon's old crew: Bob Glenn, Jimmy Gillard, Igo Kantor, Norm and Elsie Pringle, and Joe and Harriet von Stroheim. Without their recollections and grace, this book would've crashed before it began. It is with a sad heart that my book goes to print without Joe or my great-Uncle Harold being around to hoist a glass in celebration.

So many other people helped me re-trace my uncle's life. Danny O'Brien was instrumental, as were Erwin Tors, Horace Jackson, Betty Woods, and Judy's niece Karen Conway. Also contributing their precious memories were Herb Bernard, Jeff and John Bushelman, Page Cavanaugh, Hank and George Gale, Spencer Gillard, Gino Grimaldi, Stan Frazen, Michael Hoey, Bob Jung, George Mahana, Mike and Hazel Marcus, Carl Marshall, Murray Neidorf, Jack and John Perry, Teddy Phillips, Norm Prescott, Mitchell Reinis, Marion Seeman, Lou Scheimer, Don Slack and Boet Troskie. Gordon's former classmates—Don Berg, Rob Roy Bowman, Ben Gouin and Bob Wright—never failed me, nor did Normalouise Walker.

Public libraries in Pasadena, Los Angeles and El Paso deserve credit as well. I want to single out Karen Leaf and Veronica Rosenblatt of the Motion Picture and Television Fund for retrieving archived records that everybody else said didn't exist anymore. I also am grateful to doctors Keith Jamison, Bob Gustafson and Mauro Giordani for giving me a crash course on quadriplegia.

To friends curious why I'd left journalism without openly questioning my sanity—G.R. Walper, Dave Ferris, John Frook, David Bloom, Jaxon Van Derbeken, Mike Consol, Mark Arax, and John Corrigan—thanks, fellas, for sticking by me. Also lending their support were Jodie Levine and Peggy Luddington. My agent, Mike Hamilburg, and writing mentors, A.J. Langguth and Tristine Rainer, deserve special plaudits for helping me grasp the big picture.

Speaking of support, the story you are about to read would have been impossible without Erin Stalcup's wonderful editing and the can-do belief and passion of the people behind Behler Publications: Lynn and Fred Price. You both restored my faith in destiny, and the little man I was trying to portray gets to live another remarkable day because of it.

NOTE TO READERS

Although years of research and nearly 60 interviews made this book possible, I was unable to reconstruct every detail of this story, since it traces to the early 1900s. To infuse the prose with the grit it deserves, I invented some dialogue based on the knowable facts. The flavor and sequence of events in a few spots also was extrapolated. A couple names were changed to protect identities, too. When in doubt about what occurred, however, I intentionally erred on the side of caution because my uncle Gordon's journey was outrageous enough.

The chapter names were culled from the titles of a handful of the 900-plus movie-features and serials on which my grandfather, Lee Zahler, worked.

To learn more about Gordon, his family, the early days of Hollywood and my other writings, please visit www.chipjacobs.com

-Chip Jacobs

PROLOGUE
The Whispering Skull

On a hazy day long ago, my mother clenched her jaw to remind me that there'd be no escaping the little man behind the door. When the inimitable Gordon Zahler expected you, you appeared.

"And you'll kiss him hello if you know what's good for you," Mom hissed softly as a line of nurses walked past.

Her words dazed me, so I did what I could. I blinked a few times and squeezed off a zinger befitting a fourteen-year-old wise-ass. "What's good for me doesn't involve being at this stinking place. That's for sure."

Apparently, my mother appreciated my words as much as I savored hers. She pinned me along the wall in the ammonia-scrubbed corridor close enough to see her bloodshot eyes, the result of crying and chain-smoking on the drive over. "I mean it, mister. You be nice to him. Someday *you* may be in his shoes."

Of all the awful fates I ever imagined for myself, nothing — not a shark attack in the inky night sea, not secretly discovering I was retarded — compared to that. Me? In her brother's shoes? It was too hideous to even suggest.

Uncle Gordon's hospital room mortified me. Disassembled me. The last time my mother had shoehorned me in there, I'd held my breath to avoid the stench and wound up so dizzy I'd crashed into an electronic heart gizmo, almost toppling it from its metal cart. Sometimes a boy has to fend for himself. Anything was better than whiffing the flesh of my mother's fading sibling. The reek, which fell somewhere between stale bananas and a forlorn gas-station toilet, coated everything in his room, visitors included. Every time I was there I gagged for fresh air, a gust that I equated with flying downhill on my Schwinn ten-speed a safe distance from Gordon's undoing.

There was no freedom, though, not with my mom's hand clamped vice-like onto my elbow. She was doing anything to stay upright. The plastic smile she'd donned for Gordon certainly hid a baffled heart. The man who had sunk her family, and her in particular, lay dying on the other side of that wall, and none of it had been reconciled. She swung open Gordon's yellow hospital door, thrust her head into the gap and said, "Hey, Gordy," as though life couldn't be any peachier. *Boom*—two steps in and Gordon's body rot wafted into my teeth. Why couldn't I have stayed in the car? His fifth-floor room was a clammy box, all over-lit linoleum and disconnected machinery that confirmed the occupant's trudge toward death, not another miracle rebound. Its one redeeming feature, a view of sun-glistened Santa Monica beach mere blocks away, taunted me because I longed to be down there slinging my Frisbee. Fat chance of that. Mom kissed her forty-nine-year-old kid brother on the forehead and they swapped sweet, rueful smiles. In no time, she'd lowered herself into a green-vinyl chair next to his bed and nodded at me with insistent eyes. They throbbed the message I dreaded most. It was my turn to greet him. For a second, I liberated myself from this predicament, fantasizing about breaking for the stairwell on a dash for the waves. Then I realized the hell I would catch and prepared myself for *him.*

Truth be known, the revulsion fluttering in me wasn't just squeamish nostrils. I'd disliked my uncle long before his sickness. In the 1960s, Gordon could captivate any room, as long as there were grownups occupying it. Great with coddled movie stars—"Burt Lancaster, you old dog"—droll around South African muckety-mucks, he scowled constantly at little kids as if he resented their gumption for existing. Giggling, squealing—it drove him ape. During my childhood visits to his house, I used to skid along his parquet floor in my tube socks hoping he wouldn't holler at me to, "Knock it off. Get over here for a little talk." The hoping never worked. Around him, there was no hiding anything fragile. If you were homesick, he would make you spit it out. Dance around one of his penetrating questions and he would slice through it. Even as an adolescent with a flippant tongue, I shape-shifted in his presence into an insecure little boy dissolved by his barbs. "Pigeon-chested," he'd called me when I was ten. "Cowardly" he had termed my pacifism to a school bully who had bruised my arms black. Did he have any inkling how much I wanted him banished from my life? The bunch that admired Gordon as a wondrous little dreamer surfing the velvety Hollywood life never felt my goose-bumps around him. So juvenile then, how I could know that my fear was costing me a shot to learn bravery and moxie from a man who could've taught it to Neil Armstrong?

I shuffled to the left side of the bed opposite his I.V. stand wishing he were asleep. His head flopped my way and his breath was unspeakable. Up close I could see how much the disease had hollowed his cheeks. It used to be such a memorable face, Sinatra-like some said, his best physical feature easy. I already knew better than to peer down at his grizzled fingers or the shape of that so-called body tucked mercifully under the sheets, deformities that predated his illness. *Don't smell*, I reminded myself. Hold it in lest I contract that plague, which the rational part of me realized wasn't catching. Pressing forward, I tried pleasing my mom. I brushed Gordon's cheek with a glancing kiss and backpedaled.

I just wasn't fleet-footed enough, because he stopped me before I could get away. "Hold it there, kiddo," he said. "You haven't told me about school. Or what you thought about the Ali fight."

Crap, he was trying to be decent. Now I had to get a whiff of him or brace for being dizzy again. I lacked a game plan for geniality. So, I inhaled a snip of air and stammered out curt responses that boiled down to: "School's fine" (it was and it wasn't) and, "Ali really clobbered that guy," (since football was my sport, I'd forgotten who'd received the clobbering). All I wanted was to feel my age again. All I wanted was to exhale. Both I accomplished by moving away from my uncle with only cold pity for him. Every time we visited him the drill was the same. First, I'd resist being near him, then I'd fear it and eventually I'd find a corner to forget about it.

This was bunk. I should have been anyplace but the innards of St. John's Hospital. It was my Christmas vacation and I'd delivered home a novelty, a sterling report card that should've bought my amnesty from here. Hanging out in Pasadena with my pal Todd was where I should've been. Over the phone the night before, we'd penciled in a day of Beatles' albums on my stereo, submarine sandwiches at the local deli, and video Pong. Time permitting we would spend the hour before Todd's mother came for him chucking olives at passing cars. Still, Uncle Gordon was dying, no fooling this time, and Mom wasn't too sympathetic about my obliterated plans.

Off in the corner, as Gordon and Mom conferred about God and money, I tried relaxing in my patented way. I gazed out the hospital window and daydreamed of double-beef patties. Charbroiled beef held me rapt. After every visit here, Mom followed it up with lunch at Coco's, a coffee-shop chain renowned for its gooey, bacon-double-cheeseburgers. Mom called the burger my "treat," though both of us recognized it as bribery for witnessing Gordon's disintegration. (Proud of her figure, she would order cottage cheese and pears.)

In her brother's quarters that day, where the smell of his illness drifted over the harsh medicines the doctors pumped into him, that future burger played and replayed in my head. Juicier than the first tangy bite, better than the icy blast of chocolate shake washing it down, was the might of its distraction. Visualizing it kept me from acknowledging what probably frightened me the most about my uncle: our uncanny similarities.

One of the last things Gordon ever said to me came while I was in my burger trance that afternoon. He had been teasing my mom about an embarrassing episode from their childhood when he suddenly zeroed in on me. "Isn't that right, kiddo?" he roared, as if we shared a special code forged over decoder rings and oaths.

"Oh definitely, Uncle Gordon," I answered. "Definitely."

The thought of that cheeseburger had me good and numb.

Considering those poisonous feelings, how do I explain writing a book about the man who inspired them? How do I explain morphing from the helmet-haired lad indifferent to his uncle's agony to a restless young man scrounging up every breadcrumb of his existence? Was it my coming to grips with what we shared—our taxi-door ears, our obnoxious energy? Or was it guilt, life's contact cement, about missed opportunities that captured me?

The simplest explanation is that none of that mattered until a natural disaster fused our paths. October 27, 1993, the day the rampaging Altadena wildfire struck, is when I peeled my eyes backward. Until that day, I knew practically zero about my mother's relatives. To me, they were pasty faces in a moth-eaten scrapbook I couldn't have cared less about. Mom never volunteered the raw truth about them and, I never asked. Those occasions she did speak about her kin, she presented them in bursts of perfumed nostalgia around the dinner table that cast them more as cardboard clichés than three-dimensional souls in a hard-luck America.

In time, I'd realize that my mom's quaint encapsulations were fairytales that her subconscious rigged to buffer the heartache that'd strafed the family. Nowhere in her puffery were the fact that two close relatives had been shot stone-dead with disturbing similarity, or that prideful stubbornness had damned other gifted men in her fold. Gordon, as such, lived with weighty expectations on his stick-figure shoulders. He was the family's Hail Mary pass at something splendid out West, where others had run dry. The paradox made sense once you got distance from it. My uncle was the unexpected hero we needed to march from the dust. And it was because of, not despite, the sob-story that was his past. It was because he had to work harder, charm faster, inspire more and think broader than any "ordinary" man that we needed him to be *our* man.

Circumstance had assigned Gordon to elevate us, compensate us, enlisting him for a job to which he never applied.

The fire was my guide to all this -- the fallen and Gordon.

My first memory wasn't the flames themselves but what they produced: a slate-gray mushroom cloud that billowed vapor pinwheels in the sky. I noticed the action in my rearview mirror around 8:30 a.m. as I was driving to work, slurping coffee out of a travel mug. Afterwards, I couldn't wrench my eyes away. At 2,000 feet and rising, that cloud sneered apocalyptically. It had diabolical intent. I floored it to the *San Gabriel Valley Tribune* where I was a reporter and got to my desk. I checked the newswire on my computer for an update, and the words made my stomach taut. The fire was tearing east through the foothill neighborhood around Eaton Canyon, where I'd grown up and where my elderly parents still lived. Ugly visions arced inside me as I jogged back to my truck.

Figuring I had license to lead foot it home, I used the freeway's inside shoulder to bypass the miles of standstill traffic typical for L.A. disaster days. What was normally a twenty-minute rush-hour drive required half that. Yet I couldn't reach my folks' place, which was only a short distance from my house, because the roads were cordoned off. Instead I went to my own house negotiating with my panic. *Think!* My lips mouthed prayers my brain hadn't authorized. The real shock was that Mom and Dad were already in my house with their elbows deep in a box of Triscuits. They'd let themselves in with a key I didn't know they had. They were plunked on the sofa, calm about their evacuee status as they watched the blow-dried TV newscasters doing wall-to-wall coverage of "Fire '93." In all the bedlam, I'd forgotten how many close calls they had weathered in their years on Kinneloa Mesa Road. Brush encircled them.

My oldest brother, Paul, pulled up in his Corvette and together we stood on my front lawn watching the flames shoot pulsing, orange barbs fifty feet off Mount Wilson. Seeing the fire pummel that brown-violet hillside hypnotized us, condensing ten minutes of catatonic watching into an instant. According to the newscasters, hot, gusting winds called Santa Anas were whipping canyon brushfires not just in Pasadena but in Malibu and Laguna Beach as well. All of Southern California felt like it was roasting away for its suburban sins. Paving over ancient forests with primo developments touting their "environmental friendliness" was bound to tick off the land sometime. As this notion wormed into me, ash flakes sprinkled down. Sirens wailed on distant boulevards. That's when Paul and I looked at each other. We couldn't just stand there, could we? We couldn't just stare. Our decision was made in macho grunts. We were going to the Mesa to save the house. Torrid winds, a single escape road—big deal.

Paul told our dad we would wing it and I stupidly went along. The mountain was on fire.

A flash of my press credentials got us waved through the traffic barricade by a jelly-chinned cop in a bright-yellow rain slicker. Thankfully, the officer wasn't curious why a working journalist would travel with a button-down businessman (my brother) and a fidgeting, middle-aged Chinese lady (Fong, my parents' longtime housekeeper). Seconds later the cop was a speck in my side mirror. A half-mile away from him we climbed the Mesa's steep, hairpin road, eased over the old speed bump and came to a stop in my parents' pronged driveway. A surreal aura greeted us instead of familiarity. A dense charcoal fog that blotted out the sun and absorbed the mushroom cloud let you know bad things were swirling. As palm-tree fronds crackled in flames high above the blacktop I knew nothing was exempt. Everything burns. Astonishingly, the house was still intact.

Even so, that smoke bored into me. Within my first hour in it, a wispy-haired neighbor I hadn't seen since I left home at eighteen wandered onto my folks' lawn with a thousand-yard stare over his mismatched clothes. The fire had mowed up a weed-strewn hillside, hop-scotched four other homes and torched his before he could unwind his garden hose. "It's all gone," the old man sputtered. "The house. Nothing's left." From that smoke, a friend of mine in the newspaper trade walked onto my parent's lime-green Dichondra lawn seeking an interview. "How does it feel," the man from *The Los Angeles Times* asked me, "watching your old stomping grounds burn?"

While he spoke, the house across the street, Dr. Risser's old digs, sizzled on the perimeter and I wanted to punch my colleague on general principle but didn't.

At some point I scaled my parents' wood-shingle roof and screamed myself hoarse. "Where's the goddamn Fire Department? Where the hell are they when you need them?" Stretched too thin was the answer. Few fire trucks clanked up the street because there was nothing for them to do. Every drop of hydrant water already had been tapped, leaving the flames to do its neighborhood destruction virtually un-pestered. So much for fire prevention. My brother and I straggled in its failure. We hacked and rubbed eyes as the gorge that'd been the wallpaper to our adolescence burned back to its origins. Sure, water-dropping helicopters whirled occasionally overhead to douse spot blazes that presented themselves. What filled my ears, when there was anything to hear, was the *pop-pop* of manicured, ranch-style homes imploding from the heat and that God-awful crackle of fire along the ridgeline.

As the day lingered on, the smoke socked in the terrain into a near whiteout. We could barely see the pool twenty feet away. Paul had said it first after we arrived: we should scout the perimeter to ensure nothing was smoldering. I went outside my father's study, close to my dog's old pen, and it was okay. Paul, ever dapper in his pinstriped suit, skidded half way down to the boathouse and saw it was all right. Fong went somewhere else. Afterwards we joined up to patrol the southern flank together.

We walked around the lip of the Pac-Man-shaped pool, ducked under the slide and went down some stairs. You only could turn one direction, a hard right onto a concrete ledge providing access to a faded brick shed where the gas-fired pool heater sat. Directly below the walkway was a steep, weedy hill that extended thirty feet to the property line of my parent's neighbors, the Kings. They had a horse corral and a couple of restored vintage cars on their side of the gully. We, the Jacobs, had wild oak trees. A rotting plywood fence was our dividing line.

On our concrete pad, Paul, Fong and I froze. We'd been searching for a flare up and it found us. The fire had sizzled the chassis of the Kings' cars and was burning three of the plywood fence stakes like castoff Roman Candles. Sparks from them had fluttered onto our property, and a ten-foot-long strip of weeds smoked away. Boy, I remember thinking, this wasn't too safe, standing here between the shed and the hill, watching. Unwise or not, watching was irresistible. If my folks place was about to be flattened, this was the script. Between those two thoughts, precisely between them, a fire-whipped draft quivered the branches of our oaks. The wind flapped harder, and then *whoosh*. The fire lost interest in the weeds. Chalked with fuel, the fire came barreling up the hill at us on the ledge. Came at us in a spiky orange curtain fifteen feet wide. It blitzed so quickly the most I could do to shield myself was turn sideways and scrunch my eyes.

My horror freelanced from there. In my head I pictured this scene of us headlining the local news as fire fatalities with a lesson for the masses. I pictured the TV reporter doing a live remote on my parents' lawn unctuously reminding viewers "never to stand upwind of a brush fire. Be careful, people!"

Back on the ledge, the heat curtain flambéed us for a few seconds with a 600-degree spike and I expected the fire was moving in for the kill. It would accelerate so that we would be drenched in flames, the way you are by an overpowering wave, and my flesh would be singed from pink to putrescent black. If I were fortunate I could run with my clothes aflame and leap into the pool. Later the doctors at Huntington Memorial, the hospital where I was born, would shoot me up with morphine until I died from my third-degree burns. In utter fear, in only a few seconds, your mind has extraordinary ability. It can show you your doom as a little film.

Quickly as it'd vanished, though, oxygen returned. I remember cracking my eyes and looking at my brother. He couldn't believe it either. We could breathe. Our nervous chuckling reminded me of hyenas. We wheeled around to see if the fire had leapfrogged us. Nope. There'd be no skin grafts, no teary funerals. We'd been saved. The fire had mowed up to the concrete walkway where we cowered and then retreated down to the weeds. The cement had been our firebreak. When I felt my shirt, sweat glued it to my ribcage.

The three of us beat a crazed path to my truck and raced down the Mesa. The property, we assumed, would be ash when we returned. We drove to my house and Fong went inside. I had my car door open to follow her when Paul casually directed me to flip around and go back.

"You're insane," I replied. My answer made no sense because before I realized it I was already driving that direction. At the base of the road is where I slammed the gear into neutral.

"What are you waiting for?" Paul said. "Let's go."

"No!" I crossed my arms and did something I'd never done before. I yelled at my big brother, who stowed his penchant for the heroic—following bank robbers, saving drowning men—inside an otherwise unassuming exterior.

"No goddamn way I'm going up to the house," I hollered. "Understand?"

"Calm down," Paul said, hands shushing me. "We're here, aren't we?"

"You calm down. We almost got killed."

"Look, we'll just pull into the driveway. If it's hairy, we turn around. The road is clear."

"No fucking way. We don't know what we're doing. Isn't that obvious from what just happened?"

"Come on. It'll be quick."

"My wife is pregnant, remember? The answer is no."

"It'll be okay."

"Famous last words. I don't even know why I came back here."

"Stop arguing."

"Dick!"

I notched the car into drive and drove extra-slow to annoy him. Trees were burning on both sides of the road like Satan's discount landscaping. Inside, my heart swished. The closer we got to the house the less worried I was about my own safety. It was the visual that terrified me. It was the prospect of rounding that last curve, driving over that yellow speed bump and seeing the house in the throes of a mad devouring. Seeing the heat collapse the roof and everything from my childhood reduced to skeletal carbon would be an image seared into me forever.

Wishing I could cover my eyes, I guided the car up the road the fire department had evacuated that morning. Curve. Speed bump. Driveway. House. The house was okay. Jesus, it was still standing!

Paul and I got inside the main hallway and no smoke was there, either. It was when we walked the perimeter we noticed something was different. The boathouse was gone.

When the wreckage was tallied, one out of every three homes in the assaulted hills of Altadena had perished. A hundred families became instantly homeless. A half-insane Asian vagabond who'd drifted to the States and wound up living at the throat of the adjacent canyon was responsible. He'd been unable to stomp out the campfire he'd started with a cheap pack of matches, and my old neighborhood had paid.

As such, our feat was measured against others' losses. Five hours after we reached the Mesa, after our comical efforts to extinguish hotspots with jugged pool water, Paul, Fong and I had won our fight. The house survived. We said practically nothing to anyone or each other about nearly being killed, and wouldn't for years. Instead, we hoisted our pride that the single casualty was the wood-slatted boathouse. It'd rested on the lower tier of the property, at the bottom of a dirt embankment that was home to weeds and gophers. The fire had engulfed the tan, cottage-sized structure in about fifteen minutes. If something had to burn, Paul and I agreed, it was best that, definitely that. Our family's ski boat hadn't been dry-docked there for five years. The passé furniture and family heirlooms consigned to boathouse exile over time weren't so lucky.

We told our parents the good news around sundown. My dad, the Caltech-schooled engineer, smiled and gave me an, "Attaboy." Grasping the big picture always was his special gift. It was my mom, our family's theatrical one, who surprised us. She turned frigid and shuffled into my kitchen, me on her tail. Now I was cornering her. Didn't she realize she would be bunking in her own bed that night instead of a Holiday Inn hunched over her insurance policy? Didn't she appreciate the devastation she had been spared?

Yes, she responded, she got that. She spoke with a hangdog pout that she wouldn't explain until I pressed her, a trademark of mine. Finally it came out. It was the loss of her father's antique organ she mourned. When the boathouse liquefied, it was inside.

"Let me get this straight," I asked. "After everything that's happened today, you're upset about that beat-up thing?"

"Yes, I am."

"But why? It probably didn't even work anymore."

"That's not the point," my mom shot back, inhaling a quarter-inch off her cigarette.

"Then what is?"

"My dad wrote all his music on that organ. For years and years and years."

"And?"

"And that music rescued Mama Rose and Gordon when your grandfather died. That organ was everything." Mama Rose was my maternal grandma. Gordon was her son.

"I didn't know," I responded meekly.

By then, Mom wasn't listening. She was at my kitchen window wearing her own thousand-yard stare.

That evening, with the blaze all but extinguished, I plotted my return to the Mesa. I told my wife I needed to hunt for cinders that might polish off the house while we slept thinking all was saved. Kate as usual saw through my fig leaf. She sent me off. Back up the hill I drove in my soot-blasted Nissan. What had been smoky chaos before was now an outcropping of stillness. There were no more glowing embers, no smoke columns that tugged at the corner of your eye. I checked the gullies behind the boathouse. I walked our neighbors' property. Some evacuees were filtering home against police orders. If you heard their cries bang off the canyon when they saw their places, you knew all you needed. In another time, minus the Nikes, they might have been frontier refugees returning from an Indian raid. So why was I here? I had done my deed. I should have been home telling war stories between slugs off a bottle. It was as though an invisible hand had dragged me.

Before I drove off, I walked over to the heap of blackened slag that used to be our boathouse. Seeing it reduced to base chemicals hurt, especially after what my mom had just confided. I had done some serious growing up and a few dozen misdemeanors inside those walls. Now its leftovers would be trucked to a landfill. Using a tree branch, I tried identifying some of the globs seared into the ground by poking at them. It was futile, every charred bit. For an instant, I thought I'd spotted an ivory key from my grandpa's instrument near a wedge of mangled rebar and my spirit soared. Alas, it was only a band of melted steel.

As I'd learn, not everything melted. Gradually, undeniably, a strange force crept into me in the weeks after the fire. I would sense it at night when I closed my eyes in bed, a haunting pulse no doctor could measure. How would I answer my kids when they asked about my lineage? Forget that—how would I answer myself when I couldn't dodge the question anymore of what made me, me? The destruction of that rickety piano—the soul it ripped from my mom— was my starting line.

That fire peeled my eyes toward history all right. There had been ghosts around me my whole life waiting to be embraced. Brooding geniuses and Hollywood showmen, iron-willed widows and men executed mafia-style. Most had passed from this world before old age, shipwrecked from their dreams, forgotten and floating.

For all their secrets, none of them enthralled more than my uncle Gordon, the shrunken champion who saved his most improbable stunt for last. He enticed me, the nephew who'd once despised him, to reassemble him from beyond.

It'd be the hardest job I'd ever have and, unwittingly, the most gratifying. Who was Gordon Zahler? The thrill-seeking inspiration that famous faces saw, or a flamboyant nobody who tried rebuilding what his recklessness destroyed? To decide, I brought his painful ghost into my world. It would never spin the same.

CHAPTER ONE
The Local Bad Boy

The kid perched forty feet up itched to jump into history. While no one had been looking ten minutes earlier, he'd clambered into the ceiling girders over an enormous indoor pool and hid behind a column. The skinny, brown-haired boy smiled in the shadows. He was proud of his brazenness. Hell, it called for a clap. Once again, Gordon Robert Zahler, thirteen, was precisely where he was not supposed to be. The "Danger—Keep Out" signs he had read shimmying up the maintenance ladder at the Venice Plunge were emphatic about that.

Warnings for him were dares in plain sight, and that's why he teetered above the pool's frothy water. Inside of it was a collection of bobbing heads, most of them middle-aged women yammering nonstop as they dogpaddled in their goofy black and red bathing caps. Gordon's intent all along was to shock everybody, especially that fleshy bunch. For days he had planned a spectacular, high velocity dive—fifty MPH if he could attain it. His accomplishment would wipe out somebody's record. When his knees trembled high on the beam, he remembered that sure bet and his legs quieted somewhat.

Since none of his pals had reached the forbidden plateau before him, he had decided to preen before jumping. His warm-up act would involve leaping in four-foot increments from one narrow span to the next until he covered the length of the pool, east to west. Slip? He wouldn't slip. From the spans he would tiptoe to the center catwalk, bow to the spectators squinting up at him, and pull off a whistling, headfirst maneuver not unlike an Acapulco cliff diver. Everyone would be jawing about it for days to come. Gordon the infamous, Gordon the intrepid—it was all the same to him. His friends would mob him once they took stock of his deed. And yes, he understood the risk. One misstep would send him hurtling into the waters—or the concrete deck—on a lethal trajectory. His fun was brewed like this.

There was just one hitch. A lifeguard who saw him before he had his chance to preen betrayed him in the rankest way possible. He ratted him out to his mother.

Rose Zahler had already lectured her youngest child about acceptable behavior and set off for beach sun with a novel under her arm. Lee, her husband, was too busy to make the jaunt. He was in the city writing music under studio deadline, which kept a fist over his free time. It was a searing August day in 1939, the California coast bronzed shoreline to beach towel, when my uncle scampered into the rafters. And this wasn't just any public pool. The Plunge was the centerpiece of a popular, brick-and-glass recreation pavilion, L.A.'s own Coney Island, that'd been built atop a pier overlooking the green waters south of Santa Monica Beach. Salt water pumped into the pool through a warming fountain drew flocks of paying customers to swim here. The honchos who managed the complex could visualize the bad publicity and subsequent drop at the turnstile if this showoff's antics got him killed. They found my grandma down near the shore to issue her their edict. They wanted "the boy down now, good riddance to him." He wasn't welcome at the Plunge anymore.

And Rose wanted him to listen. Quickly, she was poolside, looking up at the latticework bracing the ultramodern dome roof. "Come down right this instant!" she yelled. "Do you hear me?"

He must have. The cavernous acoustics made even her gentle voice echo. Hearing the plaintive tone, many of the bathers shelved their conversations to point at the diminutive face nuzzled against the center girder. Still, the tracking fingers had no effect. Gordon refused to budge. Every time his mother shouted her command, he shook his head "No." The impasse continued until my grandma resorted to special language. "I want you in the pool, where it's safe," she said, her voice downshifting from anger to torment. "For Lord's sake, Gordon. For Lord's sake."

Brighter than the teachers who tried flunking him, my uncle recognized the gravity of the L-word. He would obey his Christian mother, yet as always he'd comply on his own terms. From the ceiling shadows, he crouched on his powerful, wiry legs and sprang. Sprang hard. A hundred bathers in the pool and on the deck froze watching as he narrowly missed clipping a joist on his parabolic descent. When my uncle splashed home into the deep end of the Plunge, it produced a collective "Oooh" from the crowd and a booming spray that sheeted ten feet. Rose gave him a tongue lashing in front of everybody after he toweled off.

Punishments for similar shenanigans came and went. Mostly they dissolved into the wreath of good times that Lee Zahler arranged for his family. The movie music he created for those grainy westerns and tearjerkers made it all possible. His pay stubs kept his wife and kids happily housed in a charming, four-bedroom Craftsman across from a citrus grove in Sierra Madre, a foothill hamlet roughly twenty miles northeast of downtown Los Angeles.

That they lived there, or could enjoy a lazy Saturday sleeping in and eating waffles, was a luxurious existence, backgrounds considered. The ditties Lee wrote and scored put floral dresses on his girls' backs, a deluxe bike under Gordon, a Filipino cook in the kitchen and a riding horse named Dixie in a makeshift barn.

Sunday nights the family enjoyed leisurely suppers at the Seafood Tavern, a local mom-and-pop. For special occasions, Lee would drive everybody to Hollywood Boulevard for dinner at the Musso-and-Frank Grill, a dark-lit celebrity hangout where my mom would skip down the aisles for laughs. This lifestyle was why my grandpa endured those Hollywood libertines. While America stood in soup lines in the 1930s, his family could relish full meals.

My mom, Lee and Rose's first-born, certainly brought her parents joy through her steadiness. By 1940, Muriel Bernice had blossomed from a gangly child doted on by daddy into a curvy nineteen-year-old hit on by young doctors, dentists, pilots and soldiers. As a teenager, she had earned good grades, submitted to church, discovered cigarettes and was named "Miss Catalina" in a hokey island beauty pageant. The height of the tiny rebelliousness she harbored was sneaking off for a screen test at Universal Pictures without her parents' consent. When she was accepted at a prestigious liberal arts college east of Los Angeles, to study music no less, Lee was incandescent with pride.

While Muriel accumulated brownie points with her folks, Gordon stockpiled demerits. A year or so before his Venice Plunge stunt, he had taken a dare and jumped twenty feet off the Redondo Beach Pier into the murky waters swirling around the pylons. He'd convinced my mom later that summer to sit on the handlebars of his bike on a speed ride down Sierra Madre's Mountain Trail Avenue. Near the bottom, the bike had jackknifed and my mom was sent flying—first onto the asphalt, then the emergency room where her bloody knee was stitched closed. Her brother felt rotten about the sutures. Nobody was supposed to get hurt.

Outside the family, Gordon was one of the area's most promising young rascals. He was nothing if not versatile in his mischief, which tended to be of the benign, "got-cha" brand that most adults couldn't stay cross about for too long. At his mother's church in nearby Arcadia, he and some friends turned profits selling "fresh-squeezed tomato juice" they concocted from ketchup and water. In the garish movie houses along Pasadena's Colorado Boulevard, he and his pals often took up positions in the balconies to hurl spitballs at old ladies' hairdos until the ushers chased them away. It was in his hometown where the authorities and neighbors that Gordon targeted discussed wringing his hooligan neck. He'd begun with your typical

high jinx—festooning newspaper shreds on the hedges of
curmudgeon retirees—until he was seasoned for more creative
missions. A favorite was taping dynamite caps to the trolley-car
tracks leading north up Baldwin Avenue. Gordon and his cohorts
knew exactly what ivy shrubs to squat in to watch the commotion
unfold without being discovered. When the blasts hit *rat-a-tat-tat*, the
older passengers jumped off their seats like they'd sat on cacti.

The conductor, plenty mad at how often this happened, would
stop the train, rip through the nearby bushes searching for the
pranksters and bellow, "I'm gonna find you punks!"

He never did. By far Gordon's proudest caper involved Sierra
Madre's uptight Congregational minister, an established teetotaler.
Gordon, acting as the man's aide, phoned in an order for a case of
bourbon from Robert's Market one weekend and had it delivered to
the minister's home, no questions asked. Being a nosey town, word
of the delivery spread. The next Sunday the minister had to ineptly
explain to his parishioners that the liquor was someone else's idea.

Shrewd about concealing his troublemaking, Gordon almost
always went un-apprehended. Those occasions he was caught, my
grandfather, a compact man legendary for his Hungarian temper,
would haul Gordon into the living room and have at it. *Thwap*—
Gordon would be vigorously spanked with the back of a hairbrush,
the number of whacks calculated by his crime.

My mother, ordinarily ecstatic to see little brother get his
lumps, bawled sympathy tears during the sternest corporal
punishment. The accused, however, bit his lip to stem any
crying. Gordon was stoic about his thrashing. It embroidered his
reputation around the block. Whatever scolding was dished up
to teach him, he came out of it un-chastened.

Once he got a hairbrush whooping he must have known he
would receive for fabricating a story at a crowded dinner party
attended by a big-wheel Hollywood producer. "Hey Daddy,"
Gordon chirped, "remember that time you were in jail and I
came to visit you?" An awkward silence built until somebody
laughed.

Though neither parent could control Gordon outdoors, they were strict about house organization. Rose ironed the curtains maniacally, sometimes late at night. If guests were coming, there she'd be on the floor, arms under sofas, on search-and-destroy missions for dust bunnies. Lee, meantime, was a taskmaster about how his children's days commenced. Rooms "immaculate" before school, he would order Muriel and Gordon. Shoes buffed so smoothly you should be able to comb your hair in their reflection.

Fiercely protective of my mom, especially with her suitors, Lee probably revised his approach to his son when traditional punishments failed to reform him. It was the long view Lee would take: that Gordon's recklessness would peter itself out before any lasting damage was inflicted. Boys being boys, it was the attention he craved, not the challenge his exploits demanded of him.

Lee's premise, if that's what it was, frayed the afternoon in 1940 when Gordon was kicked out of St. Rita's Elementary School. Certainly, this required more than a hairbrush whacking. Gordon, it should be noted, had propelled the family's move from Los Angeles to the sticks of Sierra Madre. A physician had advised them that the desiccating mountain air would quell Gordon's asthma attacks. Lee went along with the advice despite the hour-plus commute it meant for him into Hollywood. Ten years gone, school expulsion in hand, my grandfather must have been puzzled what discipline, if any, would shake sense into his son. Ground him for summer? Threaten boarding school? (St. Rita's was a few blocks from the house.) Where Lee broiled about the situation, my grandma prayed for whole afternoons. Gordon's wild streak had to be tamed, so she prayed this black mark was a blessing they'd see later.

Strides, after all, had been made. Gordon improved from a C-average in sixth grade to a C+/B- pupil in Sister Mulbuss's seventh grade. It was his misbehavior toward the nuns he called "grumpy penguins" that classified him as the problem child. In April 1940, a nun turned to write on the blackboard and Gordon seized his opportunity. He snuck away from his desk, walked over to an open dormer window and jumped out of it, celebrating his escape with a jig for his classmates to see. St. Rita's principal expelled him afterwards. It wasn't just one thing that got Gordon booted two months before summer vacation. It was his "general conduct."

CHAPTER TWO
The Lash

A surprise rainstorm barreling out of the north soaked Pasadena the day Gordon tumbled. At sunup the sky was pale blue. By the time the first school bell warbled at John Marshall Junior High, it was if night had never left. Menacing dark clouds nobody had expected lopped the peaks off the San Gabriel Mountains. An hour later drenching raindrops painted the city streets a lustrous, black sheen.

One look at the soggy grounds and Marshall's principal sent his decree crackling through the school loudspeakers: no outdoor sports today, lunch inside. The kids groaned in unison at the announcement. Being cooped up all day in musty confines with the grownups made the clocks run slower. But for my uncle and his gang, the rain was a reason to whoop. Staying indoors meant forty-five minutes to play *Tarzan: Lord of the Jungle*. Sailing through the air imitating their hero, Johnny Weismuller, giggling about the loincloth liberties they imagined he was taking with Jane, was terrific fun. The storm could last all week as far as Marshall's own Tarzans were concerned.

For all its excitement, ninth-grade gym class operated under the authoritarian regime of Coach Harold S. Turner. His boys had five minutes to undress, don their school P.E. clothes and assemble in position in the gym or the field. Any horseplay had to be done slyly because coach was adamant about locker-room protocol. Cross him and you would be doing calisthenics until the bell rang. Admire him and take a number. Turner's tough-love approach made him one of Marshall's most popular instructors, particularly among the bigger kids out to learn every play he could teach. Just the reverence in which the boys spoke of coach's football smarts elevated him to a sort of local Knute Rockne.

On this Tuesday, Turner cared more about cracking soles than halfback passes. Fungus had invaded the boys' locker room, and coach was determined to inspect every toe of every kid in his ten a.m. class for Athlete's Foot. Should peeling be detected, powder and hygiene lectures would be dispensed. Afterwards the boys were unloosed onto the gym floor until the rest of the students were checked.

Marshall's Tarzans—Gordon, Don Berg, Wally Gilmore, Benny Gouin and Rob Bowman—regarded it as astonishing fortune, their passing muster first. They were free to monkey around until coach came, and they ran out onto the hardwood floor yipping all the way. Swiveling their heads, another fact struck them about being alone. The jumping game Turner had specifically forbid weeks earlier was ripe for the taking.

Adrenaline surging, the boys set up the equipment. The object was to sprint down a line thirty yards, pounce off a springboard and clear a manmade "mountain" they'd invented themselves. The base of the mountain was a wooden-legged pommel horse central to any gymnastics competition. Prickly, mackinaw-like gym mats would be laid over the apparatus, so the obstacle (a.k.a. their mountain) grew to a challenging height. The boys would clear it by launching themselves off the springboard in front of the pommel horse and grabbing a set of hanging gymnast rings positioned behind it. While still hanging, they would uncork a Tarzan jungle yell, *AAAAH-AHAHAAAAH,* and release into a cushioned landing on the pads below as their finale. Sometimes they'd try flips on their way down. Nobody dwelled on margin of error. At thirteen and fourteen years old, they felt immune to anything of lasting consequence.

By hurrying the boys needed only ten minutes to spring over the mountain draped with one, two and then three mats. There were several near crashes, but the brinkmanship in their sweat glands kept the acrobatics moving. Besides, they were eyeing a world record. Four mats! Even the school jocks with their nickel-plated trophies couldn't outdo that. They only hoped the Athlete's Foot caseload was more than coach could handle.

Out of respect, Gordon was awarded the first stab at the four-mat record. His chest puffed out as he loped to the head of the line, confident of his skills, and why not? My uncle had wowed practically everyone except the teachers in his six weeks at Marshall Junior High. Classmates quickly learned he was funny and magnetic, a natural at pouring on the charm around the girls or bumming smokes from the older boys. Athletics also distinguished him from your average new kid. Everyone, Turner included, noticed right away that Gordon had a virtuoso athleticism that set him apart. His was a darting, shifty speed that made him difficult to tackle on the gridiron and almost impossible to throw out on the baseball diamond. Toss a ball to him and he gunned it back on target. To predict he would be on varsity squad ahead of his peers was forecasting the obvious.

If Gordon was elusive on grass and clay, he was doubly that in his indoor tomfoolery. One morning he and Rob Bowman snuck out of science class, fished matches from their blue jeans and lit a pair of long fuses they'd rolled by hand. Cherry-bomb firecrackers exploded in a hallway trashcan minutes later, and the rattling walls made some kids yelp it was an earthquake. The whole student body buzzed about it later around the lunch tables. Yet, the sweatered Napoleons who ran Marshall never unearthed evidence Gordon was involved during their investigation. They must not have believed a boy at his second-chance school would be so brash.

Under the gym's fluorescent lights, Gordon rocked on his heels, calibrating his jump. Several of his friends stood with him at the front of the runway waiting their turn. Others were at the landing zone, hands on hips, clucking for the rest to move double-time. "What are you waiting for?" somebody said. "An invitation? Go!" As the calls mounted for him to hurry, Gordon tried his best not to hear them. He realized it was pivotal he achieve maximum pounce off the board. He would be soaring higher than he had ever attempted, and being the daredevil of Mountain Avenue, that was saying something.

If only the coach had emerged from his locker-room fungus hunt blowing his whistle, my family might have surged out of 1940 unpunished. But free will is forever, and Gordon sprinted toward the obstacle steeped in his present. He blew down that runway in a blaze of pumping elbows and knees impressive to onlookers and too fast for control. *Crack.* The maneuver was gummed up from the second he touched the springboard. As his right foot pressed it, the device canted sharply to the right, chopping his speed and angling him off center. The board didn't so much catapult him as fling him sideways. With too little air under him, his left foot snagged the mat draping the pommel horse, which further reduced his momentum. There was no chance he could grab the rings to safety.

Up seven feet in the air, with gravity tugging at him, Gordon may have tried to tuck into a ball and bail out. It was too late. He landed violently—headfirst—corkscrewed onto the pads at a sickening velocity. On impact, his neck torqued to the right, compressing his cervical spine like a thick coil dropped from a roof. Underneath him, a pool of dark, sticky blood from a half-severed calf blotted the hardwood.

Pounding their sneakers to reach him, the boys who weren't there when Gordon planted himself saw that he was unconscious. More gruesomely, he was on his back and his side simultaneously. His head was ratcheted so far to one side that his hair practically touched his shoulder blade. He resembled a misshapen "S." A chilled panic swirled in his friends, who tried unsuccessfully to wake him. "Gordy, you okay? Gordy, can you hear us?" They nudged his shoulder. No response. The longer he was out, the more broken he looked. He wasn't springing up laughing, "I fooled you, suckers!" as he had after other nasty spills. How could he be playing possum with his neck wrenched so far back? Once this sank in, one of the boys ran into the locker room frantic for "Coach, anybody!" Turner came jogging in his gray sweatshirt, and immediately shooed everyone away.

"Snap out of it, Zahler," he said. "C'mon. Wake up." Coach was in a catcher's stance getting silence for his commands. "Zahler, can you hear me? Don't do this, kid." Turner rubbed his forehead in anguish, then stuffed the whistle dangling from his neck into his sweatshirt. It kept getting in the way. By now the entire P.E. class lined the perimeter of the cramped, white gym on Allen Street. The Tarzans were the only ones with the gall to shuffle close for a better peek until coach barked them away. Minutes passed. "Zahler!" coach said. "Zahler. Wake up!" Nothing. Outside the rainy skies opened up. Small, filthy rivers sped down curbs. Then there was activity inside. Gordon was suddenly awake, still splayed out but whispering into coach's ear. More time passed and Turner took action. "What the hell is coach doing?" one of the boys asked.

Turner had carefully locked his arms under Gordon's armpits, almost as if he was getting him in a Half Nelson. Next he'd lifted Gordon up from behind into a full standing position. From appearances, coach was trying to prod him to take a step on his own. Ten seconds later he dumped the idea. That's because Gordon's chin slumped into his chest and his legs bore no weight. He was like one of Edgar Bergen's puppets. All Turner could do was gingerly set him down on the floor, away from the pooled blood. On my uncle's cheeks a dusting of the Athlete's Foot powder was now visible. Coach, in his first seconds over him, had tapped Gordon's face to shake him out of what he assumed was eminently shakable.

Gordon babbled. "Coach. I can't move. My arms. My legs. I can't feel them anymore. Are they still there?"

An ambulance was called and two burly men in alabaster suits materialized at the gym's double doors. They wheeled their gurney over the floor, and it produced a frightful squeak only rubber and wood can make. One Tarzan asked another if Gordon was going to die and was told, "Of course not," with fake assurance. Some in his circle wept softly, others masked their faces. Such confusion flapped within his pals: relief it wasn't them, guilt about their game. Twenty minutes ago it had all been hoots.

At the pads, the attendants lifted my uncle up, strapped him in the gurney, and rolled him away. Through the rain he went, straight into a Shaefer Co. ambulance. Eyewitnesses said the indentation his body left on the gym pads remained for a while.

~~~

Gordon lay ghostly still, eyes closed, alone with his thoughts and the metal rods the doctors had drilled into his skull. Christ, he wanted his bearings back. Was that too much to ask? It had been days since he was whisked from school to St. Luke's Hospital east of Marshall. Gordon's drug-sluiced mind let him in on that tidbit at least. Rushed in on a gurney from the ambulance, he had heard a husky voice tell the person in charge that he had a cervical-something and a gashed leg.

The x-rays taken must have caused a commotion because before long he was returned to the same ambulance, presumably en route to where he was now. Time skittered ahead after that. It had only been Tuesday morning he was fretting the algebra quiz he was supposed to take after gym class while daydreaming which canyon trail he would pedal his bike on that afternoon. Now, as consciousness reintroduced itself, he tried to piece the shards together. What he didn't know yet were the specifics: that he was in intensive care at Los Angeles County General Hospital with bleak medical jargon scribbled on his chart.

His awakening startled my grandma, who was stiff from her vigil mashed up against Gordon's chrome bed frame. She had been praying nonstop since Tuesday, begging God to allow her to switch places with the boy and then modifying her entreaty to simply keep him alive when her plea dawned on her as cliché desperation. She had been stroking Gordon's forehead when he opened his eyes. There was such unknowing in them, such primal fear, that she had bent over him to kiss his cheek because it was vital he see her face before he saw anything else. *"Where am I? What's happened? Where's Dad? Where are my arms? What's pinching my head? Why can't I move? Am I going to die? I don't wanna die. Mom, Mommy, help me!"*

Rose pined to help, was frantic about it, even if she was unable to understand one garbled word from his lips. Gordon's broken neck had hurt his breathing, and a ventilator had been inserted down his throat. His mind hadn't adjusted to it, not yet. Sensing this in his mumbling, Rose lied beautifully about his condition. "Stay still," she said. "You're going to be fine. There's a machine helping you to breathe—that's why you can't speak. It's only for precaution, okay? Nothing to worry about. The Lord is taking care of you. Now breathe easy and rest, sweetheart. Just rest."

Squeezing his eyelids shut, listening to the respirator's mechanical wheeze, Gordon couldn't let it rest. He never could. A moment later, his memory of how he'd arrive there hardened, and it blew off the fog of why death was circling. He had been wheeled into County General emergency room half-conscious and three-quarters gone. There had been a flurry of gloves and instruments under blinding lights. Somebody snipped the Marshall T-shirt off him, and he was colder than he had ever been.

The two doctors over him rapidly spoke in a clinical, coffee-breathed lingo. One asked him whether he could feel the pinpricks on his feet. Groggily, he told them to go ahead. They said they already had. Ether—he smelled so much ether, too, when somebody clamped a mask over his mouth without telling him first. The cloying gas made the room spin until a chemical sleep snatched him away. His memory ended jaggedly.

Three lost days later, he was awake, gagging on his respirator. Soon enough he would learn that the traction pins in his head were tyrants. They had immobilized the only part of him still capable of movement.

The doctors were candid about the severity of the injury. The gym accident had occurred mid-morning and the emergency room doctors had almost lost him several times by midnight. A few days later, County General's top neurologist shepherded my grandparents into his office for the formal prognosis. Gordon, the doctor explained, had almost no chance. Few people with a smashed vertebra so high up the spinal column had lived more than a few months, let alone recovered. His type of paralysis had too many fatal complications to overcome: respiratory arrest, pneumonia, kidney failure, bacterial infection, heart failure, pulmonary embolism, and other ailments you couldn't even pronounce. The x-ray illuminated for Lee and Rose to inspect was really surplus information. The image showed that Gordon's neck was so badly fractured he had come close to decapitating himself with his jump. The neurologist's main advice was logistical. He recommended that my grandparents keep the family minister around. In all likelihood, Gordon would be dead soon. After Rose sobbed into the night, she placed her phone calls.

Between their grief and their shock, my grandparents refused to accept the prognosis. In those first weeks, they were at the hospital together sixteen hours a day assuring Gordon he was improving. After they exited his room is when their conflicting faiths went on display. Lee browbeat and stomped through the neurology ward scavenging for hope. His only boy was lying there, and he wouldn't tolerate gobbledygook runarounds from the doctors learning what he might about experimental surgeries, paralysis, nursing schedules, potential specialists and whatnot. Medicine held Lee's trust. Science had to heal Gordon.

Rose, by comparison, was kinder to the physicians and nurses and more tolerant of their "we're-doing-everything-we-can" explanations. This tolerance flowed from a reserved, albeit opinionated nature saturated by God-All-Mighty. Grandma believed the Lord, no matter the galactic turmoil facing Him, could instantaneously cure any of His children of any affliction. It was simply a matter of the right people asking Him the right way.

Rose Zahler, forty-year-old wife and mother, had made it to this stage because she had perfected burrowing into the day-to-day seeing spirituality where others saw humdrum. Her childhood had been up-and-down until it was ravaged by her father's infamous murder near the U.S.-Mexican border. She had communicated little about his slaying to her children, deciding they'd find out for themselves how cruel the world could be. By concentrating on the ordinary, be it sewing for her kids or baking rice pudding for elderly neighbors, she had been able to mothball her past. She stayed busy and learned to invoke heavenly help on a whim. Sometimes it was asking St. Anthony's guidance to help her locate her house keys. Sometimes it was quoting the Psalms in response to a friend's psoriasis. With Gordon near death, her prayers became a continuous monologue. Another man in her life was poised to leave her prematurely and that old sorrow welled up again.

The timing of this latest incident challenged her sense of rightness in the world. Gordon had been hurt two days before his favorite night for fun, Halloween. He had been crippled two months into his fresh start at Marshall. And he had landed on his deathbed on the eleventh anniversary of the 1929 stock market crash. Rose and Lee used to crow to each other how good they had had it during the Great Depression until October 29, 1940 ended the crowing with its own freefall. Nothing, my grandma saw, was more relentless than the calendar.

CHAPTER THREE
The Late Corpse

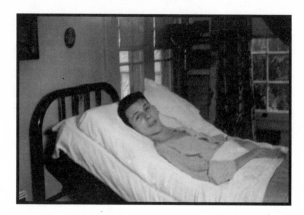

Normalouise and Mary Georgine prodded open the door to Gordon's hospital room and steeled themselves. They had waited for what seemed like months for permission to visit their friend. Now, in the corridor of the biggest hospital in the state, in a ward lined with the paralyzed and the brain-damaged, the two hoopskirt-clad tenth-graders were unsure whether to stay or hightail it out of there. L.A. County General was a forbidding place for the healthy.

The Gordy they remembered had swiped ice cream cups by the armful at church parties to please them. He dared them into the scariest seat on the beach roller coaster, the first seat, and reveled in their white-knuckle yips. When he was out of money, he wasn't below shoplifting a Hershey bar, or doing a little street conning to get two-bits in his pocket. How he committed these wrongs almost said as much about him. If a prank fell apart, Gordon refused to disclose the names of his co-conspirators.

He was noble about his crimes, never wilting under pressure if a shopkeeper threatened to phone the police because all the blame sagged on him. He'd act contrite, say what the grownups wanted:

"It'll never happen again, sir, I promise." Twenty minutes later, he'd be making faces in storefront windows and doing as he wished. Making the girls laugh was one of his specialties. Female attention was getting to be as tasty as chocolate. Normalouise was blue-eyed mischief; Mary Georgine creamy beauty. He let them tie a chain around his leg knowing they giggled hysterically when he dropped down on all fours and panted like their pet schnauzer. The three of them hiked. They cooked beans on open campfires They talked adult matters under magnificent stars, speculating on the people they'd become. The tomboyish girls were so crazy about Gordon they set him up with a Monrovia cheerleader a full grade ahead of him. Being precocious sure opened doors.

Well, the Gordy they discovered at County General had his arms and legs strapped down by thick, leather bands. A series of tubes rising from the tile disappeared under a sheet, headed presumably for his privates. There was a ventilator along the wall, comic books on a table and a morphine drip near the bed. Just seeing all the weight he had shed made them wince, because he'd been a beanpole since they'd met him.

The two girls understood traveling in from Sierra Madre they had to brace themselves for this shock. The newspaper stories told them they should. Gordon's fall had ballooned from small-town catastrophe into a major news story that shared front-page space with Nazis and school bond measures. BOY, 14, CRITICALLY HURT IN LEAP OVER GYM HORSE was the headline in the *Pasadena Post*. GYM ACCIDENT MAY CAUSE BOY'S DEATH, shouted the *Sierra Madre News*.

The worst was his head, his shish-kabob head. Metal pins a quarter-inch in diameter were harpooned into little shaved squares above his ears to pre-empt any movement from the neck up, because a twitch could be fatal. Whether he ever might be able to move anything voluntarily was a point of debate among doctors.

His visitors had their own reference marker. Just a few months earlier, after catching his reflection in a cigar shop window, Gordon had nattered on about having his protruding ears pinned back surgically once he turned eighteen. You couldn't lead the life he wanted to, he said, looking like Bambi's cousin. And taping them back didn't work—he'd tried. County General's pins were a savage contrast to this vanity. The pins connected from his head to several overhead wires strung through a pulley, which were counter-weighted by a set of miniature sandbags. Exactly how this traction gadgetry worked stumped the girls, but it didn't seem to either of them that a human being should be latched up in the middle. His brown, almond-shaped eyes were his only recognizable feature.

"So, there's nothing we can bring you? Just a milkshake from Burt's?" said Normalouise. "We could pick up a cheeseburger, double pickles."

"Just the shake. I can't have any solids yet, remember?"

"Oops, I forgot."

"Do me a favor, will ya? Lean over the bed so I can see you. These pins in me only let me look up." Both girls shuffled closer.

"If it isn't Mary Georgine. What's shaking?"

"Oh, Gordy, I don't know what to say."

"Sure you do."

"No, I don't. I feel terrible about what's happened. I still can't believe it—you're just a kid." She sobbed for a minute, breaking her hallway pledge to Normalouise not to cry. "Guess it doesn't help nobody can stop talking about it."

"Let 'em, Mary. We'll hear what they say when I walk out of here."

"See," said Normalouise. "I told you he'd be the same old Gordy." She grabbed a tissue from the wall dispenser and handed it to Mary. "Those doctors must be fixing you up swell."

"Depends," said Gordon.

"On what?"

"On which doctors you're talking about."

"You got more than one?"

"Do I. Hey, can you give me some water from that glass next to me?" Normalouise held a straw to his chapped lips.

"That enough?"

"Better. Thanks."

"Now what about your doctors?"

"You really want to hear this junk?"

"Ding dong. Of course we do. Nothing new is happening in town."

"But what about Halloween? You raise any good hell?"

"You have a one-track mind, you know that."

"Just tell me you blew up one pumpkin, Mr. Long's I hope."

"Without you, never. Now come on. What gives?"

"Since you're the first friendly faces I've seen, I'll tell you. But you have to swear not a word to anybody. Okay? That goes double for my parents."

"Promise."

"You too, Mary?"

"I won't tell," she sniffed.

"All right. When I got here, what a month ago, the doctors thought I was in pretty bad shape."

"They said that?" said Normalouise.

"Not to my face, but I could tell from how everyone acted." Gordon's voice got weak, so he closed his eyes and swallowed until his wind came back. "My dad, you know how he gets. He wanted a second opinion. So, my uncle Sonny, he flew out these doctors from New York to examine me. Supposed to be a couple hotshot back specialists."

"What'd they say?"

"Nothing. Nothing new, anyway."

"What do you mean?"

"One night the hotshots came into my room and talked when the nurses weren't around. They thought I was asleep. But I tricked 'em. I heard every word."

"And?"

"And they didn't think my body could handle it. That's what they said in a lot of fancy words. They gave me a two percent."

"Two percent of what?"

"Of living, dope. Ain't you listening?"

"Jesus," Normalouise said louder than she intended. "What happened next?"

"Beats me. I never saw them again. Guess they flew back to New York. I don't think there's much they could do."

"So that's it. You lay around all day with these things in your head?"

"Yeah, but once I can I'm gonna make the doctors eat their words. I've been thinking about this for a while. I'm gonna get out of this stupid bed. Then I'm gonna walk right down the middle of Sierra Madre Boulevard and start directing traffic. Next Halloween we'll hit the whole town."

"But what about what they said? I'd be crying my eyes out if they told me I was going to die." Normalouise looked up at the traction pulleys, then down. "Damn, Gordy. That didn't come out like I meant."

"That's okay. I've decided something. I don't believe in death. And if you don't believe in it, it can't hurt ya, can it?"

"Geez."

"Some of that Bible stuff my mom made me sit through must've sunk in. Bet you never thought you'd hear *me* say that."

"No kidding."

"Can I tell ya another secret?"

"Not if it's as big as the last one," Normalouise said with a puckered smile.

"I do cry. Lots. I just do it at night. That way nobody sees."

The girls stayed another half an hour thinking Gordon was better off than his head appeared. Out in the hallway, they surveyed where they were again, and despair socked them. Both of them wept until a nurse walked over with tissues.

As November 1940 wore on, the doctors were flummoxed. Medical-journal stories may have been planned, bets lost. Gordon, inexplicably, was alive. Almost all the specialists and the majority of literature predicted he would be gone by now. Too much havoc was stacked against him. A battered spinal column garbles the brain's instructions to muscles and organs the body needs not just to move limbs but to draw oxygen, metabolize food, circulate blood and manifold electro-chemical tasks in between. Spinal nerves are the body's equivalent of a master switchboard. The higher up the damage, the more the circuitry below it crashes. The difference here: conventional wisdom is about expectations for the average. Gordon's resolve to lie there staring at the ceiling because that's all he could stare at, grinding his teeth and urging himself to gut it out through another County General night, was the area that the doctors with all their marvelous statistical grimness could never chart.

Nonetheless, loops of complications, from seizures to infections, wracked his thinning body. There was no ducking that, no matter the staff's awe for the "Zahler kid's grit." Around Thanksgiving, Gordon was about to have his biggest setback. Near his cervical cord, bone fragments bobbed in spinal fluid and the doctors were anxious to monitor their position to keep swelling down.

So one morning, a nurse disconnected the traction tongs from his head. A milquetoast orderly with slicked-back red hair took over from there. His job was to transport Gordon in his bed-on-wheels to a lower floor for a fresh set of x-rays. Inside the elevator on the way there, Gordon made small talk with the man, who had tended him before, about one of the cranky head nurses known for snapping: "I'm telling, not asking."

The cab had lumbered only halfway to its destination when the small talk ceased. With no warning, the boy couldn't speak anymore. His chest began seizing. His breathing turned shallow. Soon no air was being sucked into his lungs. Every time he clenched his jaw and inhaled, nothing happened except a shrill gasp. His lips shaded blue. It seems the nerves that regulate chest muscles in charge of breathing had picked this location, floors away from the ventilator, to conk out. When the cab doors parted, the orderly yelled, "Help!" Gordon was asphyxiating in his rolling bed.

My uncle surely would have suffocated if dumb luck had not been there to rescue him. The dumb luck in this case was stocky, balding, Iowa-bred and, for no valid reason, loitering in front of the elevator when it opened. Joe Risser, orthopedic surgeon, remembered his trauma training from medical school. White lab coat fluffing behind him, he and the orderly hurried Gordon from his bed into an iron lung, a polished metal cylinder that uses pressure changes to help the incapacitated breathe. It was providence the machine, which resembled a barbeque smoker, was even there. Between it and Dr. Risser, my uncle's life was saved.

Or what was left of it. The tungsten-strong spirit that had amazed the nurses and tore at his parents recoiled into itself after his respiratory arrest. Stuck in traction, reattached to the ventilator, Gordon recognized for the first time how far his broken neck had thrown him from everyday existence.

There is a reaction daisy-chain people like him go through when they are ripped from the lush, tactile world to one where limbs don't work and dependence is absolute. The injury shoves them through dungeons of fear, denial, rage, and gloom. Suicidal thoughts preposterous to them in their walking days become a tempting exit. After first sticking his tongue out at his prognosis, Gordon must have contemplated asking someone to kill him with a pillow over the head.

He was smart enough to know the extent of his injury. Paraplegics have use of their hands, which equates to some self-sufficiency. He would never scratch his nose on his best day. His parents tried to convince him the breathing incident was a one-time event. Try as they did, the hurt rising out of his facial expressions let them know he didn't give a rat's ass.

Around County General, the graveyard shift was the worst time to be wallowing in one of these funks. The screams and Code Blues resonated across the ward, and the nurses were always interrupting your sleep to check some inconsequential thing or another. It was on one of these night shifts that Dr. Risser slipped into Gordon's room and squeezed down into a visitor's chair. He told the nurse stationed there as part of the boy's round-the-clock care to stretch her legs, have a smoke. Joe Risser was not Gordon's primary doctor when he invited himself in. The two probably had not even spoken since

Gordon was unconscious entering the iron lung and on the respirator for days afterwards.

In the half-darkness, the orthopedic man clicked on his pocket flashlight and reviewed my uncle's thick chart word by hopeless word. Moonbeams splashing the window helped him trace the x-rays. It took half an hour for him to catch up. Once he knew everything he needed to, he did something no other physician had. He placed the palm of his right hand on my uncle's forehead, resting it there as if it belonged there. From the doctor's fingertips, a cathartic glow warmed Gordon's body, which had been dead to the touch below the collarbone but couldn't miss this. Where needles, washrags and bandages failed, the Iowan succeeded. He made the boy feel, be it by magic or fluke. "Gordon," he said firmly, "listen to me. It doesn't matter what anyone else here tells you. Okay? It's all hooey. You're going to make it. I'm positive about it." The boy had no reason to believe him. He just did.

Tear ducts run dry, my grandparents had to think about money. Circumstance dictated it. Their son could still feel nothing below his neck five weeks after his spill and counting. No one at the hospital could tell them how long he would be in "Chinese Water Torture," Gordon's sarcastic nickname for his traction contraption. There was no predicting if his endurance signaled a long shot recovery or the flicker before his terminal-prognosis took. Most days his room felt like a disinfected battleground, other times a holding room for the funeral parlor. The only constant was the math. Everything at County General cost triple its street worth.

My grandpa, I'm sure, initially figured he could handle the bills clogging the mailbox. After all, the walls of his dingy, firetrap office on Santa Monica Boulevard were stacked two-feet high with the scores he had produced for the studios over eleven years. Since his debut as a film composer, hundreds of songs had migrated from his head, through the recording-booth glass into the theaters.

It mattered little to him that classical musicians, the ones scoring for Broadway plays and operas, viewed Hollywood songwriters as sellout hacks. Knocking out songs week after week was how independent composers like him made it, and Lee was prolific if still anonymous compared to Warner Bros' famous Max Steiner. Often, inspiration struck Lee in his Ford driving in from Sierra Madre. He would scribble notes at the stoplights, tapping out beats on the steering wheel until someone honked at him to get moving. His office was in a dumpy section of western Hollywood ridiculed as "Poverty Row" by the major studios because of the area's concentration of second-rate production outfits.

Until his son was hurt, that nickname had always felt more artsy than prophetic to my grandpa. He could afford to be philosophical. From 1937 to 1939, Lee had pocketed seventy-five hundred dollars, a handsome take-home for the era, plus cash under the table. It had been enough to fantasize about a decent retirement, maybe a round-the-world-trip for Rose and him before their arthritis set in.

Not anymore. The hospital invoices on his rollaway desk threatened to eradicate the nest egg he had built up, five dollars here, a couple bucks there. There was no health insurance then, no five-figure bank account or rich relative to tap into. Every day Gordon remained in acute care in the neuro-surgery ward scraped $4.61 off Lee's net worth. Gordon also had been in surgery twice and the plaster room three times for mini-casts. The x-ray department had photographed him on a half dozen trips at $13 a pop. The double nursing shifts cost Lee another $6 per day. While Rose's brother, Nat Ross, Mr. Perfect, had paid for the New York specialists, Gordon's two L.A. doctors (Rudolph Marx and W.W. Worster) were sticklers about collection. Poverty Row was sounding more accurate by the minute.

Six weeks after Gordon was injured, Lee had to inform Rose that their Mountain Trail house, the rental they had hoped of buying, was too pricey to lease anymore. Accessories to the good life went overboard next. Barnaby, the live-in cook who baked lemon pies my mother never tired of, was released. Sunday-night dinners out were suspended. Grandpa wanted to conserve every nickel, and if that meant they had to relocate from that spacious home with its wraparound porch and fragrant breezes to maintain emergency cash in the bank, so be it.

Rose, deferring to her nature, submitted without complaint. The way she saw it, her affection for the house, her interest in anything material, be it jewelry or calfskin books, were expendable wishes not worth mourning compared to family finances. As long as they had decent shelter, she was fine, which is why she supervised the packing with gusto, happy for the diversion. Their new place on East Laurel Avenue, a two-story Cape Cod with a latticework arch, was considerably smaller than where they'd come from. Still, its low rent made for prudent budgeting given the $1,000 they had already paid County General. Rose could do that subtraction.

As for Lee, the bad days came in bunches, as did the humiliations. One Wednesday after work found him punching his Ford toward The Motion Picture Relief Fund a few miles away on Santa Monica Boulevard. The Fund, originated in 1921 as a PR gimmick to soften Hollywood's wanton reputation among lawmakers and Bible Belt types, by 1940 had evolved into a legitimate, private welfare agency for show-biz-employed families. My grandfather's elegant writing reached its application form on December 3, and the executive action committee approved his request the very next day. That settled that—Gordon could afford his nurses. And his forty-seven-year-old father accepted the charity by slapping a binding condition on it. It would be a loan, he assured the Fund men, because he considered handouts for bums.

The Zahler house phone nearly shorted out its wiring, the ringing was that constant. Relatives, friends, musicians, neighbors, church-mates, pump jockeys—the condolences were dialed in and delivered. Between them and the newspaper coverage, a sort of vapor cloud shadowed my grandparents when they puttered down Sierra Madre Boulevard in their green swayback two-door.

But one phone conversation between them and a hard-charging lawyer from downtown L.A.'s commercial core stood out from the usual condolence calls. Maurice Rose was a cousin of my grandma and a person who would not normally bother calling. Maurice had met Lee at a family picnic near Griffith Park some years back. He knew my grandpa regarded attorneys in the same snake-in-the-grass ilk as traveling salesmen and carpet bagging politicians. Actually, everyone in the family had heard Lee's unkind opinion of "shysters" because he dealt with so many of their smarmy kind through the studios. With Gordon like this and him feeling half-dead himself, that belief, as did so many others, gave way to hardboiled pragmatism. When the lawyer phoned to extend his sympathies, Lee had loads to ask him about their options.

What choice did they have? When the Zahlers first pondered how they would make it financially if Gordon survived, shouldering the entire burden themselves was the end of the thinking. Their child, their tragedy, their dime. Not that Rose and Lee had forgiven Coach Turner. By his decision-making that October morning, he had deemed foot fungus more treacherous than letting a group of junior-high boys police themselves around the acrobatic gear. Turner, the supposed disciplinarian, had snubbed common sense. Look at the results.

As much as my grandpa fantasized about giving him a what-for and popping him in the nose, there was a reason he refrained. He and my grandma both understood the coach's misjudgment didn't undercut a more fundamental truth: this outcome was primarily Gordon's doing. Anybody familiar with the boy's past, from the dormered windows of St. Rita's to the scaffolding above the Venice Plunge, could have predicted the odds would snare him. Turner had warned Gordon about attempting that vault. He had been scolded by any variety of people to stop talking insane risks.

Lee and Rose, no doubt, felt guilt-pocked themselves that he ignored that advice. Before everything had gone south, they had given their son a wide berth to redeem himself, sure as they were of his potential. The nuns at St. Rita's, for example, had reported his I.Q. test score at 91, nine points below the average, but his parents assumed he had tanked the exam on purpose.

Behind his impishness were intuitive smarts he rarely applied at school. Others recognized it, too. Muriel took piano lessons. Gordon took apart radios to see how fast he could reassemble them. She enrolled in tap dancing. He chauffeured an elderly neighborhood couple on a long trip from Sierra Madre to Lake Elsinore out in Riverside at the age of thirteen with his parents' okay. In the crush of hindsight, that was a mistake. They bred overconfidence in him. When authority figures wagged their fingers in his face about spitballs or sneaking out, he was bound to disobey them. His sense of impunity passed through his folks. They should have reprimanded him so severely for his St. Rita's expulsion that he never would have dreamt of misbehaving again. Seeing these roots, my grandparents tried to be levelheaded about blame. By disregarding the coach's warnings, Gordon had boxed them in. Their child, their tragedy, their dime: that encapsulated their thinking at first.

Once the shock wore off, so did some of their naïveté. They discovered the accident was more complicated than an unfortunate trip-and-fall that school administrators portrayed when they visited County General, bouquets in hand. Somehow, maybe by quizzing one of Gordon's pals who were present when he got hurt, Lee became suspicious that Marshall also was culpable, and those suspicions gestated into fiery hunches. In no time he hired Maurice Rose, Spring Street shyster, to represent them.

The deep pockets of the Pasadena Board of Education were the target. Reconstructing the state of the gym the morning of the spill was how they intended to reach into them. For days, Maurice and his junior lawyers dredged Marshall's white, Spanish-stucco campus for evidence. They inspected the springboard and the vaulting horse and scoured maintenance logs by the carton. They cased the gym. They recorded Turner's deposition and that of his boss. They interviewed doctors Marx and Worster, a few of the Tarzans and Gordon, who told what he remembered laying flat. Evidence accumulated. When the school district's lawyer tried to have the complaint thrown out in pre-trial motions, Maurice bragged about how he squashed it with an "elaborate" brief.

~~~

For my grandma, the lawsuit was about survival cash, not vengeance. Whose justice was served, she asked, when a ninth grader is required by statute to hear the specifics of his abbreviated future? Maurice, swaying in his brass-appointed suite, tried explaining it was how the system worked. Rose cut him off. It wasn't Gordon sanctioning the action being brought on his behalf, she said, that put her in knots. She realized they were asking for a vault-full of money. It was her son understanding the harshness of his prognosis that twisted her up.

From the time he'd awoken at County General, she'd appointed herself the sentinel for the medical terms used in his presence. Doctors, nurses and visitors got Rose's slashing forefinger as she set down her rules in hallway briefings. Nomenclature like "quadriplegia" and "cripple" were never to be used, she'd say. Don't mention "permanent."

Now those facts had other outlets. California law mandated Gordon hear the damages before the case was filed, and doing that would tear off the protective sheathing his mother had painstakingly woven for him. It was all misguided. So when Rose finally told her son what the law said she had to, she reminded him from beginning to end not to take any of it to heart because lawyers exaggerate for a living. Nevertheless, he learned real substance from the civil complaint.

Learned he had no bladder or bowel control and never would. Learned that his limbs were useless appendages despite the phantom feelings that inspired secret hopes. Capping that, he found out his education was finished, that he was unfit for any employment, and that he'd remain a helpless, "permanent cripple" for the little time he had left.

Grandma, more than her husband, understood money wasn't justice. The $200,000 they sought from the school district would barely buy them peace. It certainly couldn't make Gordon whole.

Their case against Marshall went to the court clerk two days after a nominal Christmas. In better years, Rose would cook a sumptuous Christmas Eve dinner trimmed with exotic side dishes. Lee, bolting early from work, would tinkle holiday standards on his Baldwin piano. Before bed, he liked tantalizing Muriel and Gordon by having them add an extra layer of wrapping to their *own* presents. To crank the excitement, the tree wasn't decorated until that night. Lee, the agnostic, didn't believe in Jesus. He simply absorbed the joy the Christ-child's birthday produced, or used to. Christmas-day 1940 was mostly spent in the acute-care ward of County General, where the gift exchange was as flat as everyone's complexion. At their new Sierra Madre residence, Lee's piano was silent.

The lawsuit caused the real racket. Suing a school district for $200,000 was an eye-opener in pre-war America. The dollars sought were huge, multiple millions by today's standards. It also offered slim chance of success, whatever Maurice's braggadocio. School lawyers routinely blocked negligence suits then by waving the immunity statutes Congress and state legislatures had granted them. The basic idea was that "the king can do no wrong," the king being any government agency too integral to the common good to be easily sued. The Zahler suit was hot news however you cut it. "BIG DAMAGES ASKED FOR INJURED BOY," one newspaper announced.

Damages indeed. The charges sounded grave, just as Maurice designed. He claimed that Marshall had endangered Gordon by permitting someone of his "tender age" access to such dangerous apparatus without supervision. The school, he alleged, compounded their error by allowing him to leap off a worn springboard that should have been in the garbage dumpster. Despite supposed repairs, the jumping device lacked side supports because the original ones split wide from over-use. Un-braced, the springboard sagged, Maurice asserted, as did his client's flight path.

The same lethal disregard also enabled students to drape the pommel horse with matting that school employees should have recognized was easily tripped over. Careless thinking, he said, allowed the sharp, metal turnbuckle anchoring the high-bar to the floor to be positioned in the wrong spot, too. Set within feet of the pommel horse landing area, the turnbuckle had no give when my uncle's right calf ripped in it. He had flown two feet off course when there was no room for error.

These blunders set the stage for Maurice's evidentiary bombshell. He revealed that a Marshall staff member had raised the height of the pommel horse by ten inches—a quantum change—without notifying anyone first. Why the boys hadn't noticed the adjustment before or after Gordon broke his neck wasn't clear. Hand it to Maurice for uncovering that one.

Louis Vincenti of Hahn and Hahn, the blueblood Pasadena law firm retained by the school district, contested every allegation Maurice leveled. Two-hundred-grand was a gigantic sum likely to tempt others to sue. A message had to be sent not to even attempt it. In his formal responses, the owlish-looking, Stanford-educated Vincenti said to disregard the springboard and the rest of the gym equipment. They were in working order that day. Turner, he said, was not responsible, either. The physical education class he taught had not officially begun when my uncle crashed, and the school district had immunity against most employee mistakes anyway. To every cause of action Maurice outlined, Vincenti typed a single rejoinder. Gordon's "negligence and carelessness...for his own care" were to blame. With that, Vincenti basically dared Maurice to prove otherwise to a jury.

CHAPTER FOUR
Rich Relations

Rose should've expected that her rapscallion son someday would stick her on the blunt end of another raw deal. From childhood onward, her life was steered by duty and curbed by loss. Gordon merely continued the trend.

My grandma was born in San Francisco in 1900 as the first child of Maurice and Sonya "Dearie" Rossman. Robert Rossman, Maurice's father, had immigrated from Eastern Europe in 1876 as a newly married man with some family money in his pocket and substantial ambitions in his soul. He'd come to the West Coast to manufacture his own wealth, and manufacture he would. Using guile and grunt labor, he became a prominent Bay Area industrialist with interests in steel and textile factories.

Robert's sons, once they were grown, wasted little time parlaying their father's fortune, diversifying into restaurant ownership and second-rate apartment houses during the 1920s and 1930s. The profits ensconced everybody into black-tie wealth. One son, sizing up their corporate holdings at a family shindig, reportedly proclaimed, "Look at us. We own San Francisco!" Noveau riche elitists, they scoffed at Dearie as a peasant girl from backwater Russia unworthy of taking the Rossman name or Maurice's seed. They were so rankled that Maurice had married her against their stern protestations that they froze him out of family bank accounts.

They kept their noses up in the air about it, too. When the Great San Francisco Earthquake of 1906 slammed the region, Maurice had to leap off the front stoop with a baby son in his arms because the walls of his Oakland house were collapsing behind him. The quake left Maurice's family homeless and his millionaire relatives unfazed about his plight. They refused to give him emergency money to get himself on his feet. Out of options, twenty-seven-year-old Maurice collected Dearie, his six-year-old daughter Rose and two young boys, hauling them to Golden Gate Park. There, they resided for a whole year with thousands of others indigents in a tent city amid the damp nights and open sewers.

Hoping for brighter days, Maurice scooped his family out of the tent and pointed them toward Texas, where opportunities bade him. By 1915, their revival was complete in El Paso, a hopping border town near Juarez, Mexico. Maurice, a savvy merchant faithful to commerce and good times, had found his place. It'd been one of his brothers who'd invited him here to sell merchandise and used goods wholesale with him.

Then one February afternoon a stranger popped into the Rossman store at First and Ochoa streets. "Red" Mullen seemed an engaging young man with a tempting proposition. He offered to drive Maurice to a wooded clearing nearby so Maurice could inspect the top-grade hides Red was selling on the black market. Thinking supply line, Maurice told his clerks he would be back in fifteen minutes. He never returned. Trench diggers working along an irrigation ditch came across his buried corpse four days later. Dearie probably would have been dispatched to a Texas insane asylum had she not had young ones to tend to, her loss was that seismic. Because she was a mother with only meager savings, she didn't dare give up. Neither could she go it alone. Dearie was a busty number still in her twenties with the gorgeous face and effervescent personality that had attracted Maurice. She just had no skills to earn a living. None. The only route that made sense was for her to herd her kids to San Francisco and beg the Rossmans for sympathy. Out West, however, it was the same as before. Her in-laws were aristocratic cheapskates reluctant to show mercy to someone with her mongrel bloodline. Again, Dearie reversed field, this time moving her kids clear across the continent to New York City.

If anyone understood survival, Dearie's older brother Alexander Carr did. Carr had been an unwashed kid from Czarist Russia when he'd immigrated to America. For his first years stateside, he lived as a hobo hopping East Coast freight trains. Burned out being a vagabond, he sawed off the Semitic part of his surname (Karchefsky to Carr) and taught himself to be a traveling circus clown. From the circus tent he jumped to Vaudeville and from Vaudeville to Broadway. There, Carr refined his acting skills until he won the lead in the play *Wine, Women and Song*, which also summarized his after-hour hobbies. (Later, his Yiddish performance in *Potash and Perlmutter* won him a Hollywood movie contract.)

Uncle Alex maintained the same foghorn voice and flamboyant manner offstage as he did on, but he wasn't about to let his sister and her brood go under. He paid their rent for a cramped apartment in Brooklyn, where Dearie and her three kids shared the same bed. He showed them the sites of Manhattan, his luxury Fifth Avenue apartment top of the list..

In Brooklyn, Dearie didn't work and never dated. Mothering alone exhausted her. Despondent about her husband's killing, she sank into early widowhood growing fat, lazy, and loopy. The children handled it better. Harold, her youngest, attended public school. Nat, his thirteen-year-old brother, did too, until he sweet talked Dearie into letting him quit junior high for an entry-level job in the New York picture business. A theater-chain owner named Stanley Mastbaum had offered to pay him a few dollars a week if he sat in Mastbaum movie palaces charting audience reaction to what they saw on the screen. Dearie had to say yes for the precious dollars it would generate. Rose was the oldest child, and she excelled at school, burning through every book she could check out at the Brooklyn public library. Her mind was nimbler than Dearie's, her spirit more independent. Indeed, when Rose described the gallant Lee Zahler to her, it was as if she were telling a sister rather than her guardian.

Lee was the older brother of Rose's best friend and hardly your typical Brooklyn loudmouth. He was mature for his age. His smoldering blue eyes and his impatient shuffling on his heels broadcast aspiration. Two passions seemed to rage in him as he bumped around the Brooklyn tenements in a tweed beret. He drooled for the Dodgers to win the World Series while he cheered in the beer-soaked bleachers at Ebbetts Field. Even more, he was determined to mine his talents better than his father had advanced his.

Joseph Zahler, Lee's dad and my great-grandfather, descended from a line of affluent gentlemen farmers who had hoed the fields near Budapest, Hungary for eons. Magda Zahler, one of Europe's marquis stage dancers in the late 1900s, came from their fold. Star that she was, Joseph was expected to make everyone forget prancing Magda. He was a child prodigy who spoke and wrote five languages before he reached twenty. At the University of Budapest medical school, he hardly broke a sweat. He wasn't much physically—his pencil mustache couldn't distract from his girly lips and premature balding—but his I.Q. afforded him stature. Many educated sorts were convinced he would be the finest doctor ever to practice along the Danube River. After he wed a striking stage actress named Anna, Joseph's superior life seemed like easy destiny.

All that preceded the Austro-Hungarian draft being announced. Joseph was a pacifist who refused to join the army. He was training to heal people, he said, not bayonet them. Uncertain what to do, his parents shipped him, Anna, and their young children on a hastily arranged vacation to America. Upon his return the Hungarian military decided to make an example out of him as a rich kid shirking his patriotic duty. They threw him in prison and that is where he stayed. His parents, dignified people interested in the arts, ultimately had to bribe a pair of jailhouse officials to spring him. Afterwards they hustled Joseph and his family onto a steamship bound for New York City. The superior European life they had mapped for him had been gored by the draft.

In America, Joseph's quest to be a physician worthy of his celebrated mind died within a week. An officious bureaucrat either at Ellis Island or New York City Hall informed him that his medical degree was meaningless here. The United States had more exacting academic standards than European schools, the clerk said; Joseph's only recourse was to start over medical school from scratch. It'd be six years before he could see patients. Screaming across a government counter, Joseph said he already had his diploma. He would rather do manual labor than bow down to such Yankee arrogance. He got his wish in the years that followed.

Lee, once he was old enough to understand, resolved not to let a clerk stomp his dreams. He was born on August 14, 1893 as Leo Arthur Zahler, and brought home to 330 E. Houston Street in New York City. While there's evidence that part of his schooling was European, the assignments came as effortlessly for him as they had for his father. The teachers who skipped Lee ahead believed he was a shoe-in to get into medical school if he wanted it. Joseph may have pushed this option for a little while. Nonetheless, it was his dream, not his son's.

Lee instead dove headlong into music, his love, learning to read it, honing his scales, practicing tempo and imitating his idol, George Gershwin. His first professional gig was as a pianist in New York's swarming Nickelodeons. The flickering images of cowboys and sheiks projected onto the walls delighted the crowds, which wondered, "What will they think of next?" Scant attention was paid to the ghostly-blonde kid in the corner banging out the accompanying Ragtime ditties. He was part of the novelty. In the dawn of American cinema, my grandfather endured roaches, drunks, tobacco clouds, cheap pianos and cheaper wages to wrest his own tiny share. His years of slave accompaniment paid off. Music publishers along New York's Tin Pan Alley, in need of catchy movie tunes they could sell as sheet music, hired Lee and other young talents to compose at a factory-like clip. It was about then my grandpa, the son of a frustrated prodigy, met his Brooklyn Rose.

Their love pivoted on camaraderie and worldviews more than animal lust. Lee was certainly the better looking of the two. He was fair-skinned, bordering on albino, with prematurely white hair that he dyed blonde, then parted painstakingly down the middle. In winters, he wore a black cloth trench coat that advertised his sharp features and minimized his 5′ 8″ stockiness. Gordon, had he not taken that swan dive, would've been much lankier. Lee's head was oval, his shoulders square. To see him in pictures as a teenager knocking around Coney Island with his goofball pals boggles, for my grandfather seemed to have been born with a middle-age stubble. By his early twenties, almost every photograph of him depicts a serious-as-nails young man never without his Fedora. Rose, conversely, had inherited her mother's thick limbs and trunk, not her glamorous, high cheekbones. There was a manliness about my grandma's face, especially in the wide nose, and dowdiness in the plain, wooly dresses tugged up to her neck. When she smiled for the camera, it caught an overbite and the guarded eyes of a wallflower. Her inner grit may have been her sexiest trait.

In marrying Rose, six years his junior, Lee wed a young woman fleeing her Jewish heritage. The borough where Rose and her brothers had lived boiled in anti-immigrant hostility for people from Irish and Eastern European backgrounds. Older Jews were taunted as "Christ-killers, " the younger ones often beaten or spit on. Dearie's clan had had it bad enough growing up fatherless, poor and unwanted. To remove the Hebrew stigma from their load, they all officially dropped the "man" off their last name. *Voila*: Rossman became Ross. Rose Ross took it one further. She renounced her native religion, Judaism, which she didn't practice, for Christian Science, in which she submerged herself. Lee himself was born a Jew, but lived as an agnostic, often grumpily when Rose tugged out her New Testament Bible. My own parents would fall into that same stupefying mold.

After their 1920 wedding, Lee and Rose honeymooned by an East Coast lake. The next year they had a chipmunk-faced baby girl, my mom, Muriel Bernice. The year after that Lee sold his Model-T and hoisted his family on a sleeper train to Los Angeles. Dozens of Tin Pan Alley composers were picking up for "Hollywoodland." People said it was seventy degrees year round out there. They said musicians could make real money writing music played live with the "silent" pictures. Lee, inspired by the Nickelodeons, assumed that's where his meal ticket was.

He settled the family into a comfortable, stucco house in mid-city Los Angeles. Carthay Circle would later be part of the city's "Miracle Mile," the place to live between downtown and the Westside. In the 1920s, there was nothing miraculous about the flatland. It was a spray of tidy single-family houses surrounded by citrus orchards and gurgling oil derricks, proximate to Hollywood and that's about all. Lee's parents, sick of the East, soon joined him. They colonized their son's backyard guesthouse, and that's where they would spend their last years before they both died of bronchial pneumonia prior to World War II. Anna cooked fatty meals to kill time. Joseph, wiry and bald as a Q-tip, indulged his homesickness for Budapest. He and my grandfather passionately bickered in their homeland tongue over which country was nobler, Hungary or America, and Lee would remind his dad there was a boat leaving weekly for the Adriatic Sea if he cared to board it. One thing was indisputable: California flattered Rose. Now a wife and mother, she appeared a different woman than her pudgy former self. She'd shed a good twenty five pounds, cut her wavy hair fashionably short and smiled pretty in pictures, a wallflower no more.

Just after suppertime on February 10, 1926, Rose gave birth to my uncle at Hollywood's Benedict Maternity Hospital. With his first gulp of air, the Zahlers had the configuration they'd wanted: a girl and a baby boy growing up in a town thick with sunny possibility. Gordon Robert in a wink morphed from a curly-haired toddler with his arms around a pet collie into a pixie-eared little kid into everything he shouldn't be. At eleven, he'd already closed the height gap with my mom. His dad, spiffy in an argyle vest and knickers, enjoyed telling studio colleagues that his boy was sprouting a ballplayer's physique. "Yep," he'd say, "those legs are going to take Gordon far."

Or, Lee might've added, as far as his son's asthma allowed. Gordon's wheezing attacks occurred at night, convulsing his lungs, then his whole body, and then the entire family's sleep patterns. They needed remedies, and the doctors suggested that Gordon live in a climate dryer than even the mid-city plains of Los Angeles. Pacific

Ocean fog rolling in from the coast often seeped through the windows, and the little boy's mushy bronchial tubes shook red with inflammation. Alternative homesteads for him included Lake Arrowhead to the east, Lake Tahoe up north, Palm Springs to the southeast and furnace-hot Arizona below that. The nearest candidate was a mountain community more concept than authentic town. Not much nightlife, the doctors warned, but the cathartic air of Sierra Madre had helped others in respiratory distress. Lee, in no mood to restart his career as a resort lounge lizard, said point the way. What was a long trek into Hollywood everyday compared to Gordon's recovered lungs?

Take away the Starbucks and BMWs, add a cigar factory and train tracks, and the Sierra Madre of forty years ago is pretty much the quirky boondocks that remain today. Then as today, there is no traffic stoplight and a single gas station. Willowy Kirsten Court remains the town's axis, a good place to feel the cool shadows from the knuckled San Gabriels. Santa Anita Racetrack, where Seabiscuit would win the Handicap in '40, stands a few blocks south in Arcadia. Only Pasadena, with its much bigger population to the west, openly scoffed at Sierra Madre as backwater municipality. Just as today, Pasadena was renowned for her symphony and fabulously rich, the Tournament of Roses Parade and the county's best bowl game. Sierra Madre's civic jewels were a Wisteria vine festival and a cluster of tuberculosis sanitariums.

Oh, were Sierra Madrans proud of the comparison. They lived on juicy plots originally swiped from the Indians, cleared by the Franciscans and deeded over by the Mexican government. In the 1880s, much of the land was snapped up and subdivided, mainly by rancher Elijah "Lucky" Baldwin and the Southern Pacific Railroad. Property sales boomed in the years that followed. Rows of quaint Victorians and three-bedroom clapboards sprouted along magnolia-lined streets that took their time adding gas lamps. Above their rooflines sat vast stone canyons and the piney outer stubble of the Angeles National Forest. Up there, emerald-green mountain creeks could lure the most prudish in for a skinny dip. Coyotes and raccoons weren't shy about padding into the city during summers, either. Overall, living on the front porch of the San Gabriels was one charmed existence. People could take what they needed from nature—land, recreation—without succumbing to its extremes.

Sierra Madre's founder was a Massachusetts native named Nathaniel Carter who wrote shameless promotional pamphlets to recruit people in from the East. "It contains almost everything that mortal man would desire," Carter wrote of his discovery. Roses. Heliotrope. Hiking. Climate. Serenity. Commerce. And all only a trolley ride from the rising West Coast metropolis. Intrigued by Carter's pamphlets, the curious came: New Englanders pasty from waiting out the snow months; Midwesterners enchanted that a Kansas-like town could be found in the rich California loam. Director D.W. Griffith himself was so infatuated with Sierra Madre that he established his first California production office there. When he later relocated to Hollywood, the citizenry shrugged. They would take tranquility over notoriety any day. My grandparents never wanted to leave.

CHAPTER FIVE
Happiness C.O.D.

The nurses had heard the abuse from the other spinal-cord patients. How they were a bunch of "motherfucking Nurse Nightingales." Which of their own orifices they could shove the thermometers they brandished night and day. The veteran white-hats reminded the rookie nurses not to take the comments personally, for their floor was lined with young men paralyzed for life. It had been boozy three a.m. car wrecks or diving accidents or more ludicrous misfortunes that had stolen their legs. After a few months at County General riding out complications, many of them decayed into the sullenest of people.

Like them, Gordon's body was a hothouse for infections. Between his bladder and his kidneys, there had been five acute infections, several of which flicked his temperature above 105°F. Still, when the nurses checked on him, it was far from their typical misanthrope of the neurology ward greeting them. No sooner had they logged in his vitals signs after he'd weathered a nasty bacterium than he was peppering them with how to get a hot-fudge sundae smuggled into the joint. The bitterness that had consumed him after

Dr. Risser slid him into the iron lung had either self-dissolved or gone on the lamb. This type of movement was unusual around here.

While Gordon's spirit barged back, his sister had little time for re-acquaintances. By March 1941, my mother, Muriel, was living in the foggy spring of San Francisco in a guest-room of the enigmatic Rossmans. Her parents had plunked down the train fare. "Don't worry, darling," they told her. "Have yourself some fun up there." Normally, my mom never would have been granted such freedom, but nothing about the last six months even approached the zip code of ordinary.

Lee and Rose realized how often Muriel had been alone at the house on Laurel, or out for the sake of it, as they wore grooves into the hospital linoleum. They saw she deserved attention from their dwindling reserves, just as they saw the Bay area as a convenient getaway from an abraded home life. With her father's slaying, Rose had firsthand experience watching family tragedy devour adolescence. Maybe a break would inoculate Muriel from that same premature aging.

My mom had her own reasons for going, and double those for not returning as scheduled. San Francisco was jubilee for any footloose twenty year old. There was tea dancing at the Mark Hopkins Hotel, drinks later at the Fairmount. Even better, she could drag in at one a.m. knowing her dad wouldn't be waiting for her at the door, eyebrows in attack mode, simmering over a blown curfew. Independence aside, it minced her visiting County General. Leaving Gordon's room, she'd know that his marble collection and models would have to be boxed up. He'd never finger them again. It made her nostalgic for their wild quarrels, where they would chase each other around the house screaming holy hell over bathroom hogging or possessions gone missing. Their last tiff had occurred about two weeks before his fall. He had caught her and a boyfriend necking in the boyfriend's Chrysler down the block, and spelled out his blackmail. Either she gave him a quarter or he'd "spill the beans to Dad."

Wasn't she entitled to some grand times on account of what he had cost her *now*? Of course she was. The annihilation of her late teens warranted some self-indulgence. Her dad had sat her down before her trip and told her before he broke the news, "how terribly sorry I am about this, Muggs," his nickname for her. "This is the last thing your mother and I wanted. The last confounded thing." His remorse derived from a broken promise. He said he had reviewed their accounts again and verified there wasn't enough money for her tuition at Pomona College, the school she and a knot of girlfriends had been accepted to as juniors for fall semester 1941. He might have been able to scratch out a semester's worth, but college was about continuity. Hard as he strove to protect their savings, he couldn't beat back Gordon's hospital bills.

Up in San Francisco, Muriel stayed with her maternal uncle, Harold Ross, and his newlywed bride at their Webster Street apartment. Unfortunately, their marriage started wobbling when their honeymoon ended, and Rose didn't want my mom around the constant snapping. So, Muriel moved in with other relatives. Being in San Francisco was what counted. Among other perks, it brought her within dating proximity of one of her favorite boyfriends. Al Altfield, a sharp kid from a moneyed L.A. family, was stationed at Ford Ord Army base in nearby Monterey. Between Al and a Rossman cousin who prowled the best bars, there were oodles to entertain her.

At Nob Hill's ritzy Stanford Court Apartments, where the Rossmans occupied an entire floor, my mom unpacked her things unaware of family history. This was the same building where her grandfather Maurice was cast out from for marrying a commoner thirty-five years earlier. Neither Dearie nor Rose had recounted that story to Muriel before she left because they thought it was wiser to let the old bitterness fade. As it ended up, my mom would learn firsthand about Rossman integrity.

She whittled some of her San Francisco time in Canasta games with her grandpa. Robert Solomon Rossman, once a strutting entrepreneur, had doddered into his eighties without his wife of fifty-eight years or barely any teeth. Nevertheless, corncob pipe in mouth, he would regale my mom every morning on the veranda with the same story of how the leather army boots his company had manufactured "saved American regulars in World War I," and everyday my mom would sigh, "You told me already."

Surprises were in store for Muriel on Friday nights, when Robert's grown children would gather for a fancy-pants supper at his apartment. Highballs sloshed. Pretense ruled. Robert, the fragile patriarch, would occasionally inquire across the dinner table how an absent son was doing, and none of his offspring had the character to remind him their sibling had died of an illness some time ago. Brazenness came easier for them.. After the servants bused the meal, some of the Rossman children were in the habit of pilfering their father's curios – candelabras, figurines -- piece by expensive piece. They'd convinced themselves that he'd become too elderly to appreciate them anymore, so it was more a tacit bequest than stealing. What was once the elegant suite of the Rossman realm came to look half-burglarized after years of this practice.

Naturally, there were few references to the boys' legal difficulties with newcomers like Muriel around. Two of Robert's sons—Joseph and Isador—had been repeatedly subpoenaed before grand juries on fraud charges during the 1930s. Their shrewdest plot had been trying to outwit the feds on a military textile contract by running the old switcheroo. They'd secretly replaced some of the quality fabric their plants made with worthless scraps after the government had inspected the bales. At least, Robert by then was too senile to be ashamed. He died later with a pipe in his mouth.

If my mom accepted Rossman shadiness as the price for her escape to San Francisco, the Sierra Madre postmarks reminded of the strings attached. Three to four times every week, the mailman delivered her another letter from Rose on sepia stationary packed with censored family news and the dos-and-don'ts of her stay.

Grandma gave Mom scads to remember. "Write Gordon. Help your relatives. No wild spending. Beware of strange men. Avoid sunburns. No weeknight dates. Stay as long as you wish. Read your scriptures. Write Gordon more often—just not special delivery; the sixteen cents is extortion. Take a math class. No more plane rides. Beware of your relatives. Start planning your return..."

More bewildering to trace was what was happening to Gordon. One day Rose would write that his stomach had "revolted" and his bladder was obstructed. Other times his appetite was ravenous and his favorite goodies would slide down with homemade apple cider. Then a bad day returned, generally enema day, and he was too weak to consume anything.

In spite of the fluctuations, Rose reported, he was kinder to everybody and more like his old self. He also had a second nurse he adored, a wickedly funny Scottish woman. She substituted for the regular nurse, Jenny, an austere, big-boned woman from Sweden. Jenny had taken a leave of absence from the hospital to care for Gordon on weekdays because in him she saw a lively, special kid who needed a professional. As for Lee, Rose said little, except he moped a lot and had a new *Ellery Queen* serial about to premiere.

The savvy of Rose's letters was what they omitted. Gordon's multiple infections weren't disclosed, nor the discouraging prognoses every MD but Joe Risser issued him. The money spats she was having with Lee were blacked out. Same for the lawsuit against Marshall. Same even for the trial of the man accused of the gory shotgun murder of Rose's closest brother, Nat Ross—a death penalty case splashed across the Los Angeles papers throughout 1941. None of these details reached Muriel because her mother was convinced the girl had heard enough of them. Rose believed it was the details where life's pain resounded, details connecting Athlete's Foot to broken necks, so just forget them. Instead, trivial matters—what stores sold the best monkey-fur-lined coats—were highlighted for my mom to commit to memory.

Grandma's strangest request was for her daughter to visit a Bay Area fortune-teller to see into Gordon's future. Down home, Rose used to pay a few dollars to a two hundred fifty-pound clairvoyant whose popularity came less from her mystical prowess than the fact her cousin was czarist sage Grigory Rasputin. Rose, starchy Christian that she was, told everyone that psychics like these were "pure entertainment." Obviously there was more to the contradiction where Gordon was concerned.

Her sacrifice to him was all-consuming. Many nights, Rose would be in Gordon's room until the late nursing shift changed over. Around 9:30, she would throw her stuff into a duffel bag, speed-walk down the long corridor in her sensible shoes and catch the final outbound Red Car trolley east. The train was her only transportation this late. She had given up driving herself after she plowed Lee's car into a telephone poll during her maiden driving lesson. It was only when she arrived home in Sierra Madre after 11 p.m. that she would contemplate her own leftovers dinner.

Leaving Gordon behind every night was the worst part of her day. County General was the nation's second largest hospital, a place armed with doctors and equipment of every stripe, and mocked all the same as a white elephant of U.S. medicine. Though erected mainly for L.A.'s poor, it charged far more than private facilities. Investigators regularly found over-crowded wards, billing excesses, woeful training and graft. Conditions had only marginally improved when Gordon was brought there.

Rose felt beside herself thinking this was the best they could afford. She didn't trust a couple of head nurses, or how clean the rooms were. She was overwrought about a polio outbreak that spread from a supposedly quarantined ward to infect 300 people, hospital workers included. New reasons for her to wrinkle were always there.

On June 21, 1941, Muriel received another update from Rose:

Darlin: read your "special delivery" in care of Gordy. No need to say we were delighted to hear from you, but it's sure awful, this letter-writing business.

First, Gordy is looking better each day and continues to retain whatever he eats, for which we are on our knees in gratitude. Didn't write you what Dr. Feder had to say, because his personal opinion was not encouraging. At the time Gordon was looking very bad and vomiting, but from that day on he is decidedly on a new way...I think Dr. Feder would be pleased with Gordon's pick-up if he saw it. Someday everybody will see. I'm just waiting to hear what the fortuneteller told you about Gordon. You know we only believe the (spiritual) truth, so if the prophesy doesn't correspond, we know what it's worth. So let's have it, only send the letter "home."

I'm sorry you are going to miss Mary Georgine's wedding...I guess it's going to be a moonlight garden wedding.... One thing I can tell you right now: there will no other food than punch and wedding cake. That is supposed to be the vogue. I think it would be nice if you...sent a wire.

Gordy feels so blue that he can't be at the wedding. So Mrs. Burnell told me that...they did not let walls or streetcar tracks or anything interfere with (God's) presence. That holds good for you too if you don't get back by then.

As always, best love to you all. Mommy.

Muriel was interested in Dr. Feder's outlook. She had been dating the intern, among other boys, when Gordon was wheeled into County General in a paralyzed stupor. She wasn't so keen to relay what the psychic had foretold about Gordon. Enough doctors, nurses, lawyers, administrators and charlatans asked to ponder his shaky spine had predicted he would surely die from it.

By July 1941, when the Nazis were still Europe's business, my mom's top priority was remaining in San Francisco. Like her, it was mercurial and spoiled, naughty when nobody was peeking, sophisticated when they were. Her planned two-week stay there had swelled into months. It would have lounged into years if she could have supported herself, because her folks couldn't stomach her living off the Rossmans forever. So, she interviewed with the downtown department stores. Rejected there, she applied with the five-and-dimes. Her uncle Joe typed a letter on United Textile Co. stationary telling prospective employers what a bang-up job she would do, inexperience and all. When none were willing to hire such a greenhorn, she surrendered to the return date her parents nagged her about. She'd soon be attending Pasadena Junior College in lieu of a real university. It was all such a gyp.

~~~

Someone was dead. Gordon knew it the moment his mom's lightless eyes slipped over his bed. Yup, someone wasn't coming back, and he winced at its timing. He couldn't even comfort his dumbfounded mom, because his paralyzed arms were as useful as hood ornaments. Rose summarized for him the gunplay that'd occurred, skipping over the macabre elements the newspapers played up. He must've never wanted to stand so much, for that hug, for a chance to ram his head into the wall in frustration. But this was more than that. This was about succession. He now knew, in an ineffable teenage way, that he *had* to recover. He was the last of his family's endangered species: a breathing young man.

It'd been a short car ride from the boy's hospital room where his status was sealed. Inside a whirring rag factory along downtown L.A.'s manufacturing row, a brooding drifter had aimed a rifle at an innocent man's chest. Plant workers dashed for cover as the dark muzzle flashed: they knew this was going to end badly. The gunman's name was Maurice Briggs, and he was bent for revenge against his former boss. The date was February 24, 1941, a couple months before my mother's mercy trip up north. Two echoing rifle shots later, Nat Ross, a popular, thirty-six-year-old businessman and movie producer, lay splattered dead on the cold factory floor with his chest blown open.

L.A. now had its next sensational Hollywood murder case. Interest in it wasn't nearly as intense as the Black Dahlia killing or Fatty Arbuckle's crime, but it was a blockbuster nonetheless. Everybody — well almost everybody — seemed to have adored the victim. Put Gordon in front of the pack. Nat had been *his* favorite uncle, different than the rest. Cosmopolitan. Self-made. Whimsical. And now gone forever without so much as a, "See ya later, Gordy-boy. You get well."

Nat was also Rose's little brother, and her devastation about his violent death expressed itself in the speed by which she tried closeting its memory. After the funeral, she made her wishes known: the incident was taboo, a blight not fit for public conversation. Nat was in God's hands now, she mumbled through tear-stained tissues, so what was the point of rehashing how or why he was dispatched? It wasn't going to make him open his eyes. It wasn't going to soothe his traumatized widow, who'd fled to Europe after the shooting, never to be heard from again. Nobody, as far as I can tell, from the immediate family contested Rose's request by asking about pesky particulars. In a way it was as if February 24 was an otherwise unremarkable day.

Except that Gordon's survival felt more like the family's was riding on it.

My own mother copied the same basic heartache-repression technique that her mom had taught her. When my mom mouthed Nat's name, the facts surrounding his murder were asterisks to her montage memories of his quirky travels and rakish style. How, just for the heck of it, he used to send her classic, first-edition books; Hemingway, Fitzgerald, Keats.

If, as a curious child, I asked about Nat's death, she blunted it with a reactionary frown or a subject change. It wasn't just Nat's last moment she hushed. It was pretty much all Zahler-family pain you couldn't sentimentalize away, including some of Gordon's more unsavory exploits. When the truth was too unwieldy to shrug off, the black times were treated like nuclear weapons' waste: a history handled at grave risk. "I'm done talking about it," she'd tell me. After emotionally bottling up two murders, whitewashing Gordon's burden on the family was straight-ahead denial.

Because of this and my own smug indifference about my forebears, the past seemed to have no consequence on where my own life was pointed. I hadn't believed there was anything my mouthy uncle or any of his fallen kin could teach me.

Personal upheaval would soon enough school me. In the course of a week, family history would start mattering.

My birthday was to be a pageant of self-indulgence. There was a big USC football game on TV I was dying to watch with some coach-potato buddies, followed by a party my parents were throwing for my thirty-fourth. I never made it to halftime. Midway through the second quarter, Kate howled. We knew she had a risky pregnancy. The infant inside Kate had wanted to squiggle out four months too soon. If she succeeded, our second child would be a premature baby, all shrunken and blue, with tubes fed into her and almost no hope of making it. Things were so dicey that Kate had to have surgery to stitch closed her "incompetent cervix."

Now contractions that the operation was supposed to postpone until the ninth month doubled her over on the bed. "It hurts. God, it hurts," she moaned. "Why is this still happening?"

Kate, a strong, beautiful woman, never looked so tortured, and I certainly provided no relief. On the drive back to Huntington Hospital, a place I was growing to hate, I was lost for answers. I remember thinking this could not be as clear-cut as punishment for sins of my youth, or the people I wronged as an adult. Here an innocent was child in jeopardy, not me—or maybe that was precisely the point? Could it be my mettle was being tested? I had had your basic good life, privileged some might say, where the law of averages was always blowing through someone else's doorway

In our hospital cubicle, Kate and I held sweaty palms. We talked about everything but the obvious until the new anti-labor drugs were piped into her arm. Then the doctor, who was too laid-back for this pressure, examined her and suggested we head home because there was nothing else to do. Stupidly, we disregarded his advice. We showed up at my party three hours later in dour moods.

That all this could explode when I understood the bliss of parenthood from the birth of our first daughter, when I was supposed to be making birthday wishes not sorry-ass prayers, reminded me of something from my childhood: life pulls the rug out from underneath you with a demented sense of timing. I was an ogre to everyone around me at the party and beyond. At the newspaper I was working for, I browbeat my sources. One called me a "royal A-hole" and never spoke to me again.

The weekend after the contractions returned, with Kate stuck in bed, I went up to visit my mom. She was lying on her ocher-colored chaise lounge in a snazzy pantsuit. A *National Review* magazine flapped over her lap. Right off I told her I didn't want to talk about the pregnancy, that my head was going to explode. To fill the void I thumped on about my latest newspaper work— stories about L.A.'s corrupt subway project. That's when she interrupted. "Forget the subway. Just forget it. That's not what you should be writing about." From out of nowhere, she was acting more like my career advisor than the woman forever hounding me that my wardrobe was too dark for my olive skin. We had fought constantly over the years, Mom and I, probably because I had inherited most of her temperament but few of her priorities.

"The best story around is right under your nose," she said. "The story about your uncle. He had such an amazing life. You know he's in the medical records books, don't you? You realize what he tried to do in South Africa?"

Actually, I was oblivious. "You write it," I said, proud of my comeback. Devoting myself to write the saccharine portrait of him she wanted was laughable. His legacy wasn't worth the effort, though I didn't stress that point. *My career*, I reminded her, *my career!* I had the job I'd coveted for six years—investigative reporter at a big L.A. daily—and wasn't about to junk it.

Well, cue the next weird scene. My mom didn't dwell on my stubbornness. She began reminiscing about 1941, how her parents' fixation with Gordon greased her path to San Francisco. "You never heard I lived there, did you?" Against her parents' express wishes, she said she went up in an old-fashioned bi-plane with her cousin. Barrel rolls, loop-de-loops—the guy trying to dazzle her made her want to barf at five thousand feet.

My mom was trying to tell me something valuable in all this, but what it was I wasn't sure. Maybe she was egging me on to retrace Gordon's story as a way of delicately recalling her own. Later I'd recognize she was showing guts, pulling up some of the board planks that she and Rose had kept nailed over their darkest days because the pain from those flying bullets and crashing men had been intolerable. Now she was recruiting me to go down there and snoop around? Slim chance I'd write Gordon's story, I told myself. Slim chance as in el zippo.

CHAPTER SIX
Frontier Days

Gordon checked out of County General nine months after he checked in, still numb below the shoulders but frisky for the homecoming the doctors had once squawked was unthinkable. Showing them up was his winnable war. Nobody could forecast how far he'd take it.

Attendants strapped my uncle into another Schaeffer Ambulance in July 1941. Doors shut, they beeped the horn for the nurses waving in the hospital driveway and brought him eastward to a modest house in Sierra Madre he had never seen before. It was the house his recklessness had condemned his family to, although the joy of his return muted any observations about that.

Hearty applause burst out when his gurney was carted up the steps of the baby blue house on Laurel Avenue, which family friends and relatives thronged for the special day. "Welcome back, kid!" they said. "See how prayer works?" Or, "You hot dog, we knew you'd fight your way out."

Small gifts took up most of the free table space. The rest Rose piled with plates of hot roast beef, Gordon's favorite. He only had time for six bites with all the well-wishers patting him. Alive. He felt so stupendously alive.

Just as his spine changed the family, his return to Sierra Madre precipitated a major reshuffling of the house. My grandparents' first act was to convert the airy first-floor living room into Gordon's room, because he was too delicate to be carried upstairs and they lacked space there even if he could. His quarters were soon filled with a special adjustable bed and medical supplies, all of it subsidized by the Motion Picture Fund. Lee and Rose then adorned it with their own versions of protection. Rose hung a ceramic Virgin Mary and a picture of a winged baby Jesus on the wall directly behind Gordon's bed. Lee hooked an imitation Winchester rifle off the curtain rack. A model warplane with painted shark teeth on the nose was tacked from the ceiling.

The most dramatic reconfiguration involved my grandparents' marital bed. Rose vacated it. She was jittery that Gordon might have a seizure or another emergency during the night while they were upstairs. What if they didn't hear him gagging? So, from practically his first day home, she insisted on sleeping every night on a cot in a small alcove about five feet from his bed. A curtain drawn across the recess was her gauzy dab of privacy.

If this arrangement gutted face-time with Lee, undercutting Rose's emotional latches to him and her sexual needs, chalk it up to a mother's steel. One man in her world simply needed her more the other. There are no single-victim accidents.

Gordon's pals had their own notions about his recuperation. Within a month of his homecoming, they showed up at Zahler House with liquor, cigarettes, yearbooks, and swing records. They aimed to shake the foundation, suspecting Gordon wanted action, not congratulation. They knew their boy. As the weekend parties became bigger, rowdier affairs, the kids became bolder about doing for Gordon what he couldn't do for himself, which was just about everything. They fed him Lucky Strikes. They adjusted his neck brace. My grandparents watched how perky Gordon became when the gang knocked. They also caught on he wanted them upstairs out of the way when they did. The firewater really sloshed then— Harper's with lemon wedges, Canadian Club, Tanqueray Gin and fizzy seventy-two-ounce beers. Clouds of smoke twirled overhead. Some of the kids paired off to French kiss, others for clopping dance steps. Only able to rotate his head slightly at first, Gordon had to pick his spots in the mayhem. Usually that meant retelling a limerick or daring the best looking dame to dive under the covers.

Rollicking and wild as the partying was, it was hardly carefree, and rarely without some dispiriting moments. Gordon's buddies, who included the Marshall Tarzans and old classmates from St. Rita's Elementary, were stunned during their first visit by how much paralysis had refashioned him. His head, gingerly propped up on a pillow, was the most noticeable difference. It loomed grotesquely big over his body, which had wasted away during his months in traction. His torso cast such a weak ruffle under the sheets that you weren't sure if his lower extremities made it out of County General with him. His plumbing was shot to hell, too; a catheter and bedpan was how he did his business.

Apart from his colorful mouth, nothing moved, nothing functioned. From his neck down, he was gristle, with no suggestion he might again do what he loved best: sprinting. Limbs once in perpetual motion were dormant bamboo. The comparison was what floored his fellow teenagers. Everybody but his parents, for example, had heard about the last outrageous thing Gordon had done.

A month before he'd been hurt, he had roped five or six Marshall classmates into a five dollar bet nobody thought physiologically doable, if even desirable. After the school bell rang, the boys and girls had followed him under the tattered football grandstands, where the teachers couldn't see. He'd sat down, unbuttoned his jeans, wiggled out of his cotton underwear and contorted his hips. Seesawing them for a minute in the afternoon light, he had caught his very own manhood in his own mouth for ten indecent seconds. He'd rewritten Marshall folklore by copulating himself like that. Now the sight of my uncle's hands, more claw-like with every passing day, scared some of the girls who came round.

To my grandparents, the message of these parties was that Gordon's circle had not come round for a token visit and then ditched him for able-bodied pursuits. The experts at County General had cautioned them about this likelihood. They said Gordon would have to befriend kids in the same shape as his if he wanted lasting companionship, that invalids were his peers now.

They were wrong as could be. Something about him—his irrepressible wit, maybe his refusal to poormouth his condition with the generic "Why-me?"—made him as popular as ever with the old crowd. The apple-cheeked boys in their suped up cars peeled rubber when they left Zahler house, but they always came back (usually with contraband tucked in their waistband). Gordon was their convalescing Huck Finn. With them there, Gordon had no interest in the heavy conversations the grownups murmured about him on the periphery. Head at forty-five degrees, he jabbered about adventures past and planned as if his legs only were asleep. As Lee and Rose saw it, the underage carousing was fine if their son remained the central attraction. If he sassed them for throwing out his pals at midnight on Saturdays, they smiled thinking that hope budded from the oddest soil.

When they weren't looking for silver linings, they paced. The critical hour for the lawsuit had come. My grandparents could tell Maurice Rose to scuttle the settlement talks with the Pasadena school district and prepare for trial. Or, they could take the district's insulting offer and be done with the school and Maurice. Their lawyer had done one righteous thing in pinpointing Marshall's negligent gym program and been slippery ever since.

You couldn't choke an authoritative answer out of Maurice. Rose was leaning towards firing him after Normalouise's father, a Spring Street insurance man, cautioned her that Maurice was the wrong man to press Gordon's claim. When Rose broached this idea with Lee, he snapped at her. It would be idiocy, he fumed, to switch their attorney midstream. So what if Maurice's forte was representing corporations, not personal injury cases? They'd made their choice. More and more my grandparents squabbled behind closed doors over conquering dilemmas like this, and more and more a heavy silence hung afterwards because they hadn't been the squabbling kind. This hurt had no boundaries.

Initially, Maurice had been smug about their chances to win the whole $200,000 in spite of the immunity statutes. Between the dated equipment and the poor oversight, proving Marshall's liability would be a Sunday drive, he'd said. The sum was so large and the medical bills were so high that Lee had acquiesced to the cut Maurice demanded for himself. A pre-trial settlement would net him twenty-five percent of the award, a successful jury verdict thirty percent. Maurice blustered that was standard and not even family ties warranted a discount.

Think about it, he said. He had office overhead to pay for, just like those studios employing Lee. Once Gordon was released from County General, however, Maurice's cockiness about netting a big payout receded in the conversations. Eventually he conceded he wasn't sure that he could sway a jury about Marshall's negligence. Clouding matters, the doctors remained adamant that Gordon would die from his injuries. The district was too shrewd to approve one deal only to face a wrongful death suit if the doctors were proven right. Maurice's advice: settle.

Lee and Rose realized they'd been burned. They'd been out-maneuvered by the school's attorney and misled by their own. (It later came out that Maurice was chummy with lawyers from the school board's underwriter, The Traveler's Insurance Co.) Their options were to accept the $15,000 that was the district's final offer or take a flier on Maurice's character in trial. They weighed their choice until their instincts and logic dovetailed.

In September 1941 they decided they to take the deal. After deducting Maurice's $3,750 share, they deposited $11,219 in their savings account. The district gave my grandfather an extra $2,500 as Gordon's guardian; most of that was mailed off to the hospital. All told, the Zahlers walked away with eight cents for every dollar Maurice's brilliance was supposed to win for them.

So it went. The bad luck unloosed by Gordon's fall churned at my grandparents' heels. There would be progress in one area, and just as hopes for stability relit, two destructive things would extinguish it from opposite directions. Throughout much of the 1940s that was the pattern. Sometimes it was as though an undertow from a hidden tide was out to drown them.

For a spell, fortunes flickered brighter. Christmas 1941, while fuzzed by Pearl Harbor, was better than the Christmas before it since Gordon was home for the festivities. Lee's big present to him was a slow-speed ride around downtown Sierra Madre in a rented ambulance so Gordon could get a good look at town without the town returning the favor. It was bad enough having his friends stare at him, he told his dad. He didn't need the local grapevine pointing, too.

Home cooking helped Gordon pack on a few pounds. Determination let him regain small movement in his left arm by contracting his shoulder muscles. He could crane his neck better as well. Once in a while, if something provoked him and his legs had spasmed, he blurted out what nobody dared to say aloud. "I'm going to get up, someday. I ain't planning on being here my whole life."

When America marched into war, Gordon still could not move a limb. There was no sweeping aside of his blankets so he could take a quaking, first step toward what he'd been. On the contrary, the conflict made him bow to a kind of sad mental grounding. You can see it in pictures of him lying in bed wearing his best, staged smile. The male friends around him in these shots had exchanged their V-neck sweaters and pleated cotton trousers for service uniforms. Drafted or enlisted, they proudly wore Army khaki and Navy black when they visited my uncle, the girls smitten with the uniforms. Visually, they looked to be teenagers masquerading as soldiers, but they were going overseas to fight just as their own father had once fought. And Gordon? The most he could do was stay home in his PJs around women with whom he couldn't even take advantage.

For my mom, the home front was confusing. As she told a boyfriend in the Navy's 21st Pursuit Squadron on February 18, 1942:

> My dear Steve: I have been riding on wings all day – mother called me today at work to tell me the blessed, marvelous news. A letter from you finally arrived....
>
> Things are comparatively quiet here. Of course, there is a war air about everything and everybody. All the parks, schools, and empty areas have been converted into barracks. The streets are filled with soldiers and sailors...No more weekend passes; nothing more than six hours at the most. Of all the boys that I've ever known or gone to school with, only perhaps a few have still not been drafted. Even young kids of sixteen and seventeen are enlisting. All the women are even taking over defense jobs. Imagine, women working amidst mass production!
>
> When war was first declared, we had several blackouts. (Yes, even in Sierra Madre.) Leave it to an American to make a joke out of everything. We have blackout dates now. The minute we hear a rumor of a blackout, the fellow quickly gets a date with his favorite girlfriend and they have an enjoyable (?) evening.
>
> The boys who are fortunate enough to still be here are being entertained. I myself have gone to several U.S.O. dances – and I was thrilled to do it. We have a couple of soldiers over to dinner once in a while. Wish I could do more, but after all you know the situation my family is in.
>
> As for myself, I still have a job at Robinsons' (department store). In fact, I'll brag a little by saying I've had a couple of promotions. My life is utterly changed, too...Just recently, I've decided not to take life quite so seriously...Believe it or not, Steve, I've gone through quite a little war all by myself. (Inside, I mean.) Gordon's predicament and lots of other things have really broken my heart. The doctors still have no hope for him – even though I do believe in miracles – and it hurts. The other day Gordon remarked that the minute he gets up he is going to join the Navy. And knowing Gordy, he would....By the way, he was 16 on the tenth of this month.
>
> My social life is fun, nothing serious though. I don't think I'll ever be a war bride. I want to be a little original.
>
> Best wishes and lots of love. Muriel.

Steve never read my mother's dispatch. The post office returned it to her "service suspended," Army lingo for saying he had been killed in action. Similar wording was stamped on a letter my mom tried to send to Al, her San Francisco beau. Japanese bombers attacking his weapons depot in the tropics arrived there ahead of the mail.

Gordon's room was its own MASH unit. Glass cabinets were stuffed with gauze, cotton balls, hypodermic needles, catheters, pills, oxygen tanks, carbon dioxide canisters and special sponge-rubber bedding. Names like Owl Drugs and Western Surgical Supply Co. were inscribed on everything. Jenny, the big Swedish nurse, handled the materials constantly. Her gray hair pulled severely into a bun, Jenny had a flinty demeanor about doing tasks her way. "Gor-dun," she would say giving him a sponge bath or injection, a little Greta Garbo in her enunciation, "I van you to vurk with me."

While he trusted her, there was no disputing Jenny was the second in command. His mother was the head nurse. Single-minded in her nurturing, she was the force in that room. She became so skilled with a catheter and the different medicines she probably could've passed the nurse's neurology exam herself with minimal cramming. She'd already shaved thirty minutes off the one hour it originally took her to prep Gordon for bed. Every night, weekend and holiday, she was there, or aiding Jenny when one pair of hands wouldn't do. Tending a sixteen-year-old son who would never be healthy became what she was about.

Unofficially, my grandma had been training for this duty since she was a Brooklyn schoolgirl. Rose as a teenager had done most of the chores for her younger brothers while her mother had plunged into despair missing Maurice. Dearie's primary contribution to the household was teaching Rose how to prepare delicious meals out of tables scraps, not recipes, and then retiring to the other room. By the time she was a regulation wife and mother herself, Rose was a crowd pleaser with roasts, goulash, tapiocas and breads. Some guests swore she could make cardboard scrumptious. (Future studio-mogul Irving Thalberg, then her brother's roommate, gave her a gold watch to thank her for her marrow soup.) Her culinary skills, coupled with a spirituality that emphasized the impermanence of earthly life, probably helped persuade her that caring for Gordon was what she was born to do. If it was incarcerating for her to tend to him, smells full of his sweat and pee and stale bed sheets and spilled beer, she acted like a prisoner glad to be there. In fact, she seemed liberated in serving.

Imagine her emotions when she was the one hurt. In March 1942, a girlfriend was driving her around downtown Pasadena when a speeding sedan broadsided them out of nowhere. The passenger-side door next to where Rose sat took the brunt of the impact with Grandma's body a close second. She was led into St. Luke's Hospital with blood all over her dress. She had a nasty gash across her scalp and a hurt neck that she complained felt like it'd been speared. X-rays determined my grandma had a cracked vertebra.

Unlike Gordon's, it was higher up the spine and only marginally fractured. She was fitted with a neck cast and ordered to stay in bed for four to six weeks. A month off her feet: could this true, she asked the ER doctor? If it was, it was overkill. "Can't you just give me some painkillers? I can't be out for *two* days." No, the doctor lectured, she needed rest to let the bone heal. Lee, meanwhile, was forced to skip some work to shuttle food trays between her and Gordon. The Motion Picture Fund footed Rose's hospital bill because he could not.

The casts flew everywhere. As the plaster-of-Paris was being sawed off Rose, a lengthy immobilization was being arranged for Gordon. He was to receive a full body cast to stabilize him following an operation to fuse his spine at St. Luke's. Without the procedure, any significant jarring could re-break his neck. Dr. Risser predicted he wouldn't outlast a second fracture of it. Supposedly he asked Gordon his druthers—whether he preferred to have his back soldered in the sitting position or laid flat. Gordon voted for sitting, which was awkward for sleeping but better for daylight. Minus the fusion, it would be impossible for him to sit upright without slumping forward like a human jellyfish.

His kidneys didn't care either way. They stopped functioning twelve days after the fusion surgery. His temperature spiked and Lee phoned for an ambulance. It raced Gordon back to St. Luke's, a cupola-tipped building inspiring thoughts of ancient Rome if you ignored the dirt-clod fields behind it. Up in surgery, the doctors sawed off the cast and jump-started Gordon's kidneys. He recovered ahead of predictions. Within two weeks he was wrapped in a second body cast that entombed him from neck to pelvis. There it would stay on him, itchy and hot, for three *years* and ten months. His mouthy buddies called him "The Mummy." He wished he could flip them off.

Back home in Sierra Madre, stiff in his cast, the closest Gordon came to World War II was listening to updates from the Motorola radio on his nightstand table—or staring ahead. His dad had tacked up a large Rand-McNally map of Europe on the wall opposite Gordon's bed. Black tacks signified where the Axis was advancing, red ones for the Allies' position. Any night he was home for dinner, Lee would sit with Gordon while CBS Radio broadcast the latest update from London or the Solomon Islands. Afterwards, Lee frantically adjusted the tacks while he speculated about General Patton's tactics. Gordon even pretended to be interested in the troop movements after the novelty wore off. He recognized what this meant to his dad, this diversion affixed to the wall.

Strangely, my uncle owed thanks to Adolph Hitler and Emperor Hirohito. Had it had not been for their fascist land-grabs, the infections that regularly assaulted his organs probably would have finished him off in the recuperative stage. For Gordon and others with wrecked spinal cords, paralysis was akin to contracting terminal-stage leukemia. All it took in the good old days was a few unresponsive spinal nerves to bury you. The hospitals, other than shooting patients into morphine orbits and wiring them into traction, certainly could not offer many solutions. The inner-workings of the central nervous system were simply out of medicine's reach. An estimated eighty to ninety percent of all patients with severe spinal-cord injuries died within weeks of their injuries. If they pulled through, life expectancy was two, three years, max. The few who made it longer were considered miracle cases. Most of them lived in shaky health, generally in institutions.

Judged against modern standards, quadriplegia was a devastating word in pre-war America. Drugs that today's patients routinely receive to treat bladder infections or bedsores had not been invented. Operations to ease pressure on the cord were impossible, partly because surgeons lacked the know-how to cauterize potentially lethal hemorrhages they can staunch easily today. *Superman* actor Christopher Reeve, perhaps the world's best known quadriplegic, survived his 1995 horse-riding accident because science was primed for him. Fifty years earlier it would have stood him up. In the 1940s he would not have received the anti-swelling steroid that can preserve twenty percent more neurons than doing nothing; that fraction can be the difference between fatal respiratory arrest and ventilator-assisted breathing. In the 1940s he would not have had his lungs drained of pneumonia-causing fluids because the doctors could not suction safely.

To think how Gordon would have fared had he been hurt today instead of 1940 is to rewrite history. Yet, world history was his savior. With legions of wounded and maimed soldiers depending on them, Western scientists worked with urgency to pioneer an effective treatment for bacterial infections. The drug they stumbled across was penicillin, the world's first antibiotic. Before it, the paralyzed were the epitome of vulnerable. Pathways created by bedsores, catheters and fouled-up intestines allowed bacterial invaders easy entry. Once inside, they did much of their destructive work incognito because spinal-cord victims typically lose pain-sensitivity below the point of their injury. Thanks to mass-produced penicillin, the mortality rate for spine-damaged citizens and GIs alike plummeted within a few years of its introduction. From the little I have picked up about Gordon's early medical history, he owed his life to the drug. In this way, he owed a lot to the Allies, maybe more to the Axis.

CHAPTER SEVEN
Silly Oddities

Rose had these notions about rebuilding Gordon from the ground up. More than anything, she wanted him soldered back into civilization. The trouble was he defined civilization as the four walls of 191 East Laurel Avenue, where he had been bedridden in pain and boredom for a year and then some.

Rose, sweetly as ever, suggested he try a reclining wheelchair they had leased through Abbey Rents. "You could get some sun that way, darling, or a hamburger out with your friends. Benny could set it up."

Nope, he said, not yet. So, he stayed in bed, through lavender spring days and a sweltering Fourth of July, through bashes he might have attended and matinees he could have relished if his fear of public humiliation would have passively coiled under him. Give him credit, nonetheless. His blarney about needing "just a little more time" or "not feeling up to it" was still glossed with persuasive lament.

At wit's end, Grandma resorted to being sneaky. She spoke with her hand cuffed over the phone one evening in September '42, and the next morning a surprise face was at their screen door. Gordon recognized the man from his "y'alls" and "whatchas." Not too many Southerners in Sierra Madre, and definitely none like Father Eustace of Little Rock, Arkansas. At 6'7", pretty-boy handsome and equally literate, he had townsfolk sending him dueling dinner invitations. How he got tangled up with my family no one can say. Somehow it was tied to his job at the Passionist Father's Monastery, where Sierra Madre's hilltop runs smack into the mountain.

Inside the Zahler house the sandbagging was on. Gordon was inquisitive about why Father Eustace was there and Eustace said

surely Gordon had heard about the huge football game at Arcadia
High School that day. "Yeah, so?" Gordon said. "So, let's git you up,
boy, cuz I'm taking you with me to the game. No hemming about it. I
got to be back at the monastery for afternoon prayers." Gordon,
leaned up in bed, writhing with his ego, said thanks but no. Eustace
didn't blink; Gordon started to. "How about a rain check for next
week, Father?" Eustace just stared. "Oh, oh, I got a better idea,"
Gordon said in a nervous titter. "We'll go see their grudge game, you
know against Monrovia. How's that strike ya?"

It didn't. Eustace, who was dressed in gray civies, stood off
while my grandparents lifted Gordon out of his permanent pajamas
and bundled him in a pair of baggy pants and sweatshirt that fit over
the body cast. My grandma had handpicked the ensemble that
morning. Now, as she combed his hair the way he liked it, Gordon
snarled he didn't care about how he looked. He called his parents
traitors for ambushing him like this, popping curse words he
typically didn't use around them. "Holy shit, you think this is fair?"
His voice continued breaking with teary fury as he was cradled into
the wheelchair, rolled down the driveway and securely buckled into
the front seat of Eustace's rusty black Ford truck.

Before Gordon could fabricate another reason for a rain check,
the truck was chugging south on Grandview Avenue, backfiring
occasionally. It was just he and the Father in the cab because his folks
didn't go. Eustace had convinced them that Gordon would be better
off without his parents mollycoddling him near the bleachers with a
sweater or hot cocoa. For Rose, the restraint was enormous. In fact,
watching her son being driven off without her might well have sent
her into a round of vacuuming, which she did whenever stress put its
foot on her.

The particulars of the football outing have been lost to the years.
What everybody remembers is that a change broke over Gordon
afterwards. His paranoia of being singled out in the crowd gradually
sloughed off. After a few jaunts out, he trained himself to look
beyond the double takes and whispers he sensed trailing him. Some
of his old pluck slinked back. He began smiling and joking wherever

he went, be it a mountain drive or a brass band concert at Memorial Park that he would have ridiculed in another life. Letting that scenery rub up against his face bred a guttural excitement in him. Wherever he went was gravy compared to County General. Wherever he was meant he wasn't hopeless. The stares, he reminded himself, did nothing compared to those pins the doctors had screwed into his skull.

By war's end, Gordon was outside the house regularly despite several setbacks and his standing order to be steered wide of Marshall Jr. High. The sunshine proved intoxicating for him. Hoping that foreshadowed better things ahead, Lee designed a sun porch next to Gordon's room so his son could breathe all the fresh air he wanted in view of Mount Wilson. That mountain meant a lot, both as grandeur and memory, and Gordon lounged deckside constantly. In a glum footnote, Father Eustace probably never spent more than an afternoon on the pine patio. He was soon transferred out of Sierra Madre to either Arkansas or Alabama, and abruptly died a year or so after prying Gordon to that game.

Part two of Grandma's strategy involved Gordon's schooling. Never much of a pupil, he had been missing from the classroom for two–and–a half years when the calendar flopped over to 1943. It was more than him falling behind academically. He had been lapped. Peers too young for the draft were now in the second half of their junior year in high school; my uncle had a month and a half as a ninth-grader. For Rose, the gap was intolerable. She sprinkled it into conversations with him. In heart-to-heart talks she told him he could do anything. She remembered from her history that Edison went deaf, that Van Gogh had epilepsy. When FDR's polio was acknowledged after he died, she referenced that too, though she hated his New Deal politics. Grandma knew that America kept its handicapped in dark rooms, and wanted Gordon to pack his head with knowledge so he wouldn't be consigned with them.

Hard as she campaigned, her words glanced off him. He preferred fraternizing to algebra, beer swilling to the European Renaissance. What was he supposed to do with a diploma anyway,

he asked? Use it as his serving tray? Face it: no one was going to hire
him, so educating him would squander everybody's time. Not long
after this rebuttal an ultimatum came down, Rose warning him to
accept home schooling a few days a week or not seeing his pals
much. She'd pulled out her ace.

Flora M. Strong, Pasadena district teacher, was introduced to
my uncle around his seventeenth birthday. Both instructor and
student tried to make it worthwhile. Flora presented lectures while
Gordon fended off his daydreaming. She quizzed him about the
periodic table and Hamlet's motivations and he labored to answer
her. From February '43 to June '44 she was a fixture by the bed, which
moonlighted as his desk. Every week lessons were outlined,
schedules kept. Rose would accept nothing less.

For all the facts and figures thrown around the room, retention
was patchy. Turns out the ability to write, erase and redo with pencil
in hand oils the brain's hydraulics in a way nothing else can. Gordon
couldn't grip a pencil no matter how deep puberty lowered his voice.
Consequently, biology, chemistry, geometry and economics were
erased off the assignment sheet; drafting, too. English and social
studies, the two reading-driven subjects, were all that remained after
a few months of schooling because they could be tested orally. By the
end of her stint, Flora judged Gordon had tried hard enough for B-
grades. She trundled back to the school district with my uncle having
completed his tenth-grade coursework and, more broadly, his formal
education. There was talk he had a tutor after Flora, but sparse
evidence he learned much. In Rose's mind, at least he'd tried.

Rose's faith in the offshoot church that viewed life as a
whitewater-raft ride before the glassy hereafter was absolute. When
the unexpected struck, she would quote George Edwin Burnell, the
"Science of Truth's" founding father. Once the dire occurred, she
would be on the phone to his Arcadia home lickety-split seeking
special prayers known as "treatments." Her devotion to the snowy-
haired, stern-looking Minnesotan was unwavering, perhaps
understandably so. Rev. Burnell, then in his 70s, pushed a hybrid

Christian philosophy — "The Instruction" — that borrowed liberally from Catholicism, some from Christian Science, while jilting their most extreme doctrines for something equally assuring. Shouting from the pulpit, the reverend would exhort his small flock to discount tragedy and confusion. Heaven, he thundered, would make mincemeat out of them. The saints were ubiquitous. Hell was nonexistent. Consciousness was God's personal gift, he said, so remember your St. Thomas Aquinas. "The end of man is not death but happiness." Life, to the reverend's thinking, was a bad movie you could ignore if a scene turned vicious.

My grandma's adherence to the Instruction formed a crystalline belief system hard for outsiders to grasp. Her entire Sundays often were spent praying and reading with Rev. Burnell or his disciples. Harold, Rose's youngest brother, was among them for a bit. Lee, having little to offer in the spirituality department, sometimes felt snubbed when the Bibles rolled out onto the patio, and Rose plowed ahead without him. After Gordon's accident, her devotion to the Burnell creed amplified nearly to the point of obsession. Every day she was on the phone to the reverend or his wife, most every night with the "Axion" book he had authored. It was as close to narcotics as Grandma came.

Neither Gordon nor I wanted much to do with the Instruction except to pilfer the goodies served after the Sunday sermons. Our respective mothers had demanded we attend to upgrade our souls, and we both balked with a hodgepodge of lame excuses. For me it was the ladies' gagging perfume and the homilies everybody had forgotten by Monday. Listening to someone recite Rev. Burnell's thick prose usually coaxed me into such a deep slumber that I awoke with drool-ribbons all over my blazer. The climax of my Sunday morning funfest was being forced to sit in the front row on a stiff metal chair literally two feet from the "music." It emanated from a waxy old lady in a beehive hairdo with a tenor voice so shrill you swore neighborhood dogs ran for cover when she hit a "hallelujah."

For Grandma, though, there was a secret within the congregation. The Instruction offered the disconsolate some enthralling possibilities, possibilities not openly discussed in church sessions but there nonetheless. For Rose, it was a shot worth taking. Getting Gordon walking was her ultimate mission, and she believed Rev. Burnell could help her achieve it long after the doctors gave up. In this instance, it was the laying of his hands she wanted along with the oomph of his prayers, because the reverend practiced faith healing as if he were one of God's lieutenants raising the sick at an amen-tooting revival.

He claimed to have been rescued from a lethal illness as a baby by a faith healer, and had written of eyes suddenly sighted and hunchbacks miraculously straightened by the same technique. Rev. Burnell's wife, Mary, became a believer after a terrible scare. As a tot, the Burnell's daughter had fallen from the window of a three-story building in a drop that most adults couldn't survive. Mary had rushed downstairs uttering faith healing words amid her palpitations. When Mary Georgine's mother lifted her daughter from the hard ground, the little girl who would grow up to be one of Gordon's best friends was barely nicked.

At Grandma's urging, Rev. Burnell organized prayer groups to ask God to have mercy on Gordon's spine those excruciating months he was hospital-bound. Once Gordon was sent home, there are hints Rose petitioned the reverend to apply his magic touch to the boy. Afterwards, when her son's torso stayed anesthetized, it must have punched holes in her convictions. (My uncle probably rolled his eyes.)

Strong as a follower, not as a rebel, Rose must have pleaded for explanations. Others had been rejuvenated by contact with the flesh, so why not a teenager with his horizons in front of him? Perhaps, the reverend explained, it was not the Lord's will for Gordon to walk anymore. Perhaps it was God's wish that Gordon live for reasons that would burst forth later. How else had he overcome those pitiful odds? Hence, the prayer lobby shifted. God was asked by parishioners of the Instruction to preserve my uncle instead of the full restore. Between faith healing and fortune-tellers, my grandma would try anything to get her son up.

Her prayers had to diversify, too. In fall 1943 a sinister tumor was discovered within the tissue of her right breast. As usual, she downplayed it, telling people the lump would be benign because she needed it to be benign. She had surgery in September, ending the threat. The next month Lee reimbursed the Motion Picture Fund $1,100 for the medical expenses. While he could have used the cash, he despised taking charity almost as much as the snake-bit times requiring it.

CHAPTER EIGHT
Scenes Around Hollywood

From vacation surprises to expected celebrations, the Zahler's undertow pulled everything once golden to asphyxiating depths. Gordon's paralysis, for instance, was the dominant reason not a single retrievable picture of my parent's wedding exists today. Being in a snapshot-happy family, I used to think somebody accidentally busted the camera on Valentine's Day 1943. In my naïveté, I assumed that until I got into the teeth of this book, and came to appreciate the splatter of collateral damage.

My parents met on a set-up date arranged by relatives in 1942. By all accounts it should've been a classic mismatch. My mom, with her cigarettes and talk, was a small-town belle who acted big city. She owned a luminous smile and starlet cheekbones, both of them enhanced by mousy brunette hair clipped regularly to fashion magazine dictates. A cultured, if not overreaching sophistication, made her seem older than twenty. Boys lined up to ask her out.

My dad, three years older, tilted to the opposite social polarity. His mother was a salty, Jewish divorcee who sold real estate, bought gold nuggets door-to-door, and otherwise hustled eight to five to feed her two children. (The father of them, a bond trader, had run off years earlier for a new life in Baltimore.) Millard Jacobs's smarts earned him admission to Pasadena's California Institute of Technology, one of the country's premiere technical institutions, where he majored in civil engineering. A devoted student, he earned honors. His skills around pretty girls were remedial, if that. My mom painted him as 6' and gawky, a sometimes-stutterer with a slide rule jutting from his shirt pocket.

Logarithm lover that he was, he did flash potential. His wavy, jet-black hair and wide-arched nose reminded Muriel of a Roman centurion, not a young man from Russian-German ancestry. She rooted for him at Caltech basketball games, though he was mainly a benchwarmer, and swooned for his gravitas off-court. College for him was about acquiring a craft to build a life around (as opposed to the brain-cell genocide it was in my partying university years).

Indeed, Millard was handed his diploma on a Friday in 1940 and the following Monday at eight a.m. he was an anonymous, gopher engineer at Lockheed Corp. out in Burbank. Implausibly, he gathered the nerve to ask my mom for a second date. She accepted it and subsequent invitations. His intellect captured her. Yes, yes, she told him, she would marry him.

It'd be the last goo-goo-eyed consensus they'd reach. My mom, stoked by Rose, had always fantasized about a large garden wedding with lace ribbons splashed about while George Edwin Burnell performed the Christian honors. When the time came, that vision was gone. In her white gown, Muriel stood a few feet from Gordon's bed in her parents' rented house listening to a rabbi's strange pronouncements of man and wife. Neither of her parents had wanted this type of cheapie affair with Rev. Burnell missing, but with the undertow splashing, that's precisely what they were dealt.

My dad and his mother, both agnostic Jews, had insisted a rabbi conduct the ceremony. This irked Lee, whose possessiveness about my mom trumped the fact he resided in the same spiritual Neverland as the Jacobs. In his eyes, Millard's obstinacy about tradition upheld was costing Muriel the romantic wedding she had dreamt about since she was in pigtails. The more Lee snooped around about his future in-laws, the more this stuck in his craw. Feeling the stress, the young couple sought middle ground to pacify their parents. They interviewed every rabbi around to find one who would cotton to a joint service with Rev. Burnell. None would agree. Afterwards, my dad kept persisting about a rabbi's involvement. My mom, dejected but in love, caved to his stance. Where the nuptials would be wasn't even argued. It'd have to be at the bride's house to scrimp on money. Gordon, fittingly, was Millard's best man. Lee's blood pressure spikes became regular events after the service.

All of which helps explain the missing wedding photos.

My folks' marriage would unravel within a few years, in part due to my mom's wastrel spending at the department stores. Separated from my dad, Muriel sulked back to her parent's house on Laurel Avenue to weigh her future. When she reconciled with Millard, they couldn't find a decent place to live so my dad swallowed his ego and moved into the Zahler house himself. To this day, he swears it jabbed a dagger into Lee. His bedroom wall was up against Muriel's room, which put the nocturnal activities of his daughter and the son-in-law he felt so mortally ambivalent towards about fifteen feet away.

Being in that house provided my dad with the catbird seat on a fascinating trio. The first thing he noticed was that Rose's servitude to her son lent the place a caste-like aura. Every day, she forfeited her wants for Gordon's, and it could be painful to observe. Millard could see his eighteen-year-old brother-in-law was a party magnet/cripple not so much sullen about his condition as exasperated by how much it made him wait. Any prickliness he felt about unmet demands—a fresh bedpan, a different radio station—he zinged toward cheery Rose, who let most of it ricochet off as her as if she wore shoulder pads.

Lee was the main riddle. In one respect, he was your typical European artiste—brooding and hot-blooded, Old World about his views, wary of newcomers. He was a head-down type of man, tough to get a read on, with a booming laugh and rigid affection for family, baseball, cigars and any topic straddling music. Publicly, he was the happiest on those occasions Gordon and Muriel's pals asked him to play a favorite like "Der Fuehrer's Face" on his Baldwin, and everyone sang raucously to his lead. Lee also was one of those annoying people capable of the creative and the analytical. He basked in precision, whether it was quarter notes in a melody or diagrams in an anatomical review. To relax after work he was fond of curling up with a stogie to read his dad's abandoned medical texts.

Lee's relationship with his invalid son is harder to crack. My mom recalls they got along swell, jawing about sports, tracking the war and downplaying the paralysis with only a couple of memorable squabbles I have my doubts. I suspect their love was fierce and frustrating. A teenage livewire and his mercurial father were bound to collide.

After a tiff, Gordon was known to grumble into his bed-sheets while his dad puffed cigar clouds out on the stoop. Both babysat remorse. Before that day at Marshall, Lee had had ideas about molding the kid. Someday, he had assumed, Gordon's pranks would lose their sizzle and he would steer his boy's ambitions through college. The flip side is that my uncle had intended to make his dad proud. There were indications he wanted to be a pilot à la Charlie Lindbergh.

With those dreams gone, they had little else except for an old morning ritual starring the sports page. Lee would sit on Gordon's bed while he ripped through the morning paper to see how the Brooklyn Dodgers fared. Then he would turn to the horseracing results from Santa Anita to check on how the imaginary bets he and Gordon placed did. Sometimes the two needled each other about $10,000-payoffs and rigged races. Everything considered it might have been the most lightheartedness they could muster.

Grandpa over time sought camaraderie with his son-in-law, even if he was too stubborn to ask for it outright. My dad was glad if Lee simply mouthed his name. He almost never called him Millard, preferring a variation of "Hey, *you* there with Muggs."

During my folks' engagement, Lee's protectiveness, an emotion seared with jealousy and mistrust, rarely strayed. If the young couple nuzzled at the dinner table, he would rap my dad's fingers hard with a butter knife. "Cut that out," he would snipe. "You're embarrassing me." After my parents moved into their first house, he visited them frequently on his drive home from the studios. The open secret was that he was there to ensure my mom, who could barely boil water, was getting the princess treatment.

Lee's doubts about my dad thawed slowly and strangely. He periodically, for example, invited Millard to watch the local semi-pro baseball team, the Rosabell Plumbers, play in Monrovia. If my dad, though, weren't standing outside the house at the exact instant Lee motored by to pick him up, Lee refused to honk for him and wait. He would attend the game by himself. At the contests they both made it to, the conversations were choppy. What Lee enjoyed doing best was converting my dad's observations about the game into catcalls he hollered at the players. Mostly, my dad noticed, Lee wasn't home much. He was a musician at heart, and ten to twelve hour workdays seemed to be the standard shift in Hollywood.

Nobody in my family commuted between more dissimilar worlds than grandpa: studio hubbub by day, mountain breezes at night. Gordon's spill only accentuated the divide. My grandparents would knead their hands when one of his infections hit and the ambulance came, and they would argue around the kitchen table later when the invoices arrived. If Gordon's liquor buddies trooped in, Lee and Rose managed nice time together upstairs. Other than that, there was a whole lot of drab, smelly routine caring for the boy, all of which Rose oversaw. She had the patience for it that Lee-the-artist never did.

Out early, home late, my grandfather was a one-man music wing during the 1930s and early 1940s. He composed thousands of songs, mostly as Lee Zahler, sometimes under the mysterious pseudonyms Nico Grigor and J.H. Wood. He also performed and orchestrated much of the music he wrote or supervised entire scores end to end. His L.A. breakthrough had come as the bandleader for the Western Association of Motion Picture Advertisers (WAMPAS), a clubby, press-agent fraternity that got ink every year by handpicking thirteen luscious young women for studio screen tests. Hanging around future head-turners like Ginger Rogers was a nifty perk for Lee, but it was the networking he did as point man for the "official WAMPAS Orchestra" that hurled his career forward. In 1929, when Gordon was three, Lee earned his first movie credit scoring *King of the Congo* for flyspeck Mascot Pictures. His name circled around after that. Regular work was offered by outfits like Invincible Pictures and Producer's Releasing Corp., second-tier independents that manufactured surprisingly good B-movies in spite of frenetic production schedules that put out several new features a month. Later, some of the major studios—Columbia, Universal, RKO—hired him, mainly for serials that ran at the top of double bills. Popular series like *Rin-Tin-Tin* and *Ellery Queen* had grandpa's chops all over them.

The first notoriety Lee achieved during the glamour days of Hollywood, when studio bosses ran things, not today's cable-TV barons, he owed to little Darmour Studios. Larry Darmour, the head of the studio, asked my grandpa to make a song-and-dance man out of a clever little boy whose mother colored his hair with black school polish. The kid-actor's name was Mickey Rooney, and a whole serial was crafted around him as the irrepressible *Mickey McGuire*.

Audiences fell for Mickey; in a few years he would be America's hottest young actor. Within my family, grandpa's role training him became priceless lore. My mother recounted it so much to friends I used to think it was glued to her cerebral cortex. To me, the highpoint wasn't how Lee taught his star pupil to sing on key. It was the sideline about how my mom clocked little Mickey in the nose after he stole her baseball during a sandlot game at Darmour's studio.

Having proven himself with Rooney, Lee was beckoned onto all types of sets by all types of movie people. Directors sweating tight production deadlines courted him the most, because of Lee's ability to compose on the fly. Sometimes he'd hand Rose a considerable check, and they dreamed of down payments on a house. His only nonnegotiable stance was that he used his own instrument. He wasn't interested in some generic house piano with dull keyboard action. His organ—it may have been a portable Hammond—was his sidekick. Every scratch it in embedded character. The never-famous leaned on it. Up-and-comers like Gene Autry, "the singing cowboy," practiced with it. The organ was there when Lee scored *The Three Musketeers* with a young John Wayne and *The Galloping Ghost* with ex-football icon Red Grange. Lee toted it to the desert to compose for a train robbery scene. He sat behind it for musical numbers in a tilt-up Parisian quarter off Hollywood Boulevard. Professionally speaking, it was all he needed

As a wannabe teenage rock star in 1979, I abused that same wooden organ clueless to its origins. The instrument had been handed off from Lee to Gordon to my mom, who warehoused her keepsake under a tarp in the boathouse. The boxy thing meant nothing to me, though I'd surely heard it was my grandfather's. When I blew a guitar riff to a Led Zeppelin song my band was practicing, I'd give one of the organ's legs a swift kick. As our playing improved, its keyboard became an ivory beer coaster. That it was down there, where it perished in the fire, today seems like a crime against family.

Eventually, the genre of Lee's work changed as world affairs did. Westerns and potboiler crime stories in demand in the 1930s segued to patriotic fodder like *Bombs Over Burma* when America went to war in the 1940s. The one constant throughout was the tempting actresses around him. For the longest period, nobody suspected Lee's interest in any of these beauties was anything except vocational. The Mary Pickford knockoffs and dancers in risqué sequins were assumed to be strict colleagues and nothing more. Everyone close to my grandfather had heard his disgust for off-camera Hollywood. Stout Hungarian through and through, he couldn't stand the hypocrisy of do-gooder plot lines and casting-couch sex. Dirty money, vice cover-ups—there was no honor there. He socialized with few Industry people except for Larry

Darmour. He even made his kids swear off any career in the picture business.

Such promises were before Gordon's fall, and well before his own chest tightened up in stressful times. He tried diagnosing the compressions himself, speculating it was acid indigestion tied to money worries and greasy commissary food. After another symptom clutched him—shortness of breath walking stairs—he visited his internist. The doctor ran tests and diagnosed him with moderate-advanced coronary heart disease. Not everyone was notified about his illness immediately.

What was common knowledge was that he took Rose aside midway through 1946 to tell her they were done. Their marriage, he said, wasn't worth fighting for anymore. She was consumed with being a nursemaid to Gordon and filtering it through the Instruction and he had amalgamated life fatigue. Lee couldn't remember the last time passion kindled them. Even if old feelings returned, they would still be skidding toward bankruptcy.

Food stamps and doctors' bills were not Lee's conception of middle-age domesticity. So at fifty-four, straining to start over while he still could, he filled up his suitcases for a nondescript apartment close to his Santa Monica Boulevard office. And when he went, he went lugging testosterone and denial. The fetching younger woman with whom he had been having an affair was waiting for him to drive up. To this day, nobody knows this chickadee's identity. She may have been a contract actress or a Sam Goldwyn dancer. It was just another detail.

If my grandma was decimated, her unflappability shrouded it. If she knew in advance about the mistress, she never disclosed it to her children. Disregard anger, she was resigned. She explained the split up as a balloon payment on everything that had befallen them since Oct. 29, 1940. People around her came to accept the linkage between the accident and the breakup. There was inevitability to what Gordon's burden had exacted. Burnout had bested the marriage, no two ways about it. Living fine with denial, my mom purposely avoided asking her dad anything about his girlfriend when he stopped for visits. I can't vouch for Gordon.

After twenty-six years together, my grandparents were estranged for months—the walking wounded entering confusing beginnings. They did manage a warm hug the September day my mom gave birth to my brother Paul at St. Luke's before they departed going separate ways in separate cars. Fate being the traffic cop that it is, Grandpa's driving days would be over soon enough. His chest felt like a barbell was heaved on it one afternoon in December 1946 and he blacked out, most likely on a movie set. He awoke in Cedars of Lebanon Hospital in Los Angeles with an oxygen mask on his face, standard procedure for a heart attack victim. The nurses asked what they could do for him. "Call my wife," he rasped. "Call her now!"

At Cedars, my grandparents had their Tracy and Hepburn moment. There was no more talk about poverty and infidelity. Lee gripped my grandma's hand from his hospital bed and made his case. What did the doctors know? Remember how Gordon had shocked them. "Yesiree," he promised, he would recover. Their first order of business would be to rustle up the money for the two of them to go on a long-overdue trip to Paris, let the best bubbly flow. They'd borrow the whole bundle if they had to. Rose kissed him when he said that.

For a few weeks the reunion infused new energy into Lee. With a nurse holding his elbow, he strolled the corridor to regain his strength. When he felt spunky, he tried cajoling the attendants to let him fire up a stogie on the hospital sundeck. His ticker was uncooperative with anything bigger. It wasn't absorbing sufficient nourishment because of the plaque clogging his main arteries, and the doctors lacked options to root out the debris with drugs or surgery. Grandpa's high blood pressure and a bum kidney complicated things. No matter, he reassured everyone. He had his wife again and family around. What else was there? He called his mistress one night to urge her to take up with someone else.

Robust enough for a wheelchair, Gordon visited his dad at Cedars. The hard-bitten nurses must have fought to see that—a quadriplegic comforting somebody sicker than he. Rose was there constantly, my mom occasionally. The two prayed through the Instruction that Lee's heart would beat normally again. They encouraged him to disbelieve in his disease to chisel away the plaque. The Instruction, according to Grandma, had rescued Gordon when everything else had failed.

All the same, Lee's arteries were shutting down, and he grew sicker as the weeks progressed. He got exhausted shuffling to and from the bathroom. The most he could do was slap on a brave face when visitors came so they wouldn't detect how much he had waned inside since his early pronouncements about getting better. All he had ever wanted in California was to provide for his family by writing his music. Doing what he treasured (mostly) to support the people he loved was the formula that sustained him. Bedridden at Cedars, too frail to compose for rent money anymore, he felt dejected at the speed at which his formula had deserted him. Lying there, grandpa remembered how he had recently spurned my dad when he asked to borrow a few hundred bucks to buy land for a future house, and he was certain he was dying.

Following recent custom, Christmas 1946 was dour. Lee would've done anything to be home. When my dad came to see him on December twenty-fourth, he nicely ordered him to sit down and take dictation. There was a message Lee needed him to deliver to Gordon by nightfall. The opening was a satire of one of Lee's studio contracts:

My dear Gordon: In consideration of the sum of $1 and other good and valuable considerations, in good old American dollars that I was going to spend on you in goodwill for your happiness, I wish you good cheer for a Merry Christmas that was unfortunately interrupted due to power beyond my own control.

With God's help in the near future I will pick up Christmas with you where I have left off. Just call it a short interruption.
Dad, Xmas '46.

This cheer was relayed just as Lee asked. His pledge for a belated holiday was a reach. On February 21, 1947, right after breakfast, he suffered a major heart attack and died.

Since he had been sick for months, Lee's passing hit the family more like a debilitating cramp than a puncture wound. Rose was at Lee's bedside when he drew his last breath. If she had any solace, it was that her husband had explicitly mentioned God by name in the months before he went up to meet Him. My mom wasn't at Cedars that day. She was at her new house, hard up against the stove stirring baby formula for my big brother when one of Rose's Instruction mates knocked on the door. The woman imparted the message that Lee was gone, and my mom bawled tears into Paul's milk until she was spent.

CHAPTER NINE
Roaring Timber

Can you see them in their funeral black? Sure you can. My grandma and Gordon are in the living room of their Laurel Avenue house, rubber-faced and beat as the sun droops below the foothills. Shadows bisect the floor. A neighbor has shuttled them home from Forest Lawn Cemetery in nearby Glendale and left them a mystery soufflé next to the tulip arrangements. Rose doesn't want to sit still, as it sets her mind on her husband's coffin, so she wills herself out of a chair. Tea, she needs tea. Slogging toward the kettle, she looks over at Gordon, reclined in bed and staring at the wall where the World War II combat map used to be.

It's then that an unexpected emotion penetrates her and she can't stifle it. At first she chuckles under her breath, but this is about absurdity not subtlety, so it inflates into a snort, then a procession of them, then into a gusty hoot. Tears stream down her cheeks. Gordon asks what possibly could be funny but Rose only shakes her head. It was if she had suddenly figured out the punch line to a joke told ages ago. In reality, she is crying from laughing and laughing instead of screaming, *"What's next? Locusts? A case of the piles?"*

Almost. Bargain-basement existence loomed now that my grandfather was dead. Even with the Motion Picture Fund bankrolling the medical bills and the family's seventy-five-dollars-a-week "maintenance" subsidy, even with what remained of the settlement from the Pasadena School District, Rose only had a few hundred dollars to her name. My mother said it was so bleak that Lee had filed formal bankruptcy papers before he took ill, or maybe that made him ill. I could never locate his name in the decaying court logbooks registering his contemporaries' failures. It was irrelevant, anyhow. As my grandma wrote a Fund social worker, everywhere she went in Sierra Madre she discovered a life she couldn't afford. Hunting for a cheaper place made her, in a rare concession, "a little jittery." Gordon heard this repeatedly while she spoon-fed him ice chips during the stifling summer of '47. Price and value, she would intone, were all "out of whack."

Inside, Gordon knew they were dog meat. Outside, he pretended it'd fix itself, as if it ever had. He was twenty, and chomped to be out with the fellas. Some of it was to be with peers who he realized would soon be moving on with their lives and the hell out of Sierra Madre. Some of it was practical. What else did he have to latch onto? His home schooling was done. And the want ads assumed a prospect at least had functioning hands. Unfortunately, where he hurt his back effectively sidelined his fingers. Had he only cracked his spine a few inches lower, vital nerves would've been spared. He could've controlled his arms and fingers, maneuvering into anything from architecture to inventing. Then again, if he'd heeded Coach Turner's warning, he might be in college right now with his dad backslapping him proud.

What-if-thinking gagged him, so he deflected his guilt, hoping it'd burn off like mist, and plotted to rejoin the night crowd. He had connections. Pals like Don Berg and Benny Gouin had made it back from the service without forgetting him. Some of them enrolled at Pasadena City College, pledging the "Catawabas," a renegade fraternity that initiated Gordon as an honorary member. My uncle teased his buddies that he would divulge the names of the fastest women in town if they took him clubbing in Hollywood. Staying cooped up with his mother every night, he would say, was barely a step up from sleeping.

They hit Tom Breneman's on Hollywood Boulevard and Billy Berg's on Vine. They were repeat customers at The Trocadero with its huge glass wall overlooking Hollywood proper. These were classy, neon-lit places with headlining crooners, potent drinks, wide dance floors and the occasional actress. "That handsome guy in the wheelchair over there," needed the best booth, my uncle's friends would tell the club manager, sliding a few bucks in his palm. How many, the manager would ask? "Five couples *plus him*," they would answer.

Here Gordon received more than he had angled for. The clubs could be frantic rooms fed by whiskey and tinny music. None of it provided much normalcy for somebody slowly accepting he'd never again stand. When the other guys' dates fed him drinks through a straw during the show, he felt like their mascot. After the patrons pointed at him and his combat-vet pals grumbled about folks "who'd never seen dick," he sensed he was deadweight best left home next time. He wasn't ready. Maybe the strangers could detect the real him behind the *ain't-this-grand* aura he tried to project by grinning nonstop.

The beauty of the arrangement was that he underestimated the value of his own company. Fact was he was rarely left out. Sitting at Billy Berg's in a bow tie with a plaid blanket over his lap until one a.m., Gordon gradually learned shortcuts. Attitude, that's what he learned. *Be clever*, he thought. *Hit on the cigarette lady. Joke about my big ears, if I must. Just downplay the wheelchair — never let them confuse it with me.*

Gordon's theory on preemption was tested at the Trocadero Club on his twenty-first birthday—February 21, 1947. His favorite singer, given the heads up by Benny, sat down at his booth between sets to chatter and be photographed. The singer stayed longer than he had planned because the birthday boy had lots of opinions. As soon as Nat King Cole and his musicians jumped back on stage, he played a number for "that smilin' cat in booth number 6." My uncle saw this swagger thing had promise.

In town, some put it together. The accident. The lawsuit. Poverty. Lee's passing. Nat Ross's murder. Small towns cradle heartbreak that big cities can't, and tragedy had mauled the Zahlers the way World War II had some families. My grandma was reluctant to discuss her misfortune with strangers, this being "private matters" to her, but what could she do when the locals offered assistance? She so wished Nat was around to dig them out.

Eventually, members of Sierra Madre's all-volunteer fire department heard about the family. They were compassionate men — men with holiday charity rituals, one size fits all. In late December of 1947, perhaps Christmas Eve, two uniformed firemen with seasonally wrapped goody baskets in their arms knocked at 363 Camillo Street. (Grandma and Gordon had moved to this drab place from Laurel Street to capitalize on its bargain rent.) Rose led the men into the small kitchen. There she offered them cinnamon-spiced coffee before they extended a hearty Merry Christmas to Gordon.

My uncle was in his bed expecting pals, not surprises, when these strangers in their black rubber boots clomped in. At first he thought this was a gag orchestrated by Benny, who he guessed would be sauntering in hollering "Fire!" After he noticed the goody baskets, he knew that'd he'd guessed wrong. The strangers were there out of pity. Gordon hated them instantly for it. When the younger firefighter asked clumsily if turkey was on the Christmas-day menu, even Gordon surprised himself with his detonation. He had never had much of a temper.

"Sorry to break this to you, but you can take your measly gifts and scram. Now!" he barked. "There's no fire here."

"Come again?" the pump-man said.

"We don't want your charity, okay? What do we look like, bums or something?"

"Just one second, son," the assistant chief said. "All we brought was some fruit and candy. You can at least say thanks, thanks like everybody else."

"Thanks. Now grab your stuff and leave. I mean it. Moth-er."

Rose heard the hullabaloo and jogged in. Gordon told her he wanted to be alone, so she escorted the bewildered firemen with their unopened baskets out the door.

"You have my sincere apology for that scene," Rose said at the curb. "I haven't seen him that agitated since, well, since he was in the hospital."

"Tell me, Mrs. Zahler, what does he have against a little goodwill?" the assistant chief asked.

"I don't know," she said. "Maybe he's more like his father than I'd gathered."

Gordon was envious of people with carefree anatomies. Just because he didn't pout about wanting to feel healthy for an extended stretch didn't diminish his yearning. The organs he had lost sensation with lived under the threat of constant infection. How he had never had an attack at one of the nightclubs he wasn't sure, but this he knew in March 1948: his peeing was on the fritz. His urine either had bloody clouds in it or he couldn't go at all. Whirlwind fevers came over him, too. One evening, Rose touched his stomach, asking, "Does this hurt?" and his head throbbed. Sometimes he felt downright breakable.

The surgeons had to carve him open. They operated on him at Huntington Hospital and said, "Lookie here," no wonder he was feverish. He had calcium stones throughout his bladder. The stones were removed and he was shipped to recovery. The nurses there barely got his name.

Hemorrhaging profusely, he was wheeled back to the operating room. The doctors snipped the stitches to explore his innards more carefully, and they understood what they had overlooked before. The mouth of his bladder had swollen up so severely his urine had nowhere to go. He would poison himself to death with his own toxic waste unless something was done. The doctors recommended a risky experimental treatment developed by the Veterans Administration—that, or hope the blockage subsided on its own, an unlikely probability.

The doctors explained the odds to Rose in the waiting room and asked her how she wanted them to proceed. She wasn't sure. Lee had been the one with the medical brains. It all rested on her now. What would he do? *Jesus, what?* "Operate," Grandma said finally. "Do something!" Alcohol was injected with a hypodermic needle near the bottom of her son's spine. As it was intended, the injection prodded a nerve to relax his bladder muscle, and waste flowed again. Basically, he had survived another attack on himself.

Afterwards Gordon tried forgetting that scare. Tried forgetting that nothing was going well since his dad had died. Maybe that was why he was in bed at home on a Monday afternoon with a two-day hangover still bongo-drumming his head.

It had been Saturday that my grandma had informed him about the Motion Picture Fund letter, the one alerting them they had exhausted their benefits. "What'd you expect, Mom?" he said when Rose had brooded about the house. "They weren't going to keep sending checks forever." That night he persuaded the guys to take him clubbing, where they drank themselves pie-eyed during the show. Around two a.m., after ducking out on the tip and weaving home drunk on the zigzagging Pasadena Freeway, they stumbled from the car into Stan Lufton's house.

Early the next morning, Mrs. Lufton saw the revelers passed out fully dressed on her custom living room set and angrily went off to check the car for dings in the detached garage. *What's that in the back seat, she asked herself?* She inched close. *No, it couldn't be.* Gordon was slumped over. "Get an ambulance! And call Rose Zahler. Tell her to come over. I think Gordon is dead." Mrs. Lufton said running in from the garage.

By seven a.m. the whole house was awake, including her cotton-mouthed son and his merry band. All of them went to fetch Gordon, who was pale but definitely sentient. The boys tried explaining how numbskull it was of them. How they had been so "pooped" when they arrived home they'd forgotten to transfer him out of the car with them. Plain forgot.

"That's right, Mrs Lufton," Gordon added. "And I'm fine." He said he'd awoken around what he guessed was four a.m. and nobody had heard him call out. He'd wiggled into a half-sleeping position and hoped somebody remembered him because he was stuck with his face squished into the vinyl seat.

"But you weren't breathing. I checked," Mrs. Lufton said.

"Aw, don't feel bad," Gordon interrupted. Other people had mistaken him for dead when he slept.

Now it was Monday, and Rose was glad that Gordon was hung over. Didn't he understand how close they were edging to genuine indigence? How she had thrown herself at the mercy of the Fund administrators? She had cried to them over the phone and in person, and her sniffles didn't budge them. "Just send the fifty dollars a week for another year," she had pleaded. (It had been reduced from seventy-five dollars per week.) "We'll never ask for another cent after that. You have my word."

By late 1948, their answer was the same: sorry, Mrs. Zahler, we can't. Try the county. Squeezed by its own money crunch, the Fund had enacted new guidelines. Families had to have somebody "actively employed" in the Industry to be eligible for financial support—actively employed as in now. Rose asked about exceptions. The Fund manager pointed out the family used all of them up over the last seven years. During that time, $22,000 was dispersed to them (more than $500,000 in today's currency). The checks were over no matter my grandma's appeals.

The social worker from the Los Angeles County Bureau of Public Assistance didn't need any beseeching that Monday. She asked the usual questions. She scanned the usual financials. She looked around the front room that my grandma-the-neat-freak had purposely let get dusty for effect. Don't worry, the lady assured them. They were a lock for welfare.

Now stop where you are! Clear your head. It's here our story pivots on itself. It is here where my ninety-three-pound uncle, future comet, acquires his motivation. Their drop onto the welfare rolls was the final humiliation. Borrowing ten dollars from friends or eating four-day-old meatloaf had failed to jolt him. Welfare, however, officially placed them in the same column as rummies, deadbeats, degenerates and the chronically, happily unemployed. This was something his dad never would have abided. He would have taught piano scales to every spoiled brat in a five-mile radius rather than take government cash. Was this how Gordon would replace him as head of the family? Lying on his bony ass, getting plastered on the weekends, while his mother's white hair came in?

Two weeks had passed since the welfare lady's visit. In the interim, my uncle chased an idea he'd devised some time earlier. Friends aided him by supplying the research. My grandma was chopping carrots for stew when he decided to spring it on her.

"Mom, can I talk to you about something?"

"I hope it's not about permission for another night at the Trocadero." She sat down on his bed.

"No, it's nothing to do with that."

"Good."

"I want you to call that welfare lady."

"You mean Mrs. Harrington?"

"Yep, her."

"Okay, I'll play along. Why am I calling her?"

"To tell her we won't be taking her checks very long. A year tops. After that you can tell her we'll be paying them back."

"My goodness, this is a surprise."

"Not to me. I think I've figured out a way for us to make decent money on our own."

"I love your chivalry, sweetheart, but let's be realistic here." She swept the bangs off his forehead, assessing him for a few seconds. "Unless there's money buried under the house, I don't see how. I haven't held a job since I was waiting tables in New York. And the Fund. Well, you know about that."

"Listen—we don't need any of that."

"Oh really."

"Mom, will you let me talk?"

"Sorry."

Gordon took a deep breath. He was nervous. "I think we should try and resell Dad's old music. All those songs he wrote are worth a ton."

"A-ha! That's why you've been so secretive lately."

"Listen, we own the rights. I had one of the fellas check with the union."

"What makes you think the studios are buying? They have their own orchestras. Who do you think performed all of your Daddy's scores?"

"That's right—for movies. But the networks need music for all these new television shows they're planning. It'd cost them a fortune to do it themselves."

"Oh really?"

"It was all over the radio. I asked Benny to buy me a Daily Variety, and you won't believe this. There was a front-page story all about it. It's in my bottom drawer. I've been saving it for you."

My grandma read the entire article inches from her nearsighted eyes. Gordon tracked them moving. "Well, you're right about them needing music. It says here there might even be a strike over it."

"Wouldn't that be swell?" he said. "They'd really be eating out of our hands. You know better than anyone how many songs dad wrote."

"I can see you're excited about this, Gordon, and I think that's marvelous. There's only one piece you left out. Who's going to organize this little enterprise? I don't have the time."

"You're talking to him."

CHAPTER TEN
The Big Bluff

He kicked off with the sales pitch nuttier than any acrobatics he ever tried. If he were moving to Hollywood, he told the buddies he assembled one night, it would have to be on their backs. As much as he owed them for the camaraderie and boozing, he had never asked for anything like this. It was why he had his mother dress him executive-like in his dad's old tweed coat. Getting his family off "goddamn welfare," he explained from his wheelchair, had given him the purpose he had needed all along. It had given him something tangible to defy.

The catch was that he had nothing with which to pay them. He needed their help as a freebie, or an IOU. "Guys, think of it as the last time you let me arm twist you. In a couple of years when I'm loaded, you can hit me up. Deal?" A few of them chuckled, but the sniggers tapered off when they noticed his squint. He was serious about the freebie. He had measured its dimensions. It entailed pestering the studios for tapes, renting equipment no-money-down, doing library research, filling out union forms, making cold calls, running tape, splicing, recording and indexing, then a hundred-fold of it.

"What kind of time are we talking about?" someone asked him.
"Probably every free weekend you can spare for a year, if you want to hear it straight," Gordon said.

Sighs of disappointment creased the room. A couple of the fellas brusquely questioned what Gordon would be doing, and he answered that he would be supervising them and hunting for contracts when he wasn't. Rose, who was eavesdropping from the kitchen, would handle the paperwork. Every family friend either one of them knew would be co-opted for the effort. The boys were almost afraid to say "no." Gordon's audacity didn't recognize the word.

What they volunteered for was barely show biz. The closest they came to flashbulb Hollywood was when they would drive in from Sierra Madre, pass through a studio gate, talk to a mid-level executive, and return (usually) with the tapes that Lee had not stored in his home coat closet. Any buzz they felt when a knockout actress swished by them on the lot dissipated in my grandma's living room, where the tedium took over. Each tape had to be converted from old-fashioned optical tape to standard one-quarter-inch. Every tune had to be broken down into its musical style, its length, its studio origin, etc. The songs and movie titles were then typed in capital letters onto crinkly onion paper. Columns were added. All told, Lee had scored 915 shows, serial episodes included, my grandfather having gotten around.

Attrition among Gordon's volunteer brigade hurt the cause. Some guys shaved their hours or quit outright when they heard the workload—915 scores. The defections dragged production more than the equipment screw-ups. Most of the eight who stayed were either full-time college students or newly married men with regular jobs. The ones with battlefield memories didn't talk about them much. Some of the Marshall Tarzans were in the group. Now they had two jobs, or close to two, though nobody bitched outwardly about it at first.

When the eventual jokes surfaced in month three about Gordon being a slave driver, my grandma asked to speak with the guys one-on-one in the entryway. If they had to leave, she said, they would go with her blessing. She understood there was no logical reason they kept pulling up at her house every Saturday, generally before eleven, asking what "the count" was? They shouldn't have been in her living room sitting cross-legged in a jury-rigged recording bay with papers and musty tapes strewn across the furniture, feet from odd strangers lending a hand, as Lee's Ragtime and Honky Tonk music echoed nonstop, Gordon in the center of the chaos swiveling his jumbo-sized head to keep up. No, with all the kindnesses they had bestowed they should have been out in the sunshine thinking of themselves for a change.

But here they were, every weekend of every month. Fifty tapes to go, 49, 48…Gordon's fanaticism with the tracking—he bet someone he could memorize the entire library—probably colored their exit plan. They would finish his catalogue, however long that took, get him drunk for posterity and make him Hollywood's problem. Once he was, they would own their weekends again.

Gordon, though grateful to his core, often asked himself if it wasn't all a masquerade. Recovering from his broken neck took grit. This required courage *and* smarts.

It was a whiz-bang age, these wholesome fifties. Chairman Mao and the bomb shelter made affordable, Pork Chop Hill and TV dinners. There was Rosa Parks and Jack Kerouac, stainless steel counters and the sock hop. And here Gordon was in Hollywood sixteen months after he set out for it. Smack dab in the business Lee had warned him to avoid, his plan was to sell his dad's creations and end the handouts.

His first official office was a 1,200-square-foot bungalow on eastern Sunset Boulevard walled with chipped acoustical tiles. Hollywood's glamour set stayed on the Sunset Strip miles west of here, closer to Scandia's restaurant and the Chateau Marmont building. This part of town, next to a future freeway, was for the rest, where the dubbing houses, post-production shops and fly-by-night distributors grinded away. The real estate guys my uncle dealt with called this "grade-A back-office space." Gordon was attracted to the piddling rent. To him, the ceiling stains were invisible.

There was a reception-type area near the front door, one regular-sized office (his) and four cramped rooms just large enough for an editor and his machine. My uncle's "desk" was a rented adjustable bed fitted with a black and yellow throw-blanket. His décor was a connect-the-dot clown watercolor he had painted as a kid. The most noteworthy feature to his office was its tie-in to history. The bungalow was on the service-entry side of a stately, colonial-style building with graceful, fluted columns facing Sunset—Warner Bros. original headquarters. The first movie with synchronized sound (*Don Juan*—1926) was cut there. A few years after Gordon arrived, Warner's bugged out to Burbank, sold the complex to Paramount Pictures and a slice of the property was converted into the country's largest bowling alley. If my uncle had a responsive tendon in his arm, he could have almost rolled one of those balls into his father's old building. It was only a few blocks south.

The locale was suitable. The problem was "The Zahler Music Library" was more hope than actual enterprise. Rose and Gordon still needed to bum rides into Hollywood. Their only employees in those formative months were a couple of part-time music editors who they had difficulty throwing any work. The catalogue—no one wanted Lee's catalogue, now meticulously stored on a set of industrial shelves. Their black phone slept in its cradle all day.

Gordon, feeling especially shaky one Monday, tried to reach one of his dad's old associates at Columbia Pictures. The man had retired. The three or four commercials Gordon had picked up had been a favor from someone at Warner's. As it were, he had Rose roll him around the studio executive suite every few days in anticipation he might overhear a deal in the hopper. It was no use. Word was the networks were hungrier than ever for soundtracks. Apparently it didn't include his.

Inside he fretted his strategy was amateur hour. That explained why he had no jobs. He had tried to line up customers placing cold calls on the phone, omitting anything about his physical ruin. Face-to-face meetings were discouraged because he had experience with newcomers, not to mention small children, frightened into statues by his appearance. Parties interested in the catalogue instead would have sample copies delivered to their office. The advantage to his setup, or so he thought, was that he could keep them at a ripe distance until they were ready to sign. He had purchased a microphone headset through the phone company, something their operators might've worn, that freed him to negotiate like any other entrepreneur. A receiver went over one ear. A small boom microphone looped in front of his mouth. With a flail of the arm, he could swipe a padded lever attached to his bed frame to connect and terminate calls. It felt like progress.

When he couldn't make any, he figured someone must have snitched to the producers, who then blabbered amongst themselves. What did they assume: he was paralyzed and a mental cripple? That he would try to splice the music into the Movieola editing machine with his own teeth, thereby chancing a gruesome industrial accident, reams of bad publicity and sponsors pulling out? No, my uncle, then twenty-five, reminded himself. They had to be savvier than that. Look at their money stack.

Okay, he reasoned, perhaps he had the right product but the wrong partner. A mother-son combo was DOA in this town, especially his combo, and someone had forgotten to whisper it to him, right? They had neglected to tell him that since he was in a wheelchair with hands under a lap blanket he needed a counterbalancing front man to inspire trust. Those mornings at three a.m., when he'd slept all he needed to and would've killed for a cigarette, Gordon replayed those episodes where there had been a real meeting. It was Rose who had wheeled him into the offices, usually after struggling to get him into the elevator, and shook hands. She ran the demo music tape while he narrated and inflated Lee's career. That time he suffered a sneezing fit at NBC, she was the one babying him with his favorite handkerchief. *Jesus,* he thought, *I'm doing half of this for her, more than half. Why couldn't I only need her after work? I'm pretty sure she's the hitch.*

Besides, this was the time to pounce. The upheaval around the musicians' union had made his father's music even more valuable once producers knew it was for rent. James Caesar Petrillo, the imperious labor boss of the American Federation of Musicians, was to thank for this opportunity. Most people just overlooked it with Congress pursuing Hollywood communists.

Petrillo, a balding, ex-horn player with a phobia about germs, was doctrinaire in his economics. He railed that sound movies, big-time record labels and such had thrown tens of thousands of performing stage musicians out of jobs. Only fair, he said, their working colleagues share the wealth. In the age of Big Labor, his organization had the muscle to redistribute it. Accordingly, he taxed the record companies, depositing the money into a fund earmarked for unemployment subsidies. Next, when the studios emptied their film vaults to sell their old movies to TV, he demanded they pay twenty-five dollars to every musician who performed on the original score. Gordon and Rose must have been tooting for this charge to be implemented. If the twenty-five dollar show tax went through, they could be banking $50,000 — seed money to do something.

The 50-grand was a mirage. Petrillo soon changed his mind about who should get what, and redirected the twenty-five dollar-per-show levy into an A.F.M. fund *he* oversaw. His follow-up shakedown was so galling it became his last. After he ordered his lieutenants to slap a five percent tax on all filmed TV production, the backlash was as if the earth had belched open and out strutted Satan with a pro-union button. The major studios vowed to ignore what they called his extortionist fee. Washington threatened action. When it was divulged that the majority of musicians the A.F.M. fund was supposed to subsidize were actually middle-class doctors and lawyers who had not touched their instruments for years (or the last lodge meeting), Petrillo was accused of operating a multi-million dollar slush fund. A strike was coming.

TV producers, meantime, had their own response to the A.F.M. They would buy European soundtracks to score their shows. Why pay $1,100 to U.S. musicians and $1,400 in union levies, they asked, when they could snap up a half-hour soundtrack for $400 from England?

Jack Perry, certified public accountant, posed the question. Ditto for Nat Winecoff, promoter. They told my uncle they would chinwag with him later. For now they wanted to ask him something: "What the hell are you doing, Gordon?" He should have been flush with work, thousands-of-dollars-a-month flush. There had never been a seller's market for tracked music before. Wasn't he cold calling, they asked? TV producers were near desperate for song clips to dramatize and lighten their shows, or fill in dead air. Gordon, referred over to these men for advice by a friend at Warner's, said he was hip to that. Which circled Jack and Nat back to, "So what the hell are you doing over there?" Okay, Gordon admitted. He needed a teensy bit of direction.

Nat through his contracts generated some action. Producers of the *Wild Bill Hickok* show, a syndicated, half-hour Western in an age of them, committed to a limited, trial run of the library. The $275 was great, Gordon said. The sale made him feel better. It was just that the money evaporated after rent and expenses. Expecting Gordon would say that, Nat told him to put himself in his customers' shoes, to stop thinking so myopically about what he needed as opposed to what they needed from him, if he wanted into their billfolds. "How?" Gordon asked flailing his arms; he had gained considerable control over them by jerking his shoulders. "Spit it out." Nat explained that producers were under pressure to trim costs, so make them come to you and sway them with a bargain. After you lowball them and do a good job, hit them up for more. Make them need you. Nat couldn't have known it, but Gordon had temporarily misplaced his swagger.

On Nat's advise, Gordon encouraged people to drop by the bungalow to hear samples of Lee's work. Rose handed them price sheets and Gordon talked up his bargain. "You're not going to find a better catalogue in town at this price." Of course he knew that Capitol Records and another small startup like his were his only competition for soundtracking jobs the studios didn't perform in-house. "Give us a shot. You can't afford not to." The full press boomed from his wheelchair, which he never mentioned in advance of their meeting. With bonhomie and salesmanship, he tried distracting attention from his body in the vainest town on earth. He puffed off a cigarette that his mother put to his lips. Sometimes he queried customers if they cared for a drag.

His shtick turned some heads, mainly because Gordon framed what he was selling as transcendent merchandise, not some clunker from a used-car lot. A good half of the prospects were able to focus on the music after the shock of whom they were negotiating with wore off. By the second or third meeting, a dozen of them accepted him as the only hard-core cripple in a coat and tie they had ever negotiated with in Hollywood. And, fact was, they needed his wares.

Slowly, others came. The people behind *Private Secretary*, a network sitcom about a brassy, busty Girl Friday, signed up with him. A few commercials dribbled in. Young Gordon didn't always secure the proper legal rights for the music he sold, including a bunch of his dad's old acetates. He didn't always reimburse the obscure British composers whose songs he sliced and spliced into desirable cues. Whatever shortcuts he took, unintentional or sneaky, the copyright police never showed up; the checks did. Nat, consequently, not only decided to stick around, he invested a handful of his own money into the operation. He was a nondescript man in his thirties, 5'7" and mousy, with futuristic ideas about amusement parks and an aptitude for promotion. Spike Lee, the clowning bandleader, had turned to him for ideas. So would Walt Disney, who'd cherry-pick Nat to develop financing angles for the theme park he was building in Anaheim. In 1954, however, before he left for Uncle Walt's Magic Kingdom, Nat was Gordon's first genuine partner.

They would tool around the studios in Nat's Chevy chasing minor deals, embellishing everything, with my uncle in the front passenger seat looking sunny, if not cocky. Nat put up with the hassles lifting him in and out of the car because the little man from

Sierra Madre was a scheme-machine in his own right. Many of Gordon's ideas were harebrained takeoffs of existing programs. A surprising clump had promise. Nat helped flesh one of them out and flew with Gordon to New York City to shop it to television syndicators. Back East, Nat handled the diapering, dressing and hefting Gordon required. In doing so, Rose enjoyed her first true break from him in fourteen consecutive years, even if she worried sick about his well-being without her.

The two returned home victoriously with a signed, albeit rinky-dink production contract. Not long afterwards, Nat buttonholed Gordon in his office. How adamant was he about making it in Hollywood, really making it? Gordon said staunch. Okay, Nat replied, he had a plan provided Gordon open up on his one taboo subject.

Two weeks later, in June 1954, Gordon spoke to a United Press International reporter. A week or so later this ran in the papers.

GENIUS WHO CAN'T USE LIMBS
SCORES TV COUP
By Aline Mosby, *United Press International*

Next fall television will offer a new program that teaches you how to sew, but the real story behind the show rivals most of the dramas on TV.

Gordon Zahler, twenty-eight-year-old genius who successfully filmed and sold the interesting series, was not rich and had no experience. He is a hopeless cripple who cannot use his hands or walk.

Yet, lying on a couch in his office with scripts clipped to a board near his eyes and a telephone headset over his ears, Zahler has produced thirteen color (episodes) on sewing. They already have been sold in seven major cities to begin in September.

"Being able to sit back and observe TV a lot, I noticed every station has two or three cooking programs, but none on sewing," he explained. "There's a tremendous amount of home sewing in the United States—30,000,000 women do their own sewing. I decided it would be a saleable show."

Zahler was paralyzed at fourteen when he broke his neck....

As teacher, they hired Elizabeth Chapin, who taught sewing in department stores. On the one-woman, scriptless program Miss Chapin shows viewers how to bind buttonholes, put up a hem and other steps in a behind-a-counter couturier.
Zahler and his partners went to New York to sell their show.

"It was difficult getting around," he admitted. "When I'd phone for appointments, I wouldn't tell people I was in a wheelchair. I was afraid they wouldn't see me.

"So I would just arrive. It was a shock to some people. I worked with the hope my ability and being able to deliver a good program would overcome their feelings. I didn't work on the basis of their feeling sorry for me."

During our interview the producer sat behind his desk in his wheelchair. He paused to smoke a cigarette held to his mouth by one of his partners.
"We have two more programs lined up to produce next fall," he smiled.

Nat was right. Again. The phone did go crazy after the article appeared. My uncle's Sierra Madre friends called first to tease him and congratulate him. "Good for you, Mr. Genius," they said, "but can you show us a French hem?" Harde-har-har, he snickered back. The *Wild Bill* producers phoned next to say they would sign on for all of next season, and momentum gathered.

In the subsequent months, Gordon finalized soundtrack deals with producers of the *Ford Theater* and *Fireside Theater*, both network anthology programs, and scored more commercials. The folks at *The Red Skelton Show*, a ratings grabber, wanted a few cues themselves.

The fetching picture of Gordon accompanying the story even showcased his dimples as sort of sprinkles on the sundae.

Those victories notwithstanding, it was still a ragtag, three-person operation. Gordon could sell, but he managed impulsively. Rose, silent partner, had never worked in an office in her life, and was tasked with correspondence and answering the phones. (Gordon's cigarettes, tea, lunch, urine bag and lap blanket also were her charge.) Nat focused on his contacts. They let the temp editors be.

As the contracts came in, so did Gordon's need for guidance navigating Industry canals. Jack Perry, CPA, made headway that others couldn't. He won over Gordon with an hour-long, soft-sell argument to let him manage the financials, because my uncle knew even less about taxes and insurance than he did about precision music editing. Concentrate on wooing clients, Jack urged. Throw yourself into the mechanics of the job. Gordon went along, and not only because Jack was so brainy. They had become fast friends as only a couple of gimps could be.

When they entered restaurants, heads jerked around to watch their singular propulsion. This wasn't a medical carnival: this was adaptation into the mainstream. Nat wheeled Gordon while Jack hobbled haltingly behind on canes. Game Jack needed the crutch because he walked on a pair of plastic, prosthetic legs that at least kept him upright. He had lost his lower limbs to the Nazis at the Battle of the Bulge in one of World War II's concluding bloodbaths.

As a young GI trying to locate his unit after a furlough, he had stepped on a landmine buried on the Belgium side of the Ardennes Forest. Badly wounded, though still with his legs, he was transferred to a field hospital the Germans had baited American forces into occupying. Once they were inside, the Nazis rained down artillery shells that blew off Jack's legs and killed most of his buddies.

He was fortunate not to have died in triage. With tenacity, Jack persevered, first through the military hospitals, then through college. Some years later he hooked arms with a fellow accountant unbiased about his partner's trunk-body. They put out their shingle in a seedy part of town, near La Brea and Pico boulevards, hoping the clientele wouldn't mind the neighborhood or Jack's handicap. Like my uncle, blue-eyed Jack over-compensated for missing parts, using earnest counsel to win clients where Gordon employed ballsy hucksterism. Whatever Jack did worked, because he eventually limped his way into an expensive suite in West L.A.

It was Jack who introduced Gordon to Abraham "Abe" Marcus, a swarthy music lawyer who'd come to Beverly Hills by way of Columbia Law School in New York. He'd become the final member of Gordon's wise-man troika. Abe had a short, ramrod bearing that frequently got him confused around the golf course with a sitting superior court judge.

Away from the links, Abe filed lawsuits for the underdog. His primary clients were Hollywood composers long exploited by the studios over copyright and royalty payments. Many were irascible Europeans—guys named Dmitri and Miklos—who felt their talents went unappreciated until they hired Abe. He'd become their pinstriped Jewish hero. According to legend, Abe once hired an accordion player to perform in court to demonstrate the nuances in a song. Abe valued one quality above all else about Gordon: though green, the kid was always beating the bushes for money, and getting good at it.

During the mid-'50s, Gordon's wise men urged him to start bidding on movies, however spotty, to sock away money for when the TV shooting season went on hiatus. Gordon heeded their advice after witnessing the checks it brought in. One of the first was from director Edward Wood Jr. Not long afterwards, Gordon dictated a letter he'd been dying to send. It notified the county welfare department to stop sending any more vouchers to the family. Gordon and Rose could pay their own way now.

CHAPTER ELEVEN
Here Comes Flash

My uncle was comfortable with Edward Wood Jr.'s movie-screen aliens. If they wanted to conquer mankind by raising the dead and acting uppity it was okay by him. He was just the music guy. Here was the material:

BRAVE AIR FORCE COLONEL: Why is it so important that you want to contact the governments of our Earth?
TESTY HEAD ALIEN: Because of death. Because all you of Earth are idiots.
AIR FORCE OFFICER NO. 2: Now you hold on, Buster.
ALIEN: No, you hold on!

Only Wood, the big-hearted hack, could write such garbage and film it worse. When his lead actor, the aging, strung-out Bela Lugosi, died just *after* shooting had commenced, Wood found a replacement and filmed the back of his head. Under his direction, day and night shifted within the same scene, and extraterrestrials recruited vampires to do their dirty work. His terrifying U.F.O. was a hubcap that someone spray-painted silver.

By the 1990s, Wood's *Plan 9 From Outer Space* was a cult classic beloved for its schlock appeal. But in the sci-fi 1950s, Wood had trouble getting it reviewed. Some critics trashed it as the worst picture ever made. So why did Gordon's name appear as music supervisor when the credits rolled? Why did he sign up for future Ed Wood/Atomic Productions like *Night of the Ghouls* after he had better gigs? Because a job equaled distraction. Yes, the plots crumbled and Wood was a drag queen with a fetish for angora. It was still a subject Gordon could wrap his mind around instead of fixating it on his iffy life span.

In the summer of 1957, before Ed Wood called him, Gordon's belly was shutting down again. The telltale signs returned — the headaches, the sweating. Dr. Risser was contacted. X-rays revealed stones all over his left kidney and a few in his bladder and urethra. It was best they come out now, Risser said, preferably at Huntington Memorial. Gordon, contemptuous of most doctors, considered Risser a shaman. If he said you would recover, you'd better start healing.

The hurdle was the expected medical bill — $300 he didn't have. Headset secured, he dialed the people at the Motion Picture Fund, whose last check to the family had arrived six years ago. Now that he was in the Industry, he inquired if they would finance his surgery. Fund administrators said they would.

By all rights, it should've been Gordon's last earthly request. As the surgeon that Dr. Risser had recommended slit open the bad kidney, Gordon's blood pressure fell in precipitous drops. In a couple of minutes, the needle was at zero. His breathing stopped, then his heartbeat. Technically, he was dead.

Forgetting the kidney, the lead surgeon grabbed another scalpel. He sawed an incision a few inches wide through Gordon's sternum, wiggling two fingers into the cavity and poked around. There was the heart. It was limp, jelly-like. The surgeon rubbed it and massaged it and prodded it to restart, this being the age before cardiac-shock paddles.

"Beat!" the surgeon said. "Beat, God damn it." It didn't move. The surgeon massaged the organ harder now. If he didn't get the heart pumping soon, Gordon's oxygen-deprived brain would be so scrambled it wouldn't be worth the resuscitation. After a minute, he withdrew his fingers. Everybody in the operating room watched the incision. *Boom.* The heart twitched. In a minute it regained its normal rhythm. Breathing kicked in, his blood pressure surged. Gordon was well enough in two weeks to have the stones successfully removed. He was ornery enough after that to whine about missing work. Once again, his impossible life was saved.

Far from leaving him gun-shy, the near-death experience produced an opposite and equal reaction. He felt elation to recover, a dedication to it, not depression his heart would stop again. Sitting in front of his reel-to-reel tape machine while a part-time editor scored *Plan 9* with heavy organ music, he reorganized his mind. Any movie job, even an Ed Wood stinker, was advancement. His health stabilized with him proud of this breastbone scar. It'd take a lot more than that to plant him in the ground.

Being my uncle's clerk nine to five, then his home attendant every night, had not done my grandma's battery much good. At fifty-five, her hair was a tangle of dull gray locks, her eyes strewn with wrinkles customary for someone twenty years older. She walked constantly. And when she wasn't moving, she was either parked in front of the stove, hunched over Gordon's bed, or typing letters for him hunt-and-peck style at a desk inside his office. Rose was on her feet so much that the svelte legs her husband used to rave about swelled up nightly, painful and stiff with elephantiasis. Every week of every month she only had a few hours to lavish on herself, usually late at night when Gordon was snoring. A long bath or some late-night reading was her equivalent of me-time. The caretaker's existence was devouring her incrementally.

Certainly, nobody could have faulted Rose for throwing a hissy fit those times Gordon unloaded on her for not being his hands when he needed them. The more successful he became, the more his impatience reigned. "Hurry up, Mom," he would shout from the other room. "I don't have all day to go through the mail, you know." How she must have wanted to throw down her spatula, in moral protest if nothing else! "That's it. I can't do this anymore! Call one of your friends. I'm taking the week off." Could have but wouldn't.

Grandma absorbed most of his snipes with the passivity of a Buddhist monk. In her heart, she was convinced it was the tension between his dependence and his ambition that was flinging them, not his core being. My uncle had leapt from kid-businessman to full-throated capitalist in a matter of years. Rose welcomed the change, although the change came at her expense. When dejected about it, she'd slather niceness on the closest person. It was rather exhausting.

And, perplexingly, undervalued. Mama Rose's nearly-unimaginable sacrifice to Gordon's gangbuster ambitions remains legend, even today, to the outsiders slack-jawed to be around it. Just the endurance it required for her to stick to his side morning-to-night, a pit-boss to his whims, smacked of the super-human. A thousand meals standing up; friendships lost; arthritis gained; holidays on bedpan detail; no time for church? You got a couple hours? While she handed over more of her lifeforce to Gordon than anyone in my family has given to another, this duty flowed organically through her. Mama Rose was never happier than when she was serving others, and her service was never more needed than it was for a son as pitiful as a legless lamb. She didn't need a platinum charm bracelet with her name on the back as thank you. She needed more sleep.

As I tried reconstructing how such a star-crossed old lady weathered that beastly load, it troubled me that her self-deferment for the greater Gordon was not better honored within the family. This, naturally, trained a bull's eye on her daughter. Beyond an occasional teary nod to Mama Rose's endurance, my mom withheld virtually every anecdote and any "I remember…" specifics about Rose's slavishness. "Saintly" — that's all she could muster. "Now please pass the potatoes." Was this because my mom had been so whipsawed by her own family problems that Rose's commitment to Gordon felt suddenly blasé? You decide if that's possible.

In 1941, my uncle resided on death's prickly doormat, seeing more doctors than kin. By the mid-1950s he was a Hollywood player slinging small talk with Desi Arnaz and Red Skelton.

If my mom had been too preoccupied to seal this inside her, she had a passable explanation. But if she was aware and just couldn't say, a vast, terrible truth had to be imprisoning it. It was on my shoulders to liberate those memories, or all I'd have was generalized nothings about a lucky gimp and his bedraggled mommy.

Back in her era of servitude, Rose eventually let it slip: she needed a breather. Now that she was speaking her mind, she could use a regular day off and a short vacation, too. There had to be someone dependable they could hire as a part-time attendant. When she brought out the Yellow Pages and pointed to the employment agencies, Gordon thought he misheard her. His mother: on a trip? Impossible. To him, she'd discarded self-interest so long ago it was hard to remember when she requested anything more personal than a neighbor watching him for a few hours so she could go to church or, occasionally, out to buy undergarments. By voicing she needed a break, Gordon understood she must've been gasping for one. He could see she deserved to relax. All he had to do was study her poor ankles. If only the timing was better. "We can't, at least not now," he'd say when she tried finessing the issue. "We've been over this." Her rest time, he said, would jeopardize what little savings they'd compiled if he had to pay someone else to care for him. Two hundred bucks was too much. Hell, one hundred was.

Gordon's blunt no was squashing. But surrender? Not this Rose. The lady in the black granny glasses, the woman who preached pacifism as the way to stomp evil, was in actuality willing to confront some very influential men. In 1957, she filed a $300,000 lawsuit against Columbia Pictures for stiffing her over Lee's royalty payments, a choice that didn't come easy. Grandma had always been sentimental about Columbia; the studio had been the first major to hire her husband. Perhaps, Abe Marcus offered, there were different executives in charge now. After *Crime Takes A Holiday*, one of Lee's old Columbia movies appeared on local television, Abe wrote the studio to ask where the Zahler's compensation was. No response came. Other films Lee scored trickled onto late-night, L.A. television, and Abe sought a meeting to discuss things. His request was ignored. Injunctions were threatened. They were disregarded.

At issue were my grandfather's intentions. After he had scored a film, he used to bang out a *pro forma* license granting his studio employers the right to play his music in movie theaters with the picture. For symbolism, he had charged them $1 per synchronization license. The music was his. Nothing had been negotiated about TV. How could it be? Beamed electrons didn't exist commercially until after he died.

Abe wrote Columbia for months on end that they were violating their side of the bargain. Lee's art was being recycled, so where was the cut for his survivors? Columbia, by ignoring Abe's letters, signaled Lee's heirs to get lost. Indeed, the studio bulled ahead to auction 300 of my grandfather's films and Abe had a drawer full of unanswered communiqués. A suit was discussed, and Gordon and Rose asked about consequences. Abe explained that their chances of victory were remote because Columbia would go all-out to fight the suit, if only to deter the families of other dead composers from staking claims. After the lawsuit reached *Daily Variety*, Abe speculated that the rival studios would close ranks around Columbia. The company, he added, might portray Rose as a greedy widow. For the prospect of $300,000, enough money to retire tomorrow, both mother and son nodded they would take that gamble. Rose never used to say that.

It was a jittery period all around for them. The standoff between the studios and the musicians' union was even more make-or-break for the Zahler livelihood than the Columbia suit. If soundtracked music were abolished as part of a new labor pact to protect Hollywood orchestras, they would be promoting a tape catalogue that no one needed, not *Wild Bill Hickok*, not Ed Wood. Their venture would be over and they would probably be reapplying for welfare checks within three months.

Fortunately for them Big Labor was still posturing. When the major studios ignored the A.F.M.'s levies, Petrillo tried smoking them out. He ordered a nationwide musicians' strike, expecting it would freeze movie production in its tracks. This time the majors called his bluff. Paramount and Twentieth Century said let the musicians picket, they would jack up their use of cheaper European and Mexican players. (All the studios were on a cost-cutting kick because of competition from TV.) Fearful of extinction, L.A. movie musicians took bold steps themselves. They voted to abandon the A.F.M. for a new, democratic organization.

By doing this, they ended the strike and essentially the reign of James Caesar Petrillo.

Show biz music would never be the same under compromise agreements. TV producers only needed freshly recorded music for a portion of their shows. Studios that had employed their own private philharmonics since the Golden Age of film would disband them in return for musician pay raises. Films would be scored on a project basis or with soundtracks. No two ways about it: Petrillo's botched shakedown led customers directly to Gordon's cashbox.

Gertrude Ducrest, Gordon's new secretary, called out there was a Mr. Fields on the line. "Who?" Gordon asked. He swiped the lever and spoke into his headset. Twenty minutes later he told Gertrude to have his mom drop everything and come in. The *Howdy Doody* grin he wore for that UPI story had reappeared.

"What is it, Gordon?"

"Mom, take a load off." She did with a frown. "Remember how we were talking about finding new jobs? You know, now that Wild Bill and Ford Theater are being cancelled?"

"Yes. But you said we'd get picked up by the Ann Sothern Show." (It was the spin-off from *Private Secretary*.)

"That's small change compared to the appointment we have in Culver City next week."

"Culver City? What's in Culver City?"

"Oh, I don't know. How about a little company called MGM."

"Gordon, I'm too tired for this today. Just say whatever it is you called me in here for."

"Maybe this will make you feel better. Our appointment is with Joseph Fields. He's producing the next big Doris Day movie. And he want us—us—to score most of the movie from the catalogue!"

"I don't believe it. You're pulling my leg."

"No, I'm not. Not when it's MGM calling. We have to cover about forty minutes, give or take."

"Why us?"

"I don't know. Maybe we're getting a reputation. We'll find out with Mr. Fields. He's taking us to lunch to sign the papers."

"This sounds too good to be true."

"Tell me about it."

"Did he say who else is going to be in the movie?"

"Richard Widmark. Gene Kelly (the actor) is directing. His debut, I think."

"Do they have a title?"

"*Tunnel of Love*. It's based on a play."

"Gordon, I'm speechless. This is the best news we've had in, gosh, I don't know how long."

"It's better than that. With the four-thou we stand to make, we should be able to put down a deposit on a house around here according to Jack. No more back and forth everyday. It'll be sayonara, Sierra Madre."

"Don't speak ill of Sierra Madre. It's been wonderful to us."

"Loosen up, Mom. I'm only saying that since we work here, we should live here. Anyway, I'm sick of living there. Hey, are you listening?"

"Not really. I was thinking about Doris Day. I just love her movies.

"I'm going to love the check."

CHAPTER TWELVE
The Little Big Top

That morning Rose wept. Gordon beamed. Moving day was here. The money from *The Tunnel of Love*, the story of a suburban Connecticut couple bumbling their way through conception, did finance their down payment. After five rentals, each one more ramshackle than the last, their name was typed, notarized and duly recorded on a deed. Hectic as it was amid the stuffed cartons, their first night at 8979 Shoreham Drive, Hollywood, was a night inside enchanted walls. Grandma cooked roast beef with Yorkshire pudding for everyone who helped with the relocation.

And Gordon had a request. Someone lift him out of his wheelchair and grab the camera. Someone snap his picture sitting in a regular chair, which the doctors had cautioned him against, to commemorate the milestone. If he tumbled onto the floor, he would be all right. He would laugh his ass off inside his new house and slurp another cocktail.

The cream-colored place was in a dense, blue-collar neighborhood in the hills above Sunset Boulevard, west of Laurel Canyon. The TV detective show, *77 Sunset Strip*, was supposedly set right down the road. Inside was a basic setup: a small kitchen, two back bedrooms, a vanity nook, a brick fireplace and a bottom-level garage. Floor-length mirrors made the living room, where Gordon's bed sat, appear bigger than the precise square footage. There was a bright aura here owing to the beige carpeting and lavender parlor couch, and a bay window that beckoned in the sunbeams. From his bed, my uncle had a clear view of western Hollywood, particularly the skin joints and neon-splashed nightclubs anchored south of him on Sunset. Perfect! The structure cost $22,700. What the bank didn't own, mother and son split fifty-fifty.

Under the existing pecking order—Gordon the boss, Rose the bossed around—not much else was split. Where Gordon was once content to run the office, he began to assert control at home as well. Things he had never cared about before—how the furniture was arranged, mortgage rates, nursing bills, custom-tailored suits— mattered now. At thirty-two and self-assured, he wanted to rule the details. My grandma, too winded to fight much, let him. Parts of her were so relieved she sometimes went to bed humming.

It wasn't like she could keep him corked up, anyway. She had been there when people scoffed at his ideas, the ideas of a cripple, and saw how it locked his jaw. She had seen it again when my dad, the civil engineer, admonished him at a family gathering about trying to chisel an elevator into his new house. It would be a technical loser, my dad had warned, a potential hazard. Get a ramp. "Guess time will tell if my way's better, eh Millard?" Gordon had answered, smiling between spoon-fed bites.

He had his own engineers. Okay, they were sound and recording technicians he met on some dubs, plus Nat, but they were a wily bunch and only a tad vulgar. "Stuff it," they said when my uncle tried to pay them. They liked the challenge and the free beer. Using new parts and cannibalized ones, evading city inspections along the way, they built him an illegal, two-person lift between the bottom story garage and the main house. A shaft appeared where a stairwell used to be over the course of two weeks. It was Gordon's vision. He willed it. He argued with the guys about electronics and the winch, as if he knew. He cheer-led them on amid the flying plaster. Scavenging a war surplus store for supplies, he found a jet-fighter pilot seat complete with ejection handle and bought it cheap. *Bingo*—there was his custom elevator chair. (The phone-booth-sized cab was too small for his wheelchair.)

Trial runs were tense. Without some means of transporting him in from the garage, they might have to sell what they just purchased and pin themselves into a modest single-story place. Grandma couldn't lug a wheelchair up those stairs a single time, let alone twice daily. Regardless, Gordon was positive it would work out. But what if the cables snapped and the cab plunged, Rose asked? What if she went deaf? Nobody had expected the jackhammer vibration the elevator engine would send through the stucco walls.

Then too, nobody expected the contraption would run so dependably with practically no maintenance save for lubrication over the years. It was a point Gordon reminded my dad about over chess games and dinners for years to come.

This was making it. Buying trips to London and New York. Ed Wood doubling what he paid last time. A music deal for 195 *Crusader Rabbit* cartoons. Watching secretaries who'd once fabricated excuses why their boss wasn't in welcome him with a supple, "Good morning, Mr. Zahler. We've been expecting you."

It was all good, all bizarre evolution, but he was working such long hours overseeing the edits and stocking new music that he sometimes broke into unexplained sweats or felt weak by eleven a.m. Gordon's head whirled in business twenty hours a day and his body suffered. Rose badgered him to be careful. "You're going to work yourself back into intensive care if you don't take it easy," she would say on the drive home to Shoreham Drive. CPA Jack had his own opinion. The TV-shooting season was over, he said. Take a little vacation.

Tell that to the quiver at the base of Gordon's skull. *Be content you're making money,* the quiver lectured in tight situations. *Stare in the mirror if you get antsy for more.* Why shouldn't he look? Existing above the neck, Gordon felt severed from the thrills that were once his stipulated daily requirement. No mischief, no speed, no double-dares, no girls. Paralysis demented him with boredom. Others were in charge of his every damned wish. By the time they fulfilled it, the new items he thought of were already green with mold. About the only action he enjoyed was traveling, which he couldn't do enough, and pitching ideas.

Too often, watching the blood drain out of people's faces when they caught site of him for the first time constituted the dramatic part of his day. Then he'd have to calm them down by acting casual. If that failed, he found it helpful to repeat stories about his wild childhood — old stink bomb attacks or riding bikes off roofs. Their knowing he hadn't always been a quadriplegic seemed to offset their shock, though it didn't quell the twitch inside them they were one bone-crushing fall away from being him.

As if the comforting did him much good. Twenty years of sponge bathing had pancaked expectations. In that time, there had been two thrill rides and one genuinely interested woman. The club hopping — that was adolescent stuff. Now that he was in Hollywood, around soundstage gunfights and peroxide sex kittens, he saw how frustrating it was to be numb in a touch-me town.

He wanted to cavort. The Sunset Strip was right there. He only needed a shove. My grandma said she was baffled. Why, she asked, couldn't he be content with what he had accomplished? Everybody was so proud. "Remember the article (that called him a genius)?" Because, he said, that wasn't enough. Watching Milton Berle on TV in his new house after work left his juices cold. She reminded him of the fun he had at that costume party, when a friend had dressed him up as Whistler's Mother and he took first prize. "Couldn't you be satisfied going to a party once a month?"

He looked up at the ceiling, disgusted. "Mom, you haven't figured it out, have you? We both know I'm never getting up. But getting cheated when there's a lot I can do? If you want to know the truth, I'd rather be dead."

Neither of them plied the subject further. In the silence, Rose thought about what that physician who had given him a checkup a month ago had predicted. She had called Dr. Risser at home for a second opinion that night when Gordon sacked out early. Was it true, she had asked? That he couldn't possibly live another five years as the other doctor had told her privately? Depends on him, Risser had responded. He had never heard of anybody with a cervical injury like Gordon's who made it past thirty-five. An orthopedic journal had already published a story on how surprising it was he'd lasted.

Ultimately, it was Rose's mother, the fat, folksy Dearie Rossman, who bestowed on Gordon the adage he had been waiting to hear. The occasion was the party for his thirty-third birthday, and most of the guests had surrounded the coffee urn in the kitchen. While they were away, Dearie leaned in close and whispered to him what she told her neurotic pet dachshund. "Don't strain yourself. You're here for pleasure."

Pleasure. Early one Friday evening, a month after his birthday, Gordon sat alone in the rear seat of a Chrysler ragtop gunning along Interstate 10. He was being driven to Palm Springs, a desert playground 100 miles east of L.A. Samuel Bronston Jr., the son of one of Gordon's independent-producer-friends, was behind the wheel. His actress-girlfriend was nuzzled up close to him on the front seat. It was to be a relaxing weekend of poolside card games and indulgent, four-drink dinners. They had the radio turned up and Sam let everyone pull swigs from his silver flask. Anybody mentioning business got the evil eye.

Sam Jr., however, was more interested stealing looks down his girlfriend's blouse than concentrating on the one-lane road. He never saw that rut in the highway, the one about the width of a pizza box. Twenty miles out of Palm Springs, the Chrysler's left front wheel clunked into the hole and the car veered violently off course. The rut sent it skidding right toward the highway shoulder wholly out of control. Despite's Sam feeble attempt to brake, the car plowed into a dirt mound at about twenty-five mph. The next sensation was after the crash, when both Sam and his girlfriend felt the pinch of whiplash in their necks. Here was the other shocker: Gordon was missing from the back seat.

Night was coming. So was the weekend traffic. Sam Jr. flashed ahead to what he might be facing—manslaughter charges, his father's wrath. This was supposed to be kicks. So many disastrous events start that way. "Gor-don," he hollered. "Where are you? Gordon-don. Where in the name of Christ could you be?"

To be specific, seventeen-and-one-quarter feet up the highway. Gordon, as he would tell and retell in vivid reconstructions, wasn't in the backseat because he'd been launched out of it. Sir Isaac Newton could explain it: a body in motion tends to stay in motion. The moment the car slammed into the embankment, there was nothing restraining Gordon, certainly not any car seatbelt, which wasn't standard then, or his own scrawny body mass.

He was jettisoned, catapulted like flaming ammo during the Crusades, probably a foot over the door-lock if he had to wager. Along the way, he blacked out. He remembered nothing about being airborne or the landing. His memory reset when a car close to where he landed tore by. That was because he saw it from the tires up and assumed he was dead.

Actually, lying face down on the asphalt he was sure he was dead. He wasn't just on the asphalt—he was just outside the narrow, white line separating forty mph oncoming traffic from the shoulder. The light wasn't terrific for motorists, either. Twilight speckled the desert in amber hues and deceiving shadows. Pointed northwest, Gordon could see what was coming towards him. And a large set of headlights, possibly from a big rig a half-mile away, was coming. Whatever it was, the headlights shone a lot brighter now.

"Help," he called out.

"But where are you?" Sam whimpered. "Jesus. I killed Gordon. I can't believe it. I fucking killed him."

The headlights wound around a little bend and then caught Gordon 150 yards away.

"Over here!" Gordon shrieked, his voice cracking on the vowels. "I'm over here. Near the white line. And hurry up. I'm begging ya."

Sam ran over and scooped him up in his arms. His passenger was royally peeved. "Nice driving, Sam," Gordon said. "Five more inches over the line and a car would've squished my head like a grapefruit."

The marvel was that he hadn't shattered his fused spine on impact and died like road kill. Incredibly, his neck was undamaged. His face was okay, too, if you excluded the purple knot engorging out of his left temple. It wasn't until Sam laid him in the car that Gordon said he was feeling lousy. He was nauseous, and it had something to do with his arm. It'd spasmed. Sam said hold on. He backed the Chrysler out and floored it east on Route 10. This time his girlfriend sat in the rear with Gordon.

At Torney General Hospital near Palm Springs, Gordon suspected his arm was fractured and said so. The E.R. doctor, a freckled young man not long out of medical school, was skeptical a quad could detect limb damage. His hunch was that the patient was woozy from a minor concussion. "Just grab my elbow and pull up if you don't believe me," my uncle countered. Ignoring him, the doctor asked the male attendant to assist him removing Gordon's sweater because it kept getting snagged along one of the sleeves. It came off, and his shirt was bloody along one inseam.

Seeing what lay underneath, people in the room felt their bile surge up, everybody that is but Gordon, who was accustomed to medical drama. This was a new one. The bone in his upper-right arm had snapped cleanly in two with a compound fracture. The end closest to his elbow had punctured the skin like a twig poking through snow. Inside, viscous, yellow bone marrow oozed around the blood. Suddenly there was a dull *thunk* behind the examining table. Gordon asked Sam what happened and Sam said the attendant had taken one peek at the bone and fainted off in the corner. The doctor apologized for the incident and then shipped Gordon up to surgery.

A couple days later at work, wearing a sling over his arm cast, Gordon told Nat that Palm Springs could wait. He had come up with something even better. A speedboat—that's what he needed.

CHAPTER THIRTEEN
It Happened Out West

Josef "Joe" Von Stroheim was getting courted whether he asked for it or not. Gordon had convinced himself that Joe, the affable kid in his late twenties, was the editor to pattern his workforce around. Whenever he spotted Joe on the Sam Goldwyn lot, Gordon had whoever was pushing him make a beeline in Joe's direction. The headhunting was relentless. Gordon would yak that there was a better post with him than the one Joe had with *The Roy Rogers Show*. Huge upside: $150-a-week, ground-floor potential. Why the full tilt for a sound editor, a technical job as unglamorous as can be? Joe had the acronym credentials my uncle revered (MGM, NBC) and a smart-alecky personality he enjoyed being around. Joe also was hot into sound effects, which Gordon wanted to package with his music. All that lore about Joe's dad, the maverick silent movie director Erich von Stroheim, was incidental. It was his son that Gordon coveted.

Tempted about the job, Joe still had his reservations—about his prospective boss, about this buttering up. It would be risky jumping ship for a small outfit run by a cripple. Having been reared in a showbiz family, where Clark Gable sometimes gave him a lift to school on his motorbike, Joe knew the terrain. And when he spotted Gordon laying it on thick to an executive interested in his catalogue, his uncertainty grew.

He deduced what others later would: my uncle was as much bullshit artist as overachiever in his quest for contracts. If you had something he wanted, he was a pit bull in a poodle's body. In those early days, Gordon was known to stalk his contacts and then feign surprise when he ran into them. By the way, he would ask, "Anything new on that show? They need music?" Joe supposed his pursuer was overdoing it, trying not to be felt sorry for, but eventually people would wise up to his deal-pouncing act.

The unknown was *when*. Joe had a family in the San Fernando Valley suburbs and the $150-a-week was substantial. Joe also assumed he could find another studio gig should things with Gordon blow up. "Okay, you got me," Joe told him in so many words in the late 1950s. "Will that shut you up?"

Not really. But they made quite a duo. Joe, with his thick chestnut hair and colorful roots, could hardly believe he was in a dumpy office on the wrong end of Sunset for twenty-five bucks more a week. Gordon, his black hair now receded into a widow's peak, his aquiline face dashing above his brittle frame, had a hard time believing it himself.

Jimmy Gillard, thirty-five, was easier to bag. He needed my uncle's money far more than Joe. Out of work, living off unemployment insurance, he had five kids and a wife to think about ahead of his pride.

He had driven out to the West Coast from his hometown near Shreveport, Louisiana in the late 1940s with tempered ambitions and a soft, handsome face. Lovella, his country-girl wife, and their children traveled out later. Jimmy's father had been one of a handful of prosperous black farmers in the Jim Crow South, harvesting crops from okra to peanuts to cotton and raising a barn-full of livestock.

Jimmy himself couldn't wait to be outdoors. Playing hooky from school to loll, swim the bayous, ride horses or swill moonshine if his parents weren't there was good-time rebellion. He was the fourth oldest in a family of ten, and the freest spirit among his brothers, all of whom outsized him. Many of his siblings went to college but not Jimmy. His talents were mechanical. He excelled fixing anything with gears. By his mid-twenties, Jimmy had heard stories about there being jobs galore in California, even for a Negro who dropped out of grade school. He was a natural with machines and L.A. was supposedly a city of factories.

Out West, though, none of the top plants had any openings for him. Scraping for rent money, he took a low-paying job at a metal works. It was as greasy and dead-end as what he left behind in Louisiana: changing out tires on Greyhound buses. He thought he'd escaped that by moving to California, but he hadn't. So he poured iron. He melted pipes into fittings. He did just about everything at the Compton foundry except have steady employment. The company was choked by labor disputes, and the workers were constantly walking the picket lines with no money in their overalls. Once more, Jimmy, grandson of a slave, did what he was accustomed to: he secured another paycheck. He climbed aboard an L.A. trash rig as a garbage man and prayed nobody he knew recognized him. When that job ended, it was back to the metal works. When it went on strike, it was the unemployment line. Ten years in creamy California and Jimmy Gillard was going in circles.

One morning, Isaac Ross, a mailman friend of his with a Hollywood route, mentioned he had a customer who needed a driver. "Here's the number in case you're interested," he said. That night Jimmy drove to Shoreham Street. My grandma trusted Jimmy's face before he conceded he had never spoken with anybody in a wheelchair before. "Don't be apprehensive," Rose told him. "Treat him like he's permanently seated. Before you meet him," she asked, "how about some coffee?"

Introductions made, Gordon was all business. This job was about doing the things he couldn't, not mere chauffeuring, he explained. Another man who had tried out hadn't embraced that. It was about rotating him on his office-bed to forestall bedsores, feeding him a sandwich at lunch and swabbing him down with hydrogen peroxide at night. It was about grabbing tapes and holding papers for him in meetings with important people and fading into the scenery during contract talk. It was about mastering traffic shortcuts. And don't expect to be home before seven-thirty; there were no set hours. "Think you can handle it?" Gordon asked, no doubt seeing Jimmy was a small-built 5'7". "Absolutely, Mr. Zahler." The negotiations proceeded. The job paid seventy-five dollars a week to start plus free meals and Sundays off. Probably some travel involved. Jimmy said it all sounded great.

"Can you start tomorrow, say at ten a.m.?" my uncle asked. "It's Saturday, you know."

"I can be here at 8:30 if you want," Jimmy answered.

And so it began, my go-getter uncle and his proxy legs. Jimmy wasn't complaining. His maiden weeks on the job put him in a dubbing room at Desilu Productions, one of America's hottest studios, in his only dark suit. He fed Gordon tea and, as told, said nothing. Doing that got him introduced to Lucille Ball and Doris Day as if they were his neighbors. Kept him in Gordon's graces, too. Jimmy, meantime, made himself a pledge. Someday he would understand the secret of what was happening here—how scratchy, old songs could be reborn to make foolish stories better than they were.

In those early years, Jimmy's brothers whooped when he phoned them on Sunday afternoons to describe his Hollywood job. "What's it like?" they asked. "Strange," he would answer. Gordon was cool, but the money was nothing special. He got to drive a light blue Cadillac convertible, but Gordon called out lane changes as if his foot were on the gas pedal. "It's clear on my side," he'd say aggressively when he wanted you to speed up and switch lanes. Already, the boss' forehead had thwacked into the glove compartment at four sudden stops. Jimmy said he'd learned to stick out his right forearm at unexpected red lights and "Mr. Zahler was mighty appreciative."

Strange—Jimmy said he could handle strange. Gordon had asked him in an alley on the Paramount lot if he'd mind jumping into a smelly, gray dumpster where producers were known to toss rejected screenplays. Jimmy hopped in holding his nose and his straw hat. A month later Gordon requested he tend to him on a recording trip to Stuttgart, Germany and Jimmy said he would do anything to go, having rarely gone anywhere.

Carrying Gordon up the narrow Pan Am airplane ramp was treacherous because one slip backwards and it would all be over. Once seated, the flight over the Atlantic unlocked a happiness Jimmy hadn't known. They then checked into their German hotel, a drab place with geraniums in window flower boxes, and Europe didn't seem so different anymore. The concierge surveyed Jimmy like a side of beef and in broken English mouthed that blacks weren't allowed there.

Quick as he came in, Gordon canceled the reservation. He had Jimmy connect him with the house operator and he hunted down another inn. "I didn't say nothing," Jimmy told his brothers. "Was afraid to." Later, pushing Gordon around a cobblestone-lined street on a sightseeing trip near a castle, he heard voices and snapped around his head. A group of German kids in cloth jackets were following behind them about twenty-five yards back. Every time he stopped, so did their German entourage. From the children's gestures, Jimmy surmised they had probably never seen a black man up close before, maybe they thought he was an American ballplayer. Gordon agreed. In London, he bought Jimmy a Bola hat that he wore the whole trip, never wasting another breath on that hotel.

From Europe they stopped off in New York for meetings with the big media outfits. Jimmy described it as a haze of skyscraper offices and exhilarating side trips to landmarks like Radio City Music Hall. He felt electric weaving his boss through the suited crowds of Manhattan. After they concluded their meetings there, they rented a car and drove through upstate New York and into Montreal because Gordon was aching to see the World Fair. Who was Jimmy to object?

Gordon's "sewer line," he admitted, was the one chore he could have done without. Every other night after work, if the nurse was off, Jimmy couldn't just rush home to his family in Compton. With Rose supervising, he had to press down on his boss's tummy to knead it. The object was to "wake up Gordon's bowels" to force him to poop out his food.

"Strange" just about covered it.

My grandma assumed she was free to plot her own East Coast holiday with Jimmy on scene. "Vacations are for other people," Rose used to say. She felt rejuvenated being in their category now. In November of 1960 she phoned TWA and made plane reservations to visit Lee's sister in snowy Springfield, Massachusetts. That night she informed Gordon, whom she hoped would be pleased. All the arrangements were in place, she said. The male nurse hired to deal with his catheter and other tricky medical issues would stay with him at night for the roughly two weeks she would be gone. Rose would freeze a couple of casseroles just in case.

"You'll be in good hands," she said. "Nothing to worry about at all."

"Fine," Gordon said tartly. "Stay as long as you want."

"Oh Gordon, don't be this way. I'm not made out of iron, you know."

"I can't believe you, Mom. You're jetting off for two weeks and you expect me to be glad. You know what the nurse is going to cost me?"

"Us, you mean."

"Whatever. You know what it's going to cost—the nurse *and* the plane fare?"

"But you've taken trips. And you managed some fun for yourself."

"Those were for business. Besides, I hired Jimmy so you could have your breaks."

"Gordon, you're trying my patience. Enough."

"Tell me this then, Mother. Who's leaving who?"

They didn't speak much about the trip until the eve of Grandma's departure. She was zipping up her Samsonite on the dining room table when my uncle announced he had something imperative to share with her.

"Let's have it," Rose said blankly, sitting on the arm of the couch. "You're obviously angry."

"I'll make this short. While you're gone, I plan on using every free second I have to find you someplace else to live. Nothing personal. We've just been roomies too long."

"Roomies?"

In Springfield, the pampering spun her around. She was shown the town sites, plied with Maine Lobster, caught up on Lee's family and told not to lift a finger around the house in preparation for Thanksgiving gluttony. She would be meeting Lee's other siblings later in the week, and was promised a gourmet dinner and Broadway show in New York City. "Oh Happy Day," Rose wrote my mom, hinting at her depression two days into the trip. In the letter, she chided herself for not booking a shorter stay.

Left unsaid was how antsy she was un-tethered from her burdens. Grandma's anxiety was relaxation because she had never practiced it. She'd learned long ago to occupy herself with chores and mothering and favors and the Instruction as her homemade recipe for memory repression, because there were things to bury in her most unreachable spots. Her father had been killed. Her brother had been murdered. Her husband kicked too early. Her son probably wouldn't make forty. Idle time drew into her a black-edged despair that made her struggle for deep breaths. She'd forgotten that until this vacation.

Time had done what she had asked of it. It had softened her pain into a manageable throb while she cared for the son she was determined would outlive her. As much as she needed her rest in Massachusetts or anywhere, her palms moistened thinking about her son's nursing 3,000 miles away. She paced in her guestroom. Nobody from Shoreham Street was answering her letters. It had been all of a week since she'd left.

She pressured my mom to spy. "Darling," she wrote, "find out what you can if his bladder equipment is being sterilized." Jimmy, she said, can't yet be trusted to handle Gordon's body. Gordon recently returned with him from a business trip to Phoenix with a rump full of pressure sores that took weeks to bind. "How can I have a free mind if I'm not kept informed? In fact, I don't know if he's alive from day to day. It isn't as if he is a normal, healthy human being...I sleep very little." She acknowledged in a follow-up note that she was bracing for her homecoming because Gordon was tired of cohabiting with an old prune like her. "You cannot possibly imagine how uneasy I feel."

When she did walk in from the airport, Gordon admitted he had blown his stack before and asked about the snow.

Soon enough he would be steamed at her again. Consciously or not, he resented his mother for being the only female on the North American landmass willing to be seen with him. Since arriving in Hollywood, he had flirted with any number of eligible women. A few studio secretaries he charmed had almost agreed to a dinner date with him, too. In the end, the pressure was too much. Their vanity about being caught in public with him, combined with their uncertainty about what possible future they might have, strangled any odd temptation they felt about saying yes. Usually, they vamped see-through lies about having boyfriends. "Got it," Gordon would tell them. "Understood."

His sole adult relationship was in the mid 1950s with a lanky, brunette divorcee named Marilyn Seruto. Marilyn was a fun-loving chiropractor who lived next door to my mom and dad in the leafy Pasadena suburb of Hastings Ranch. Marilyn supposedly jabbered to friends she could fall in love with Gordon's personality if she allowed herself. They dated for a few months. Nobody knows why they stopped seeing each other except to speculate that Marilyn ended things after concluding Gordon would be no easygoing, second husband. Excluding her, there was only one other woman anyone can remember designated as Gordon's post-accident "girlfriend."

Connie was a pixyish girl from San Marino with shimmering raven hair and a cache of lewd dating jokes. She hung out with him regularly in Sierra Madre before he started the business. Then with no explanation Connie stopped dropping by. Gordon later heard she'd gotten herself engaged to the scion of the Coronet five-and-dime-store fortune, and he couldn't blame her.

There's a snapshot of how Gordon's libido strained for the female attention his physique repelled. The photograph was taken at the wrap party on the set of *26 Men*. The syndicated Western about lawmen in turn-of-the-century Arizona had lasted a year before being yanked. Gordon had done some of the music for the producer, Russell Hayden, a thickset real-life cowboy who'd broken into Hollywood as "Hopalong Cassidy's" sidekick "Lucky" in the movie serial.

The picture of the bash shows the actors drinking liquor out of paper cups around a checkerboard table. A stunning brunette in a slinky white dress is seated among them. The men are all ogling her with testosterone eyeballs, none more than Gordon. He is in a starched black suit smiling an overeager smile. Jimmy, standing behind him in the group of doughy, white faces, has his left hand on Gordon's shoulder as if saying, "Down, boy." Gordon has apparently said something clever to this bombshell and everybody is gauging her reaction. When the woman pursed her mouth coquettishly at him, it was as good as it got. Scorched history had taught him that someone like her would never hand him her phone number unless she mistook him for a feature producer.

All he really had was his mother. How much he relied on her and his frustration in wishing he didn't have to was the movie-trailer of his life.

Paralysis, nonetheless, did offer benefits in the business realm that Gordon exploited as his exclusive advantage. While his able-bodied rivals navigated stop-and-go traffic or fixed a house water heater or chased illicit sex at the club, Gordon's mind could whirl. Among other tricks, he trained himself to recall everything he couldn't physically get his hands on. He started with his thousand-song music catalogue. By staring at lists on the music stand by his bed for an hour a day it was fairly easy. From there he memorized which of his dozens of tapes the songs were recorded on, then their order on the tape.

When he was through with that he absorbed music-publishing contracts and other documents. By the early 1960s, his mind let him recite those same contracts, cue sheets, negotiating memos and tapes in such crisp detail that outsiders suspected it might be a parlor trick to impress them. Jimmy knew it was no hoax. The boss's recall and energy fed off each other. It always had. Because of this, Jimmy watched clients from Piccadilly Circus to Melrose Avenue express their astonishment about Gordon's data-gobbling memory after appointments with him. How so much focus got packed into so small a space seemed to violate the laws of nature.

What was it he wanted, an associate like Nat Weincoff might ask, besides being filthy rich? Sometimes he would answer, "One great thing, that's all. One great thing no moron can ruin." Obviously, he was hedging his bets.

According to the legal documents he filed with the state, my uncle envisioned himself someday in the corner suite of a mammoth corporate conglomerate. He planned to promote, produce and record anything on stage or film. He would conduct real estate at home and overseas. He would publish educational music, trail blaze photographic techniques, print books, traffic in patents and licenses, invest in oils, minerals and hydrocarbons and sell retail merchandise on the side. His niche being entertainment, Gordon expected to preside over a multimillion-dollar portfolio bulging with whole movie studios, radio stations and TV franchises he could sanctify as his great things. At the extreme, Gordon expected to be a upstart tycoon or a well-rounded flake. He had listed thirty "primary" purposes.

Even the corporate name he selected belted out his aspiration: General Music Corporation. It came off his lips like a Dow Jones company. The $400 worth of seed stock was evenly divided among three people. My grandma was the titular president, Gordon the Vice President and Abraham Marcus the secretary. Abe, as others did, discounted his hourly rate in return for a slab of Gordon's future profits. The kid's upside was worth the gamble.

Nobody was going to give them a damn thing. On January 20, 1959, the day director Cecil B. De Mille passed away, so did any chance for Rose and Gordon's financial justice. A superior court judge deciding whether Columbia Pictures had cheated Rose guaranteed that. Abe had marshaled the strongest argument he could, citing case law and reading aloud what my grandfather had written his studio employers. "*This license shall apply only for public reproduction and performance in theatres or other places of public entertainment...*"

Columbia's attorneys counterpunched deftly. They argued a broader interpretation was the correct one; Lee Zahler was a studio contractor, they said, and he had been compensated for his work. TV was not part of it. When the honorable Kurt Kauffman sided with Columbia, it was proof that movie songwriters were still algae of the Hollywood food chain. There would be no $300,000 for my grandma, as if she were that surprised anymore.

CHAPTER FOURTEEN
The Fine Art of Kissing

Summer 1961. It began harmlessly enough: about cash, not the heart. An Air Force colonel from Mira Loma Airbase near San Diego had contacted Gordon to inquire if the company could insert sound effects onto a new pilot training film. The subject was dry—how electronics in Soviet MIG fighters reacted to American radar—yet timely. A U.S. plan to topple Fidel Castro had backfired at the Bay of Pigs two months earlier, and Berlin was looking like the tripwire to a Superpower collision.

The colonel used a lot of big words to explain that his job had to be executed discreetly. Any General Music employee working on it required a security clearance vetted from Washington, D.C. People could never reveal what they saw afterwards, either, because they would be viewing pictures of enemy cockpits someone had bootlegged out of the Iron Curtain. Gordon was fascinated from the first word. Overloaded with campy sci-fi movies, he got a buzz off the idea of being a Pentagon contractor.

Until, that is, he was one. It was hard enough making payroll.

Now he had a sneering military guard with a sidearm loitering around his secretary. When the footage arrived, an Air Force mechanic wrapped an industrial-gauge chain around the editing-room door. Office windows were covered in aluminum foil. File cabinets were secured with fist-sized locks. To Gordon and others, the sex appeal of national security barely seemed worth the $1,000 the Air Force agreed to pay. Ed Wood owed General Music more than that.

After a few weeks of editing, the colonel tapped Gordon on the shoulder. "Outstanding work, soldier," he said, and drove back to San Diego with the master tape tucked under his cobalt-blue uniform. In phoning a month later, the colonel had a new request, a personal one.

"Son," the colonel said, "I was so impressed by the work you did on the training film, I was hoping I might steal a few hours of your time for you to talk to some men out at the Van Nuys V.A."

"The V.A.?" Gordon said. "I don't understand. I don't know anything about the service."

The colonel chortled. "Soldiering is not what I'm looking for. I've talked this over with my commanding officer and we both agree it'd be a real boost if you'd give some of the wounded men out there a little pep talk. Tell them how you overcame your adversity."

"I don't know, colonel. It's not something I like going into."

"Talk to them about the picture business, then. Explain how you get your workers to stamp sounds onto the right spot."

"You mean splice?"

"Exactly. And let them know how you keep from feeling sorry for yourself when you're not 110 percent. They could really use advice in that department."

"Colonel, I'm flattered you're asking me, but I'm awful busy right now. I just got a new show and the producer's a real jerk. Besides, you can do better than me."

"Don't be so coy, son. This can't be the first time someone has asked you to do this."

"Actually it is. Sorry."

"Well, I don't have to tell you how devastated the mind can get from a bad wound. These men at the Birmingham center have had a pretty rough go of it."

"I bet. But you're asking the wrong guy."

"Can I be totally blunt, Mr. Zahler?"

"Uh, yeah."

"If the men out there see all the piss and vinegar in you, their situation won't look nearly so bleak by comparison. You'd be doing me a favor."

Sometime later, my uncle's wheelchair was parked center stage in the recreation room of a U.S. Veterans Administration Hospital in the western San Fernando Valley. The décor was government-issued bland right down to the ratty gray curtains with the cigarette burns in them. Gordon was here to tell the patients the sky was the limit if they drove themselves. He was here sticking to his Hollywood adventure for what was supposed to be a quick forty-five minutes.

Predictably, the soldiers he was intended to inspire greeted him as they did other civilian guests: they rolled their eyes and snickered. A fellow named Barney, who had come home from Korea without his right arm, was their ringleader. He dreamt up a swipe custom-made for Gordon, chanting it several times: "Lights, camera. Inaction!" The vets' favorite activity was coughing "horseshit" under their breath at keynotes in the speech, which became choppier as it went along. If these men hungered for a role model, they had one sarcastic way of showing it.

Gordon seethed on the drive back to Sunset Boulevard with Jimmy, his face resembling an allergy patient in a pollen field. "I knew I should have told that goddamn colonel no. Nobody could get through to those...people."

"Don't beat yourself up, boss," Jimmy said. "You're done."

"You bet I am. I'm calling the colonel when we get back to tell him I ain't doing no second pep talk."

"Want me to take Laurel Canyon to the office?"

"I don't care."

"You want to stop at Pink's for hot dogs then?"

"No! Aren't you listening to me?" In a couple minutes he spoke softer. "What I want is for you to follow one simple rule from here on in. Don't get me within 100 feet of another cripple, okay? You see another wheelchair you get me out of there. I'm not like them."

"What about Jack Perry?"

"Jack's okay…Can you believe what that one idiot said? How I didn't know anything about suffering. What do they think, I enjoy this?"

Gordon stayed quiet the rest of the drive, which left Jimmy nervous. When they turned into the parking lot, my uncle was halfway back to his old self.

"I've been meaning to ask you something," he said.

"All right."

"How would you feel about a little beach time?"

"Does it involve your boat?"

"No."

"I'm all for it then."

The idea was to force the world to study his ideas instead of his anatomy. The plan was to stop waiting for scenery and reap the outdoors.

It was my mother who had recommended he and Jimmy cut out Friday at noon for an early summer weekend at Laguna Beach. My dad had rented the bottom floor of a beachside duplex for a week's vacation and the extra rooms had pinned thoughts in her head. "C'mon, Gordy," she'd said. Between his work demands and the trauma surrounding Peter, my mentally retarded middle brother, they had not seen that much of each other. (As the mound in Muriel's stomach, I would be along for this trip.)

There was a spare bedroom for Jimmy, she'd said about five times. Perfect weather. Green seas. "Remember how Mom would have to drag you out of the water by the ear, you loved it so much?" He remembered, just as he remembered Muriel hadn't seen him in a pair of Bermuda trunks lately. He said count him in, anyway.

The beach was packed, umbrellas dotting the coast, when my

uncle pulled up in a terrycloth robe and Wayfarer sunglasses. In the crowded parking lot he sniffed the saltwater air and allowed a goofy expression to laminate his face. Let's hustle he told Jimmy; they would find Muriel later. He had gotten geared up about reaching the sand. It was important to be a little delirious, too, because he knew the other beachgoers would be commenting on his motivation for coming someplace they suspected he was incapable of enjoying.

Jimmy, as usual, was responsible for whatever enjoyment was attainable. He sweated through his T-shirt slogging Gordon's chair 100 yards through Laguna's pristine white sand. Jimmy's next assignment, lighting Gordon's cigarette in the breeze, creamed his last pack of matches. Some vacation day for him: in two years in my uncle's employ, he had never had more than a weekend off.

At the shoreline, Gordon felt the ocean spray tingle his scalp, heard the transistors blaring the Everly Brothers and watched a thousand wild-eyed children romp and splash. It was hard to fathom he had once been one of them, harder still to believe no amount of willpower by him could reanimate his legs for a second adolescence. After ten minutes orbiting those regrets, he glanced over at Jimmy. Sweat poured off his face. "Jim," Gordon said. "Go cool off in the waves. That's an order. I'm not going anyplace."

The men divided along capabilities. Jimmy jogged into the foamy surf, flopping about like a dizzy sturgeon, while my uncle tried imagining how the cool water must've soothed. It was in this yearning for little pleasures that the cosmos delivered for him — with a fifty-cent hunk of plastic. Round and innocuous, the hunk pinged off the right armrest of his wheelchair and spun itself a divot in the blazing-hot sand. When Gordon glanced down, he saw a tri-color beach ball the size of a pumpkin resting there. When he blinked again, an ash blonde with catlike eyes was bending over to scoop it up. She wore a beige one-piece suit that appeared painted onto her along with a lovely smile. "Sorry about that," the woman whinnied. "My friend doesn't throw very well. She almost beaned a seagull yesterday."

Gordon was unsure what to do with this rare opening except not to blow it, so he engaged her in a hasty conversation to corral her from walking away. This woman's eyes shimmered possibilities. He blathered out his name and other basics and learned hers. Judy — it fit her. Judy explained that she and a girlfriend had driven down from the city, Hollywood to be specific, for the break and a tan. No diamond ring snugged over her finger. They chatted for five minutes, mainly about their favorite local restaurants. Gordon had his prelude to ask Judy out for next Saturday night, which he was assembling the courage to do, except that he'd blathered too long.

A tall, featureless blond woman named Gail walked over, tugging at Judy's elbow until Judy scowled at her to stop. "I'm sunburned," Gail said. "I thought we were heading in." Gail's eyes bulged when she spoke, as if she were doing Judy a favor extricating her from this awkward encounter. "All right, all right," Judy said. She handed the beach ball to Gail and stroked my uncle's shoulder. "Very nice meeting you, Gordon Zahler." The women went to their towels, collected their stuff and left. He had squandered his possibility. His body had shooed away another sweetie.

Now he could relive it the rest of the trip. Before he had met Judy, he had planned on having Jimmy dunk him in the surf to see what would happen, but it sounded asinine after his overture was shot down. At 4:30, Gordon said, "Jim, wheel me in, will ya. I've had it." Inside the rented duplex, my mom cut the two off at the hallway. Join us on the patio at six for cocktails, she said with perky obliviousness. Sure, Gordon exhaled. A double, no triple, whiskey sounded useful. Why did he even have to meet that broad? He arrived thirty minutes late, punctual for him given the grunt labor required to shower and dress him, with a tan across a face that'd checked its smirk at the door. Noticing he looked downcast, my dad asked him his drink order, and Gordon heard himself stammer, "Huh?"

Lying on a plastic recliner, cattycorner to him on the concrete patio was Judy in a green-and-yellow polka dot sundress. "Why, hello there," she said, putting down her paperback when she saw him wheeled in. "You didn't say you were staying here, too. We're on the second floor. Can you believe that?" She came over and gabbed for two hours.

Judy Marie Wetzel, it'd come to be known, was a bubbly working girl who probably should have been someone's wife in the suburbs by now. She was thirty-one and lived with her mother and an older lady above a quirky weight-loss clinic on Commonwealth Avenue in southwest Hollywood. Judy, being mostly around dowdy women, exuded sweetness about her view of things, not thrusting sensuality. Likable? Yes. Gullible? Absolutely. She operated from the presumption her existence was dishwater-dull compared to anybody in the Industry. Gordon never had a better audience for his anecdotes. Judy Wetzel was a pushover for celebrity.

Physically, she was a mixed message. He prize attribute was a dazzling, cheek-to-cheek smile whose power Judy relied on as her ace card. Surrounding it was gossamer blond hair cut shoulder length, a delicate, trim nose like Jackie Kennedy's and gorgeous pale blue eyes spread far apart. Gordon observed that she walked with a slinky grace that accented her neck, and held her cigarette with the arched wrist of a debutante. This was no accident. It had been taught. Similarly, without that smile, her attractiveness melted into the ordinary. Judy, in fact, could have been a Midwestern beauty queen's Plain Jane sister, the one fated to be the town's spinster librarian. There was an androgynous quality about her, what with her flaxen skin and a tomboyish frame that made her solid legs seem bolted to the wrong gal. Theoretically, Judy's parts were there but the proportions were off. Still, Gordon didn't care that much about her body. How could he? It was her face that bowled him over.

Never married, Judy supported herself in the fashion trade. Clothes—she adored clothes. She reveled in fabrics. She loved circling dresses in *Vogue* she couldn't afford. She sketched her own designs. Being offered the job of assistant buyer at Bullocks-Wilshire, one's of the city's upscale department stories, was a godsend. Her specialty was wedding dresses. And here was the kicker: she might be buying one for herself. Judy told Gordon on the patio that day in Laguna she was dating someone and that it was serious. Said the guy was "a real doll."

Gordon, upon hearing this news, refused to sulk as he had on the beach. *Don't get cheated,* he reminded himself. *Act like you have options.* He stuck to making friends with her, gleaning what might be. The whiskey my dad served him had his confidence high. After Judy left for upstairs, he re-traced their time together. If she were in love, where was the stud today? And if she were so head-over-heels, why was she so touchy-feely toward him?

My uncle treaded cautiously when he returned to the city. He visited Judy a week later at Bullocks-Wilshire, where he played it cool. My mom later ran into her on a shopping trip to Bullocks and Judy admitted she'd had a major spat with her boyfriend — know any cute bachelors? If she had been on a blind date, it was a dud, because Judy and her boyfriend made up. Gordon assumed she would be nothing more than a pretty acquaintance that got away.

Then out of the nowhere she phoned. "You terribly busy?" Gordon invited her over to his cramped office on Sunset, which she immediately termed "quaint." It was there Gordon let slip the number of network shows he had going. Did she watch *The Wrangler* Thursday nights on NBC? He and Loren Ryder of Ryder Sound, *the* Loren Ryder, had dubbed the sound together. It had been astoundingly complex, and they liked it that way. It was the first television show recorded on videotape using a new film-to-video editing technique invented to give TV a movie-screen appearance. To synchronize everything, they needed to stretch the film out on a straight line, which involved un-spooling it from inside the dubbing booth all the way into the street. "People were looking at us like we were lunatics," Gordon told her. "But, it was worth it. The critics loved what he did. It was the show's plot they hated."

Judy was speechless. To impress her even more, my uncle pointed to the wrinkled blueprint tacked on the wall. "Interested?" he said.

"Oh, yes."

"Well, me and Nat Winecoff, he's one of my partners, we're kicking around the idea of building something really unusual." He described to her a themed amusement park catering to newlyweds and tourists near either Niagara Falls or Yosemite. The motif would be Old Testament meets Disneyland, though cash-carrying pagans would be welcomed as well. Visitors would enjoy a "Tut's Tomb ride," a "Dead Sea cruise," a Noah's Ark attraction and other brimstone thrills. "We'll have to do it in stages. If we get investors, I'm telling you it'll be a goldmine."

"Do you have a name for it?"

"Bibleland. Or Bible Storyland. Catchy, huh? And if that doesn't pan out, I've been thinking of doing a Hollywood Entertainment Museum near the (Hollywood) Bowl. You'd take a cable car to get up there."

"I don't know what to say," Judy sputtered, "other than my goodness. By the way, I was wondering if you were free for dinner next week?"

Recognizing he struck the right note, Gordon strummed it while Judy wavered over her emotions. Mostly during the next couple weeks he listened. He learned that Fred, the man she was supposedly crazy about, was an upstanding Catholic who worked in stocks and bonds. He wasn't well off, as Judy calculated Gordon certainly would be, only healthy. She and Fred played tennis. They waltzed. He opened car doors for her. She blushed.

The longer Judy spent around my uncle, the less Fred existed. The more Gordon spit out ideas in front of her, the less intimidating he became. (A young sci-fi director who met Gordon about this same point compared him to a wounded Prussian general.) When he became frustrated Joe and the other editors weren't cutting on his schedule, she saw that was him talking, not his condition. Judy also fixed her eyes above his collar. She decided my uncle had a chiseled face, part Sinatra, a smidge buccaneer.

Girlfriends heard her glowing reports about his dimples and get-rich schemes. "That's great Judy," they'd say. "But what good can come out of this? What tomorrow can you have with someone like him?" Before she knew herself, romance bloomed between them. With café dinners and backseat necking while Jimmy waited outside smoking, their hearts pounded as their minds peered ahead. This wasn't going to be fairytale love of the Camelot sort. No, it was ardent, practical affection. Each saw the outlines of a possibly fabulous arrangement. Judy could have her security and glamour, Gordon his show-wife/companion.

But a dozen dates into their courtship Gordon considered killing it. Judy was half-inventing her past to hook him, he was positive of it. She tangled up the facts of her own story — what year she graduated from college, names of past boyfriends. Then, over iced tea, Gordon was introduced to Judy's mother, a folksy sparkplug of a woman, 5'2" in heels. Obviously, Judy had learned from the master.

"Billie" Willie Mae Wetzel, Gordon would discover, had a personal mission she expected her daughter to fulfill. In her honeyed Southern drawl, Billie leaned on Judy to marry upwards, preferably within the film community, and the sooner the better as Judy was north of thirty. It was Judy's solemn obligation to wed the right man. Not only would he have to provide her with a feathery lifestyle, he had to elevate Billie from working class to *nouveau riche* where she reckoned she belonged. She had always pictured middle age in a classy Westside apartment, as the nine-to-five life was for pedestrian gals. After all, she had grown up in a venerable Tennessee family that owned a willowy plantation and, once, a battery of Civil War-era slaves. The best Southern finishing schools had educated her. Or so the legend of Billie went. Pour a little bourbon into her milk ("mother's milk") and she would proclaim she deserved to be a lady of importance, "don't you know."

Here is what's known for sure. Billie and her first husband, a dark-haired man she was nuts about, had a little girl, Anna Katherine, in 1913 and all was well. A few years later, when her husband was twenty-five, his car was mangled between a pair of Southern California railroad cars and nothing was the same. Seeking financial cover, Billie remarried a gas company office manager, a geeky fella with a Neanderthal forehead, and they conceived Judy.

Billie knew she'd made a poor choice as the years sped by. The accountant was a rotten spouse and a worse dad. They divorced when Judy was twelve.

And the splintering accelerated. Billie, a single mom again, had to pound the pavement selling goods door-to-door in Long Beach. There was talk she had to work after her ex stole Judy's college money to spoil his new wife. Inside the Wetzel household, there was a different kind of trouble. Anna Katherine, Judy's half-sister, had lapsed from a problem drinker into a full-blown alcoholic. No one was positive why she drank, just that she did. Billie, of course, wanted her eldest daughter sober, wanted her healthy for all the right reasons, and yet awash those hopes was paranoia the drinking would dump shame on the family. She couldn't have that stigma, not after the others. Consequently, people aware of Ann Katherine's skid into the bottle were instructed by Billie to maintain strict silence about it.

To some extent the cover-up succeeded. Anna Katherine married and presented Billie with a granddaughter. Happy as that was, motherhood couldn't stop the inevitable. Anna Katherine's pickled liver caught up with her, and she died at thirty-two. Not much prestige in that.

Billie changed addresses to help buffer her grief. She and Judy relocated from Long Beach into the upstairs apartment of a Hollywood Victorian with a spiral staircase. On the building's ground floor was an unorthodox fat farm that Billie managed with its owner, an entrepreneurial widow named Sadie Cosby. Their secret weapon was a row of vibrating pulley machines that customers belted around their flabby waists and thighs. Actors, some famous, were repeat-customers and that at least pleased Billie.

Judy, like her mother, glossed over the details that didn't suit her. She told my uncle she had graduated from UCLA when she had only taken classes there. She said she had joined a sorority when she hadn't been initiated. In polite language, she claimed she had been de-flowered at a raucous frat party and that a horde of good-looking boys pursued her. In truth she was infrequently asked out.

Gordon, with his own gift for bullshit, could have confronted Judy with her fabrications and still gotten her to marry him. Judy was hardly coy expressing how much she wanted him to propose. All they needed was a champagne dinner at Nicodell's, his favorite grill, to pop the question. Gordon, using the opportunities that came from being on his rump all day, analyzed the situation from every nook and derived several conclusions. One was that Judy's embellishments were no longer an issue; he reasoned they were the scaffolding she needed to reinforce her own ego as much as to snag a man. He aimed to spell out his broader feelings about their relationship on a date off the Sunset Strip. Judy assumed they were making it official.

Nope, he said, they would never survive as a couple. It was insanity for her to think she could be content with someone like him. Had he reminded her that Dr. Risser was the only doctor he'd even seen who predicted he would live this long?

"I don't care about any of that," she said. "You're stronger than most men I know."

"Come on, Judy," he retorted, "let's not be naïve."

She asked why he was so pessimistic and he enumerated his reasons. Cubing his steak and feeding it to him bite-by-bite at the Brown Derby amid all those luminaries would have been barely tolerable. Eliminating regular sexual activity and any hope of children was bad enough. Now lop off midnight strolls, spontaneous weekenders, card games and pillow fights. Take away doubles tennis, back rubs, gardening, opened car doors, mercy screws and Judy was looking at one sterile union—a marriage by conversation really.

He couldn't do it. She would be clawing her way out in two years, resentful over the love she had tossed overboard with boring Fred, and he would be worse off than if he had stayed a single man living with his indulging mother. Go to your other boyfriend, he advised. Go dancing. Savor the normalcy. You'll thank me in the long run. Fred is your life.

Thank him? Judy wanted to brain him. She didn't want to be Mrs. Fred So-and-So, she said, tears smudging her blue eye shadow.

She didn't require conventional. She needed him. "Don't you trust me when I say I love you for what's inside? Isn't there another way? Isn't there?" After twenty minutes of her beseeching, he said stop. He would make her a bargain he never expected to be consummated. They would go their own way without seeing each other for an entire year — not six months, a full calendar year. If she was still interested, and he was still around, they would know their future.

CHAPTER FIFTEEN
What's Your Racket?

Where money used to be Gordon's handy temptress, it was now one tempting distraction from the woman who made his heart cha-cha. Self-exiled from Judy, he chased the almighty buck around town cutting sound effects into commercials and animation work, including *Mr. Magoo*. He searched for investors for Bibleland and beefed up his music library with regular acquisitions. In between he cloyed to the same daily routine as an insurance policy against surprises.

By nine a.m. Jimmy had him dressed, usually in dark, cuffed trousers and quality white or blue button-down shirts. His hair had to be parted just so using his special comb, his blanket positioned symmetrically on his lap, where his briefcase would rest during appointments. No one except Jimmy and Rose knew he wore an adult diaper and sheepskin-lined chest brace under his clothes, or that after his Palm Springs catapult, a rope was laced around his ribs when he sat in the car. Around 9:30, Jimmy would steer his boss's Cadillac into the parking lot. With steady hands, he'd ladle Gordon out of the front passenger seat and into his wheelchair, a top-of-the-line, collapsible Everest and Jennings that Gordon insisted Jimmy keep spit-polish clean. From there they would roll into the bungalow. Most of the time my uncle conducted business from bed. Should there be calls to return, Gordon's headset was fastened. It was only when he was meeting someone new he was wheeled behind a desk to reduce the shock factor.

Jimmy was on guard when clients came by for music. Gordon might say, "Tape 54, Cue 21," and Jimmy had to scribble it down on a notepad and yank it from the racks in another room. Customers happy with the selection would depart with a tape canister and a license/invoice. When they preferred a different track, Gordon would call out another cue, sending Jimmy on a second (or more) jog to the rack. At least once a week he would push Gordon around the MGM and Desilu lots to troll for new pilots needing music. Jimmy would have a smoke or wash the Cadillac with a chamois during down time.

The work relationship was instant. The friendship of Gordon and Jimmy simmered slower. On the commute home, they might relive a particularly lame scene being edited, or compare the peculiar assortment of customers wading through the door. One memorable Wednesday began with a chintzy clown/producer (minus the red nose and floppy shoes) whining he couldn't afford Gordon's prices while leering at the secretaries' legs. In the middle was a dandified European film importer named Hugo who feted every woman he met with, "Well, hello there, my dear." The final two appointments were with an ex-mercenary in alligator-skin boots trying to make it in TV and a visit from *Mr. Magoo* himself, Jim Backus. After they discussed such moments, employer and employee began detailing their own lives.

On Saturdays, Jimmy would drive my uncle to Orange County's Balboa Bay. Around the salt air and fiberglass, Gordon could block out second-guessing about Judy with his hankering to cavort with the fellas. The twenty-four-foot powerboat he and Joe went in halves on was a moderately beat-up Chris-Craft "Overnighter" that boasted a Chrysler inboard engine, a white hull and a galley that slept two. Each man ponied up $1,500 to buy it, plus more for repairs. They christened it *The Take One*, and had a motion-picture clapperboard painted on the stern above the propellers. Equal ownership ceased there.

The Take One was quickly reborn as Gordon's weekend party hangout, then his ocean hot rod. Joe had to battle to schedule time for his own family; Gordon's guests always seemed to be pouring tourist-style through the marina gates. Jack Perry liked bringing his kids, and if he scolded them for too much grab-ass, everybody else on the boat watched. Jack would trundle after them on his stump half-legs, drawing comparisons to a gorilla in a Hawaiian shirt, because his prosthetics wobbled too much to wear on board.

Nathan Jones, a cannonball-shaped real estate man with dense, black hair, was another regular. He was the loud one of the group, a little tragic inside, and a lover of drink. Nathan was particularly adept at gunning the boat in the open sea, so when it hit a wake *The Take One* sailed airborne ten feet before a riotous crash that made Gordon howl. (He wasn't so enamored with the slight crack in the hull that resulted from it.) Composer Walter Greene was another hard-drinking pal who, according to Jimmy, "drove the boat like a bat out of hell." *The Take One* was docked at Stephen's Landing, where Southern California's moneyed set rented slips. Most boat owners there favored puttering around. Not my uncle and Joe. He drove full throttle on trips to Catalina Island. Gordon said faster. Joe spun the boat in tight circles ("water donuts") outside the jetty. Gordon convinced him to spray bayside diners inside the five-knot zone. Arrested development put the starch in their sea legs.

Just one more item, Gordon informed Joe, a Cheshire smile on his face: he'd decided where he planned to sit onboard. He didn't cough up this money to recline daintily in his wheelchair. Joe winced hearing the plan, and the next weekend a marina handyman spent half a day bolting and hammering it to life.

Gordon's "boat chair" was an old TWA jetliner seat he got an airline buddy to donate. It was bracketed on top of the engine casing, a boxlike structure behind the wheel console. The chair was aerodynamically unsound, but what Gordon lost in knots-per-hour he made up for with his seat elevation. It instantly rendered him the tallest person on board, a status he never felt on dry land. Once he was accustomed to his perch, he shouted speed and coordinates with a peppery sureness that grated the nerves. "Port, port, port, port, now starboard. Swing it, but watch the buoy. Joe. It's coming up hard. You see the buoy, Joe?"

After a few outings, Joe summoned Jimmy over to the wheel to clue him in on the obvious: they had a Captain Blye on their hands.

"Think he'll buy that we can't hear him?"

It was Los Angeles that had thrown these men into close quarters. There wasn't a diploma among them.

Joe had grown up in Beverly Hills as an easygoing, adventurous kid into surfing, cameras and girls. Mesmerized by the Old Hollywood his father showed him, Joe dropped out of high school his senior year in the late 1930s for a job photographing stars in MGM's publicity department. His career was ahead of him. His father's was dust. Erich, who had directed *Greed* and other silent picture epics, had been blacklisted into professional castration. Louis B. Mayer and the other studio bosses had grown so disgusted with Erich's spare-no-expense approach to moviemaking and his chutzpah in publicly questioning studio management they collectively refused to assign him any more big-budget films.

Hence, where the von Stroheims once had lived sumptuously, they struggled to get by on Erich's lowly screenwriting jobs. Where they once could sprint off on extravagant European trips, the family needed the collection plate taken up for them by William Powell, Myrna Loy and others stars after Joe's mother was critically hurt in a freak beauty parlor accident.

Joe left MGM and his family problems behind once war was declared. He joined the Marines, where he trained as an army combat photographer. For the next four years he traveled between the Pacific Theater and Europe with a 35-mm in one hand and a M-1 rifle in the other. In between battlefield assignments, he drank hooch, ran wild with his buddies and almost got nabbed by the Germans at the Rhine River. (The Nazis had a bounty on his head because of his father's sadistic portrayal of them.) Near the end of the hostilities Joe snapped pictures that graced national magazines — of a German P.O.W. camp where 1,110 people were incinerated; of Japanese war criminals who'd mugged for his lens. Once stateside, he went straight to his girlfriend's apartment and discovered her banging his best friend.

After that, landing jobs in Hollywood was a breeze.

Jimmy had survived by keeping his eyes open and his opinions to himself. His dilemma all along was being too smart for the jobs people offered him, yet lacking the skin color and formal qualifications to show them up. If there was anything Jimmy learned from past mistakes, you had to suffer to get what was due you.

His dad had forced him to quit school in the fifth grade to hoe the fields alongside him. Toby Gillard needed aid with those forty acres. His wife died of TB when Jimmy was little, meaning Toby had to rear ten kids on his own. He accomplished it with a fair hand, on top of preaching at the Methodist church and working back channels to maintain racial peace in town with its liberal white banker. Considering the time and place, the Gillards had it better than most, though not as good as the white kids, who were driven to school in buses instead of having to walk dusty miles. All of Toby Gillard's kids spent time planting and harvesting. The fields were their livelihood, and it usually provided them with more bounty than it demanded, but not always. They all were in the cotton fields that day a furious storm seized the sky. Before they found shelter, a bolt of lightning zapped Jimmy's ten-year-old sister with such energy it nearly broke every bone in her lifeless body.

As he got older, Jimmy was determined to leave. Maybe it was sheer restlessness. Maybe it was when another boy, a white cracker angry that Jimmy had spoken with a black girl he had a crush on, shoved a loaded gun in his face and said, in essence, "Nigger, don't ever try that again" that fueled his wanderlust for other parts of the country. Midway through World War II he took off. Jimmy and a cousin enlisted with the Marines, believing no woman would be able to resist them in uniform. He was assigned to a segregated unit in North Carolina, where the Marines expected to rebuild the farm boy into an efficient killing machine. Jimmy realized his mistake in signing up within days. Nobody at the recruiting office had informed him that ten-mile runs and five a.m. wakeups, not to mention the Salt Peter, were job essentials. He needed an escape route from Fort Lejeune, North Carolina.

First, he pretended to suffer chronic headaches, knowing they were hard to disprove. The drill sergeants were dubious. Switching ailments, he started peeing in his bunk at night to fake a malfunctioning bladder. The sergeants said nice try. Well, Jimmy was dogged. He persisted with the bedwetting for three months, sleeping on the cold barracks floor after he let loose. He cleverly hung his soiled sheets off a railing where he knew the sergeants took their smoke break to make it appear he was embarrassed about his secret. After a stint in the infirmary, where he continued his midnight whizzing, Jimmy received the general discharge he had sought. He'd urinated his way out of the Leathernecks in roughly three months.

In L.A., Jimmy's touch with women as a backcountry Romeo was something to behold. Once his marriage with Lovella came undone, Jimmy frequently drove to the dance clubs and bars of South Central straight from a ten-hour day with my uncle. These nightspots were his happy hunting ground: he almost always came home with someone. Getting through the next workday on a few hours of shuteye took more practice. Even so, Jimmy wasn't much for braying about his conquests or the relationships that flowered from them. They spoke for themselves. By the time his libido receded in the late-1960s, he'd fathered, depending on who you ask, anywhere between nineteen and twenty-seven offspring with a gaggle of wives and girlfriends.

Some of these things the three men confided to the other. Mostly they kept it light. Neither Jimmy nor Joe ever heard Gordon describe how his accident pulverized his family. Neither of them heard him bellyache he didn't deserve what he'd been dealt. What he might say in an offhand moment over a drink was that paralysis was his salvation. "Without it, I'm telling you, I'd be dead or in jail."

The vision of an incarcerated Gordon sometimes was a pleasing image. While Joe was hosing down the boat one Saturday, Gordon noticed a distinguished, balding gentleman with a thirty-five-foot yacht seven slips from his. He had seen the man's face dozens of times, never in person. Gordon whistled for Joe to come over for a look-see himself. "You know who that is, right?" Gordon said excitedly. "You know what's he's worth?" "So?" Joe said. "So push me up to the marina office. I want to see about moving our slip next to his."

A month later Gordon was back in his element: dockside at Balboa, yanking friends' chains. It was summer 1962. Joe and Jimmy were painting the cabin of *The Take One* and drinking Budweiser while Gordon observed their effort through a porthole. The boat was in its new slip.

"Joe," Gordon said, "you've got the imagination of a house fern. If we can get a man in space, anything's possible. That's it. With the grain, back and forth."

"First off, I don't see what rockets and you water-skiing have to do with the other. Second thing, quit telling me how to paint. I know what I'm doing."

"Sure doesn't look that way from where I'm sitting. I can see little bubbles under the paint. It's cuz you're not going with the grain."

"Oh zip it. For once in your life, can't you sit there and enjoy the air?"

"No! Now let's talk about putting skis on my chair."

"You're insane. You have about as much chance of water-skiing as I do getting rich off you."

"Just do me a favor and paint right, okay. Why'd we prime the thing first if you were going to do the rest half-assed?"

"Why did we prime the cabin? *We?* I'm warning you, Gordon. It's half my boat, remember?"

"Jimmy," Gordon said with an alligator grin. "Talk some sense into him."

"No thank you. I'm trying not to listen to you boys."

"Come on, be a sport."

"Naw." Jimmy took a long swig of Budweiser, malty in all the paint fumes. "I've learned."

The banter should've stopped there, but Gordon never knew when to shut up. "You know what I think? Jimmy should be a diplomat and Joe should keep his day job. He couldn't paint a flower box."

That last dig hovered in the fumes. A buoy clanged and Joe's eyes narrowed into felonious slits. He dropped the paintbrush in the can and rammed his head out the porthole. "That's it," he said. "I warned you." He stomped out of the cabin, around the deck, jumping off the bow to within a few inches of Gordon's roundly bronzed face. "Listen," Joe grunted, "I gave up Saturday with the family for your precious paint job. I didn't think she needed it, but you insisted."

"Easy Joe, you're gonna pop a blood vessel."

"Good."

"Maybe you should take a walk to cool down."

"No, you're the one about to cool down. The next pointer you offer, I'm pushing your chair off the goddamned dock. Then you can tell all the fish about *going with the grain.*"

"They'd get it faster than you. That's a joke, Joe. Laugh."

"Keep it up, man. Keep it up," Joe said, storming off the dock toward the smoked-glass marina building.

Before he got inside, Gordon yelled: "You're not going to strand little me here, are you Joey?" Joe shook a balled fist from behind.

A minute or so later, a sixty-three-year-old man in khakis and a blue plaid shirt peeked out of the cabin of his yacht, which made *The Take One* look like a dinghy. "Excuse me," the man said, "but I couldn't help but overhearing your tiff. I was wondering if you needed a hand."

"Very nice of you to offer," Gordon answered, "but I have someone else here. And I'm going to apologize to my friend when he comes back—if he comes back."

"Here's hoping he does," the man said.

They talked cross-ship for a while before the man insisted, absolutely insisted, Gordon and Jimmy come over for martinis and his wife's fresh-grilled crab cakes.

When Joe returned to the dock twenty minutes later with level blood pressure, Gordon gestured for him to join them on the man's yacht. Joe nodded. He recognized that Gordon had made his move. Walking over, Joe studied the cartoon bird painted on the back of the stranger's yacht. The bird with the spiky red mane was known around the planet for his machine-gun laugh and acerbic wit. *Woody Woodpecker* had made millions for Universal Pictures plus a load for its creator. Joe climbed up the ramp. Jimmy shrugged at him.

"Joe von Stroheim," my uncle said confidently, "I'd like you to meet Walter Lantz."

"Nice to meet you," said Joe. In his head, he debated if Gordon had engineered the fight all along.

"Likewise," said Walter. "May I offer you a drink?" Joe said please. Walter's wife, Gracie, put a Tiffany martini glass in his hand. "Gordon here was telling me about your dad. I'm sure I spoke to him at Universal a few times. Incredibly talented man. I was sorry to hear he passed."

"Kind of you to say," Joe said.

"Joe," Gordon said. Another smirk had settled into his right cheek. "I have some amazing news. Mr. Lantz, I mean, Walter here, wants us to do the postproduction on the new Woody cartoons he's planning. Music and effects."

"Tell him what else," Walter said.

"You betcha. We're going to organize a music company for him so he can collect the royalties instead of letting Universal hog them all. Should be quite a take."

"I meant to ask you before, Gordon," Walter said. "Do you think Universal's lawyers will try to block us?"

"Let them. As long as you didn't sign away the original rights, they're your property. If they own the rights, we can easily record new material. You'd own it outright."

"You can do that?"

"Absolutely. I know about five composers who'd do a tremendous job. Top-notch."

"Sounds good. Can I get samples of their work?"

"Whenever you want." Jimmy gave Gordon a sip of his martini. "Hey Joe, aren't you going to say anything?"

"Yeah," he said chomping his martini olive. "Does your deal mean we're done painting?"

~~~

The seedling was jumping into business as Walter Lantz's music man. A slow, molecular-level change rumbled through my uncle. Lawyer-Abe heard it in private conversations. Secretaries captured it in confidential memos. Now that he was around an authentic Hollywood success, waiting for his one great thing struck him as too passive an objective. Gordon, thanks to his association with Lantz and his own emerging studio connections, was meeting men with vacation homes and executive assistants. There was no reason he shouldn't have their spoils. He didn't have to con his way around town anymore as an oddball schmuck peddling his dad's stale songs. He didn't need sympathy-work. A stable lifestyle for his mother and him had been his goal and he had licked it.

A decade after leaving Sierra Madre, he was a small valve in the creative engine. Soon that wouldn't be enough. He'd move beyond the postproduction grind to his intermediary target, producing movies himself. Doing that would position him for what he wanted most: inventing something the entertainment world would ask how they had managed without. He wasn't sure what that something would be—a stunning piece of equipment, a technical process—but the vision "put his heart in his mouth." He'd had always loved that phrase. To burrow into his new mindset he dictated grandiose memos about financing packages and "four picture deals with Desilu." In flying to Germany and Austria to record new music, he began staying at the finer hotels regardless of the cost because you had to act prosperous to be it. Occasionally he even felt sorry for the bullied production assistants and chain-smoking directors scurrying around the sound stages of the movies he was sound-editing. He assumed these people had rejected saner professions like dentistry or taxidermy because they felt as vulnerable on the inside as he looked on the out. Recognition as an Industry Somebody was how they medicated their self-doubts. Considering his journey there, recognition alone just didn't cut it anymore.

There had been that time with Joe after they had cruised Balboa Bay. Joe was pushing him up the dock ramp to the car when they spotted a prominent, married producer named Roland on his eighty-foot yacht. Roland was crawling out from underneath a deck tarp with a voluptuous blond adjusting her black panties. They were giggling. Champagne glasses clinked. "Keep your fucking mouth closed," Gordon warned Joe. "You didn't see that." But for months afterwards, my uncle saw it. He wanted to be Roland, not the adulterer mind you, but an independent man with a yacht and a blond as his party favors of success. His assurance he was on the correct path soared when filmmaker Sam Fuller cold-called him. Fuller, who'd later become a good friend, was a cigar-gnashing, little fireplug known for his corrosive depictions of the American psyche. Soldiers got shot in the head in his movies, and the good guys were never all good. He needed music and effects for *Shock Corridor*, his upcoming picture about an ambitious reporter who goes undercover at an insane asylum to ferret out a killer, and had heard of General Music's bargain prices. Gordon saw himself in Fuller's movie, which, incidentally, the critics slammed as a cornball descent into madness. Saw himself going undercover into a nest of crazies to wrest his own greatness. Hollywood became his one welcomed infection.

To me, his town was a swamp of phonies. To me, the jaded Angeleno, only a rube confused about heroism genuflects in the presence of the celebrity stretch limo. I began believing that after my parents took me to a dressy Sunset Strip restaurant, the kind no kid enjoys until dessert, following a visit to Gordon's. Sitting at a nearby table was an aging French actress we'll call Leslie. She was eating a Cobb salad with another lady. Both of them were elegant and fastidiously coiffed. "Go ask her for her autograph," my mom urged me. "She'll be flattered." Why did I go? Blushing to the collar of my Navy-blue blazer, I shyly approached their table. I sputtered my request, handing one of the women a pen and paper. It just so happened I handed it to the wrong lady. I will never forget how Leslie glared at me, surprise pollinated with indignation, a look that said, "*You twerp. How could you not know who I am?"* I was eleven years old. The actress snatched the pen from her friend, scribbled an illegible autograph and gave it to me without glancing at me.

Before I knew anything about my own family's Hollywood registry, I'd rip friends seduced by celluloid fiction. "What's wrong with you?" they would ask. "Relax." In my bones I couldn't. So it was to be expected, I guess, that when I broke into reporting at the *Los Angeles Business Journal*, the first investigative piece I ever wrote was on a $1-million pork-barrel museum dedicated to movie lore. Its name was the Hollywood Entertainment Museum, the same concept my uncle took at stab in the early 1960s.

Years later, when I was first wrestling with this book, I freelanced for CNN when it was planning an expose on the phoniest of all Tinseltown creations: the Hollywood Walk of Fame. The Walk is a strip of sidewalk on Hollywood and Vine boulevards where stars and quasi-stars pay upwards of $15,000 apiece to have their names enshrined in terrazzo squares for posterity (and free publicity for their upcoming projects). You don't have to be talented to get your name in the concrete, merely connected. To me, the Walk of Fame is a sham in a town of them.

It's probably fair to point out, too, that for a guy as cynical of Hollywood as I am, I sure do write a lot about it.

CHAPTER SIXTEEN
Ladies Crave Excitement

My grandma, a sixty-one-year-old conservative in J.F.K.'s America, was being shunted to the margins. Her caretaking wasn't needed much on the weekends, not with Gordon's maritime outings with Joe, or nights out with buddies like Nathan Jones. Travel-wise, Gordon bumped around Europe and Manhattan just fine thanks to Jimmy. Rose was being frozen out at all levels. When Gordon listed directors for Sunset Music Inc., a second company he was establishing exclusively for music publishing, her name was nowhere around.

As always, Grandma tolerated Gordon's snubs and went about her chores in a bright, floral apron that shouted Cézanne on Quaaludes. Being his mother was tricky, because it was so often un-maternal. Sometimes she was his punching bag, and sometimes a dissenting voice roping him off from adult desires. Rose knew she'd earned her say, so she kept opinions ready. She agreed with Gordon's breakup with Judy. She told friends how uneasy she was about him being ground up in an untenable marriage or exploited by Judy and Billie as their sugar daddy, if that was their intention. The couple of occasions she tried consoling Gordon he had been smart to end the relationship he clammed up. Could it be he was really in love with Judy? Or, Rose questioned, was it he was thinking past her? Whatever it was, the notion of him marrying anyone made her feverish about what she would do the rest of her days.

Frankly, mother and son had wedged each other into lumbering stereotypes. They had successfully warded off poverty, and their equilibrium as a tandem now slanted decidedly toward Gordon. He hustled. She cooked. He wanted serious money. The hunt didn't wow her. He adored gadgets. She pestered him about his catheter. He trusted salesmanship. She harped on him to "Put his trust with the Lord." Rose had tried surrounding Gordon with the trappings of an otherwise ordinary lifestyle. Pork chops fried to perfection, slacks crisply ironed. Her miscalculation was in overvaluing those trappings, because he yawned at them now that he'd had a whiff of grander things. Consequently, she had won and she had failed. By submerging her own needs so he could be "normal," she had inadvertently aimed a bulldozer named Gordon at herself.

Gordon was stuffed inside his quandary as well. His throat turned dry picturing his mother years from now fussing over his every whim. Paralysis had such staying power in what it demanded of others. His father had been yoked by it, and it was the same for his mother times ten. She should've been in the arc of leisure, feeding her grandkids baloney sandwiches in the park. Opportunities missed, caring for him was all she had conquered. Opportunities lost, she refused transitioning into the retirement he dangled in front of her, or the apartment he offered to rent her as a pension. It was the status quo she hugged. Until this living arrangement changed, Gordon understood his own Big Life would keep eluding him. He assumed it was why he lashed out at the mother that so many people wished were theirs over the silliest issues. Everyday he resided with her and her 499 worries cast her more as a martyr and him as the heel. They crucified and protected each other on a rotating basis.

~~~

Ornery about his home life, Gordon buried himself with film work. When Hugo Grimaldi approached him in early 1962 about doing the postproduction on a schmaltzy space movie, Gordon said let him at it. Neither of them had delusions the film was Oscar material.

My uncle couldn't get enough of Hugo. Compared to his lunch-pail editors, the man was Monsieur Debonair. Hugo wore smoking jackets and foppish ascots if he was gassing up the car. He spoke flawless English tinged with an Italian accent. A painter and sculptor, he spent hours high up on a ladder chiseling grape leaves and family crests into the exposed beams of his legendary living room. His house was actor John Barrymore's old hilltop spread, and its history was as intriguing as Barrymore's bad-boy reputation. The seven-building estate, which Gordon waggled as many invitations to as he could, luxuriated with towers, lily ponds, secret passageways and a rathskeller where Barrymore had stowed his booty and scribbled women's phone numbers. During Hugo's ownership, Katharine Hepburn rented one of the chateaus without worry about autograph-seekers. Hugo, after all, was accustomed to famous people. He could captivate you with stories of how he and his brother were the legitimate heirs to the Monaco throne instead of that poser Prince Rainier, who Hugo was a dead ringer for with his pencil mustache. It was true: the Grimaldis were royals. Denied his birthright to be king, Hugo had emigrated to the U.S. from Italy with dreams of being a top MGM producer. When that didn't happen, he adapted. Tapping his contacts, he made himself an expert importing and dubbing European sci-fi movies into English. It was a living, though epicurean Hugo didn't need the money. His wife had plenty.

In the early 1960s, Hugo phoned Gordon about an East German movie that had leaked out of the Soviet bloc. He drove to General Music, where he laid on Gordon's office bed to watch a rough cut of *First Spaceship on Venus*. Unfortunately, it was too late to export it back. The storyline was passable enough: an international team of astronauts setting off to Venus to unlock her secrets. Once the spacecraft lands, the stupidity ensues. The explorers encounter a creepy quartz forest, ward off metallic insects, flee villainous sludge, and wonder where the natives are. The cliffhanger twist is that the visitors are in a dead civilization. In preparing to irradiate the Earth to soften it up for invasion, the Venetians had accidentally nuked their own planet. A film critic called it "post-dubbed, pseudo-scientific gobbledygook" filled with anti-war propaganda. He was being generous.

Thinking salvage job, my uncle applied the same technique he learned from Ed Wood's movies: the more wretched the screenplay, the more smothering the music. The term was "Mickey Mousing" it. Amazing what it could do. On *First Spaceship*, Gordon had his staff composer, Walter Greene, insert up-tempo horns to accentuate plot surprises and background strings and bass drums to dramatize the dialogue. As the crew bickered about aborting the mission a wall of violins moan behind them. Joe went heavy with the sound effects and the net result wasn't as half bad as the directing. The same technique extended to scores of other low-budget films General Music did. On *Navy Versus the Night Monsters*, a "thriller" about man-eating shrubbery attacking a Navy airbase, it's rumored the producer uttered into Gordon's ear: "Save this turkey with your music."

In the pre-digital age, success as a music editor or an effects guy meant being an improvising craftsman. The director would sit with you viewing a cut of his denuded product, where dialogue was the only sound. He would say, "Insert something in this scene, not that one," and you would visualize how it would flow with a stopwatch in your hand by a time-honored process called "spotting." If this were a soundtracked job, you would scan your music library and pick out candidate cues stored on ¼-inch master tapes. It would be trial and error, hours of fast forwarding and rewinding, until your eyes watered. Once you had the cues arranged, you would transfer them from tape to film at a sound lab like Ryder's or Glen-Glen. Then you would break down the picture on a cutting bench and synchronize your product to the nth degree—that or risk an outburst from the director about a sound effect where there was supposed to be a syrupy ballad. Your butt was on the line to create a flawless strip of effects and music that would be super-embossed next to the dialogue on the finished sound reel and run with the movie. If you were in this for the girls and glory, reconsider. It's at the end of credits, after the picture editor who makes more than you anyway, where your name finally rolls.

Gordon, wheeled into editor cubbies to either approve the work or direct it, became expert at calling out cuts himself, even if deal making titillated him far more than audio-visual harmony. He had spent hundreds of hours observing editors make music waltz with on-screen action. Remembering their tricks, he could watch a film segment on the Movieola and in a few minutes of directing a splice here, a change there, usually unscramble what had given others fits.

For all these distractions, Gordon couldn't erase Judy's image from his thoughts. Jimmy was petrified to let on he had seen her on an errand off Sunset. My grandma confided to Abe Marcus's wife that Gordon was unbearable to live with. Everyone around agreed. My uncle was as miserable as only love can make you.

At dinner at my parent's house, Gordon slouched low in his wheelchair dwelling on what he'd blown. "I must've been brain dead running away from her, Mur," he told my mom. "The prize was right there and I got spooked. It's over." Muriel took pity on him; little bro dejected? She asked him if he wanted her to try patching up things girl-to-girl, and he dipped his oversized noggin up and down. His forced, yearlong separation to test Judy's sincerity had lasted eight-and-a-half months.

Judy was nibbling a tuna fish sandwich in Bullock's paneled tearoom when my mom approached her. The vibe between them was artic. My mom asked her how her Catholic boyfriend was doing and Judy said curtly, "Fine, just fine." (In reality, Fred's mother resented Judy, who she considered too strong-willed and conspicuously non-Catholic.) "I suppose you expect me to ask about Gordon, now," she added. Maybe not, my mom answered. He was a wreck. "Well, he deserves it," Judy volleyed. "The way he dropped me was one of the worst things I've ever gone through." Give him a second opportunity, my mom said. He's sorry. "You ought to see him."

Now Judy chewed it over. She did love him for who he was in his depths; well, his depths first, his future tax bracket next. Okay, she told my mom, have him give me a call in a few days. "I'll see for myself how sorry he acts."

CHAPTER SEVENTEEN
Pasadena's Rose Parade

The getaway was as unconventional as the couple. On a Thursday afternoon in late August 1962, in the days after Marilyn Monroe overdosed, Gordon and Judy sat contentedly in the backseat of the Cad with the roof down and the wind mussing their hair. Jimmy was hotfooting them up the Ventura Freeway, the hillsides and farmland blurring into earth-tone collage. They were headed for Santa Barbara, a sleepy, coastal town dotted with eucalyptus groves and bohemians 100 miles north of L.A. There was a reason for the rush: Gordon and Judy were marrying. Trailing behind was their wedding caravan. Joe and his wife were in one car, Walter Greene and his spouse in another, editor Axel Hubert next, with Dorothy Chester, one of Gordon's secretaries, bringing up the rear with Hugo. Technically, this was more of a road-trip wedding than an elopement. The main principals missing were the bride and groom's mothers, and they'd been strategically excluded.

The reverend at the First Methodist Episcopalian Church performed a no-nonsense, ten-minute ceremony. The couple celebrated with a short, deep kiss. Gordon wore a dark jacket with a white shirt and matching tie, mobster-suave. Judy was in a cream-colored wool outfit with red and blue trim on the button line. Her hair was done pageboy. On her wrist was the Rolex watch Gordon had given her as an engagement signing-bonus. On her finger was the modest diamond ring she received for going through with it. Gordon looked electric in post-ceremony pictures. Judy radiated blissful relief. Afterwards, everybody checked into the beachside inn where they were staying to guzzle Dom Perignon out on the balcony as the setting sun melted orange into the Pacific. They all worked up a good high. That night it was Gordon's treat for a first-rate dinner at Victor Hugo's restaurant in nearby Montecito. He ordered tender veal medallions, Baked Alaska all around. As usual, he only ate about a fifth of what was set before him. A "kiddy" portion stuffed him.

Joe, meantime, never felt so bittersweet about love as he did on the first night of Gordon's nuptials. On the drive up from L.A., he had turned to his wife and told her what he had been waiting for months to tell her—they were through. Phyllis, a plump, bull-necked woman with round cheekbones, reacted calmly. She knew her drinking had eroded their marriage. At a party at Gordon's six months earlier, she had gotten hammered and spilled a plate of potato salad onto her lap. "I think you ought to take her home," Gordon whispered to Joe, shooting him that look. Not long after, when Phyllis had departed for a long stay in the Hawaiian Islands with the kids, Joe had fallen for a cute interior decorator with a '57 T-bird and a minor prison record. Certain that he and Phyllis were done, Joe brought his girlfriend around Gordon and Judy for little parties. They accepted her and, being discreet people, kept mum about it.

So there was Joe, happy-go-lucky and a free man again. He was leaned up against the balcony of his Santa Barbara hotel room, which was next door to my uncle's, having a smoke and pondering it all. (Phyllis had arranged her own hotel room to weep in private.) The stars blinked overhead from the black velvet sky when a curiosity engulfed him. How would Gordon spend his honeymoon night, specifically, that is? Joe assumed it couldn't be anything sexual; they were probably watching TV. Yeah, that had to be it. He tried mightily not to peep in. Willpower, he thought. Common decency. He smoked a second one, deciding halfway through it that willpower was overrated. He heeled out his cigarette, and tiptoed up to the sliding glass window of the newlywed's room. He studied the action for a minute. Next he rubbed his eyes. "Oh?" he said, "Ohhhhh." Gordon was lying on the bed, except his face was obscured, for which there was a logical reason. A naked Judy had climbed on top of him and was straddling his hairline.

Joe crept back to his room shaking his head. You had to give it to Gordon. He used what he had.

The wrenching tug in my grandma's abdomen was like nothing she could recall. In all her years with Gordon, she had always assumed the good in him would, when it really mattered, transcend any petty impulse for him to act too big for his hemmed-in britches. All she wanted to do was be there when he wed. Considering the sum tonnage of her sacrifice to him since 1940, an invitation was the least he could provide.

Rose had known in advance about the elopement. Gordon had informed her about it matter-of-factly on one of the hottest days of the summer. She had heard the other half of his intentions a week or so before the ceremony. He'd told her to begin searching again for that new place to live, because there wasn't sufficient room in their house on Shoreham for the three of them. To have Judy brushing up against her mother-in-law in the earliest stage of their marriage, he explained, would be claustrophobically unfair. "You can understand that, can't ya, Mom ?"

What was there to understand? She'd been betrayed, and her anger at being replaced like some kitchen hand blew over the empathy that made her tick. It wasn't that she expected Gordon to remain a bachelor forever. It was learning she was being ejected on two-weeks notice from the house that had defined them in the years after Lee's death that she was unprepared for. Who did Gordon think he was fooling? His excuse about the cramped living conditions was a smokescreen for his new order. Grandma knew that. She splashed cold water on her face before she rebuked him. "God help you, Gordon, if you're capable of doing this to me...." When he wouldn't reconsider, Rose defended herself with fangs you wouldn't think she had.

While Gordon was at work, Grandma phoned my mom with the news. Within twenty-four hours she was living with us in

Pasadena, where my mom wanted to tar and feather Gordon for the eviction she ranked with treason. Two weeks later Grandma leased a one-bedroom apartment in Sierra Madre a mile away from her old Mountain Trail place. My dad parachuted into the fray next. Rose needed him to distill her share of the assets from Gordon's so she could sustain herself. Gordon, keyed up about his upcoming event, had assured my dad before the wedding he would negotiate. He had a heart, and asked Jack to draw up an offer. Gordon would pay his mother $260 per month less what she received from Social Security, and forty percent of the house when sold, provided she waived her interest in the company. If he died suddenly, which seemed both impossible and imminent, she would inherit half of his music royalties, or about $10,000 a year. Next thing my dad heard, Rose had dolefully signed some papers before Gordon skipped off to Santa Barbara.

Grandma had a surprise for Gordon on his return to Shoreham Street. With an attorney counseling her, she wrote what she never thought she would:

The purpose of this letter is to call to your attention that on Friday, August 31, Gordon Zahler did extract from me my signature on several documents that I herewith repudiate and renounce.

These signatures were obtained as a result of a series of threats and extracted from me under extreme emotional duress. Gordon Zahler did not explain to me the nature of the documents he demanded that I sign and I did not understand their content or the significance of my signatures. I now believe that the purpose of the demanded signatures was to obtain my release of any claim to interest in the stock of the General Music Corporation – an act that is exactly contrary to my wishes and desires.

I was paid nothing for my signing the stock release (if that is what it was) nor did I receive a copy of what I signed. I hereby put you on notice I do not consider these signatures binding on or of any affect whatsoever.

Rose Zahler.

The unintended effect of this schism gift-wrapped a tremendous present for me. It gave me a grandma who lived nearby. Pretty soon,

"Mama Rose," as we called her, was inviting me over to her apartment for regular visits. Where my parents would say no to treats, she invariably said yes. We had a ritual where I'd spring up and down on the daybed near her front window and beg for Crackerjacks. "What do you like best," she would ask, "the popcorn or the prize?" "Both!" I would say, giving that box spring a beating. "Both." She'd then grab my hand and walk me down the block to Reece's Market, where I would wheedle her into Crackerjacks and Bazooka bubble gum.

Deep down, though, my visits only brought her vapory happiness. She had been a caretaker so long she was rudderless when there wasn't anybody to tend to except her measly self. It was a breather she wanted. Summary retirement was too harsh. Sandwiched between them, she gobbled up periodicals and dove back into Instruction classes. She mailed dresses and brass tie tacks to distant relatives and came by our house for supper. She became interested again in politics as a Goldwater Republican, but still a loneliness draped her. Over time, Gordon and she reconciled, and she babied him when given the opportunity. She accepted Judy as her daughter-in-law, too, because she accepted everyone. Nonetheless, Grandma had lost her *raison d'être*.

One day she couldn't muffle her lonesomeness any longer. She gathered my mom onto our living room couch and outlined an idea that'd she been nurturing. Would my mom be willing under any circumstances, she asked, to bring my brother Peter back from his live-in school? Mama Rose wanted to raise her special grandson. If she could handle a grown man alternately helpless and obnoxious, caring for a little boy would be a breeze. Everybody would win: Peter would be five minutes from home and Grandma would have a reason to get out of bed. No, my mom answered, that wouldn't make sense; Peter had already been ripped from home twice. Grandma stared into the white shag carpeting hearing this latest rejection. First Gordon, now my mom: she'd been decommissioned. It could make a person ill.

Peter, my middle brother eleven years ahead of me, didn't vacate my mother's womb for his grand entrance in February 1950 the way he was supposed to. The obstetricians dealt with it. They clamped forceps on his temples, as they routinely did during arduous labors, and suctioned him into the delivery room. They gave Peter Millard the once-over and pronounced him normal except for a seemingly trivial defect: he was missing a toe on one foot. Other than that, everybody assumed he would be a fine, little brother for Paul to harass someday. Both had the same puppy-dog, brown eyes.

After Peter's first birthday, that comparison died off. My parents' second boy was a late walker, and would only drink milk. As a toddler, he didn't cry and wouldn't laugh. As a little boy, he careened behind troubling stoicism and repeating the same sentence endlessly until being quieted. Later, an inscrutable rage burned in him. He expressed it by kicking gaping holes in the plaster or running away to horn-honking Foothill Boulevard. Something was most definitely wrong, and his stunted development was first pinned on those barbaric forceps. In later years, the more basic was blamed. It was genetics, a microscopic strip of jumbled chromosomes, that'd messed Peter up.

In the conformist 1950s, raising a mentally retarded child was stigma on top of hardship. My mom, lover of convention, was buffeted as a result between two different existences. There were summer pool parties for Paul, her first-born, and secret doctors' appointments for Peter. When Paul's elementary school mates caught wind that his little brother was a "freak" prone to unstoppable tantrums, the secret got out. Some days, Paul's ego was only as stable as Peter's behavior, which was anything but *Leave-It-To- Beaver*. A few of Paul's friends were warned by their mothers to steer clear of the Jacobs's house, because you never knew what "that retarded boy" would do. Sharing the same room with him, unsure whether to defend him or ditch him against neighborhood bullies, Paul survived adolescence longing for other kids' problems.

My mom for her part tried pretending it away. If Paul brought home a pal to build model airplanes with, she'd grab Peter and lock herself in the bathroom with him for the duration. Chatting with her friends, she occasionally gave the impression she had one child. Gordon had his millstone. She had hers.

Time didn't pacify it. After my folks moved to a bigger house on Kinneloa Mesa Road, Peter promptly christened the property by lobbing the family basset hound off a twelve-foot concrete ledge. The child psychiatrists tried drilling into my parents that this was their future. There were no wonder drugs that would realign Peter's misfiring brain. They recommended he attend a school for the retarded in Santa Barbara for a six-week trial. "Why not give it a try, Mrs. Jacobs? It would be best for him." Feeling poisoned, my parents released Peter's hand.

At the end of the six weeks, my folks had lunch with the head of the school, Mrs. Devereux, while Grandma occupied Peter in his spartan dorm room. Mrs. Devereux was blunt. She recommended Peter reside there permanently. He would be with others like him. My parents countered they couldn't do that. He was their child, however imperfect. He belonged at home with them and that's where he went.

Up on the Mesa nothing changed. One day, Paul had a friend over and my mom and Peter hunkered down on the bathroom tile for the entire afternoon. That day she knew. She dialed the local child psychiatrist and told her she was ready to bundle Peter off to Devereux School as his new home. "When can you have him ready?" the psychiatrist asked. "Oh, in about a week," my mom said. "How about an hour?" the doctor replied. My dad, who'd traded in engineering for more lucrative real estate as his career, rushed home from his Los Angeles office to say goodbye. Peter was six months older the next time they saw him.

The doctors cautioned my parents not to have another child after that trauma. My mom had already had a few miscarriages. It would be a giant risk, they said. You might well give birth to another Peter. This explains why I was an accidental conception, just not why I was "normal."

With Peter lassoing my parents' attention, my oldest brother found refuge in Gordon and Grandma's house. Paul could ride his bike from New Haven Road close to where I used to live to the old house on Laurel Avenue. There, Grandma spoiled Paul silly while Gordon shouted out, "Hey kiddo, whatcha know?" After Gordon and Rose moved to Hollywood, Paul made it there, too. Gordon's attitude was to treat Paul, then twelve-ish, as a pint-sized adult. If Paul acted squirrelly, Gordon faked a sneer to imitate Ralph Kramden. "Do that again and I'll send you to the *mo-on*." Paul soaked it up: being introduced to Lucy, Ann Sothern, Bozo the Clown and TV tough guys on trips to the set, hearing about wrist record player Gordon wanted to patent. On Friday nights, they watched the televised boxing matches together on Gordon's bed munching gooey Hamburger Hamlet cheeseburgers while screaming for blood. Nobody had an uncle like this. You couldn't beat him at gin because he would memorize the deck. He even let you drink coffee and hold his smokes if you showed guts.

Later, as Paul grew into his teenage ears, Gordon hired him during the summer as an apprentice music cutter. It was there he learned what the regular editors already had: the boss was a perfectionist who bird-dogged your work. Be off a hair on a cue and you might have to re-cut it endlessly, even for a *Popeye* cartoon. If Gordon felt a rifle-shot sound effect sounded too much like a fart, which he often did, you might be in the desert sun with him the next day to fire a real shotgun next to a portable microphone. His meticulousness not only provoked snide comments among his crew, it had instigated a fracas at a sound stage. About a year earlier, he had asked two actors in *Young John Dillinger* to re-dub a fight scene because he was unhappy with the take they had. "Fellas" he said, "I want to hear a pow. One of you slap the other guy with an open hand. Put some muscle behind it." One of the actors, however, had walloped the other when he wasn't ready, and the two had briefly duked it out with a live mic between them and Gordon saying, "Cut, guys. Cut!" You knew you were in dutch when Gordon had the editing machine wheeled over to his bed so he could inspect your progress. If he liked your effort, he would promote you to a more important show instead of extolling your skill. On payday, everybody complained and few got raises. Paul himself barely earned minimum wage.

Gordon, though a skinflint, disliked administrative duties of being *the* boss. It tapped the wrong side of his brain. His apathy about the little things also showed up in his attitude about his body's maintenance protocol at work. Bedsores—he could barely be bothered with sterilizing them. "Just leave it," he would tell my grandma when she approached with gauze. Bladder infections—he would take his medication if he had a second between appointments. Once Paul felt nauseated after spilling urine on his hands emptying Gordon's pee bag, a tapered, rubber container connected via tubing to his catheter. Gordon glared. "If that's the worst thing you ever get on your hands," he said, "consider yourself lucky."

After work, Gordon's attitude was to hell with the splicing. He wanted to cruise! One Friday evening around ten, he ordered Paul to load him in the Cad and hop on the Hollywood Freeway. "We're going to Newport to check out the boats." "But," my brother stammered, "I don't have my license. And I've never driven on the freeway before." "Who cares?" Gordon said. "Can you handle it or not?" "Well, yeah," Paul answered, sweat dewing on his fifteen-year-old neck. "Then, punch it, kiddo!"

Paul chummed around with a version of Gordon I never did.

Then again, we all shared Grandma, who plunged into her last phase in the same mossy, Mayberry town she held dearest of all. She hadn't wanted to depart Sierra Madre when MGM gave Gordon his big break, but she knew she must to unleash his talents. It cost her a lot. She replaced her view of the purple San Gabriels, which had made her feel God when he didn't seem to be listening, with the backs of trashy Hollywood nightclubs. Now she was home.

Being minutes away, we spent holidays with her and basked in her compliments. We watched her in action with my mom, over whom she still could fluster when etiquette was involved. Who else did Mama Rose have? She and Harold, her baby brother with a San Francisco business and family, had long been on the outs. She disapproved how Harold changed faiths from the Instruction to Buddhism the way some people switch diets. Harold had his qualms about how she handled the past. Rose and her mother, Dearie, were never close either despite their proximity. Rose was the grounded one, Dearie the Damon Runyon character. Dearie lived out her old age in a convalescent home near downtown L.A.'s MacArthur Park, a half-hour ride from Sierra Madre. Near the end of her life, she became companions with an old man preoccupied with feeding pigeons. The "pigeon man" may even have converted her to Christianity before she died of an enlarged heart. Crushed twice by the killing of her husband and a son, that heart, I guess, could take no more.

Mama Rose was just assembled differently. In the mid 1960s, for instance, Paul, then seventeen, walked out into our driveway on a foggy Christmas Eve to find a spanking new red MG sports car with a giant bow on top. Every fiber in him wanted to take it for a spin. If only somebody else in the family would oblige. Tomorrow, they yawned. It's too late tonight. That's when Grandma flung a shawl around her. "What are we waiting for?" she asked. The two of them screeched around the winding roads off Eaton Canyon in the night chill for half an hour. Paul sped like Gordon taught him while Mama Rose mouthed a prayer to the Virgin Mary about keeping the tires on the road.

CHAPTER EIGHTEEN
Code of the Fearless

Fall 1964. Marriage agreed with Gordon, both as aspiring mogul and as a man arrived. In those formative years with Judy, Gordon monitored the clock as he never had before. Jimmy's standing order was to deliver him home every night before seven p.m. along insider shortcuts south of Sunset Boulevard, can't-miss meetings notwithstanding. Judy, vying to be the perfect spouse, wanted him home. When he rolled in off his elevator, frazzled, she was there with freshly applied rouge and his scotch-rocks prepared. (Jimmy would settle him in bed, grab a bite and drive his own car or Gordon's back to South Central.) "Meet anybody interesting today?" Judy would ask, pampering him with a warm towel. "Anything new on that foreign deal?" she would inquire while basting the rosemary lamb chops. Sometimes, if affections moved, she slept in his orthopedic bed with him, tugging a pillow over her head at four a.m. when Gordon's compact metabolism usually woke him.

This Big Life of Gordon's gravitated to two poles: grooving a domestic rhythm with Judy as a married pair, while slaking his appetites away from her. Together they hosted regular dinner parties with Judy's cooking garnering praise. They attended private meals with the Lantz's in Beverly Hills. Before long, he arranged a trip to Acapulco, where he chartered a fishing boat to "teach" Judy how to catch marlin. Jimmy held the pole; Gordon said when to reel. If a pressure deadline was met, Jimmy and he might sneak away on a Friday afternoon to throw down fifty dollars at Santa Anita or make a Dodger game to see Sandy Koufax pitch. Unshackled at last, he was making up for lost time.

Judy was on the receiving end herself. Her hubby put money in her designer bag, though not enough to go bananas on Rodeo Drive. He parceled out an allowance for Billie, who half-kidded she would have married Gordon if Judy hadn't. He let Judy quit Bullocks, too, and after she bugged him, permitted her to fool around with song lyrics with Walter Greene for a half dozen *Woody Woodpecker* cartoons. What Judy sought most—to be romanced Gordon-style on a trip to Europe—he aimed to give her in spades.

The money was there. His employees just didn't see a whole lot of it. Gordon's philosophy was to operate lean, nothing unaccounted for, while maintaining a fat cushion in the bank. It worked smoothly because the accounting and payroll minutiae were handled by his CPA. Jack Perry served an important role beyond his green eyeshades as well: he made for a convenient scapegoat. Gordon reflexively invoked Jack's name if an editor doing so-so work cornered him about a raise. Blaming Jack, to Gordon's mind, was slick management. "Sorry, I can't bump you up," he would say. "Jack's orders." Some employees grew to doubt this was the truth. They carped about being underpaid. The few who droned on about it when they should've been cutting music or sound effects in their cubicles were invited into the boss's office and reminded they were free to apply at the competition.

Gordon's hard-knuckle approach had some merit. Several of the network shows he stripped music and effects onto had been cancelled. General Music also was owed big, maybe $25,000 or more, by B-movie outfits like Crown International and San-S Productions. Hang tough, company lawyers would advise him. The producer absconded with the cash; we'll have to pay you in installments. The other legal claptrap thrown at him also begged patience. He'd get his money—after they convinced some theater owners to air the rotten film. Gordon's response to the excuses can be summed up as think again. His psychology was a throwback in this company town. Either you made good on every promise or you were a skunk. It was one thing for him to lowball his way into a contract or fudge a song ownership, quite another to shirk written money commitments. Abe Marcus dispatched dozens of pay-up letters on his behalf.

Gordon and his deadbeats became a long-running saga often more entertaining than the project in dispute. Ed Wood Jr., into General Music for thousands, claimed he "was not personally responsible" once his company, Atomic Productions, went belly up. Charlie Dean, a smaller debtor, pleaded for understanding. Dean had tumbled from writer-director-producer of TV and film to a substitute mailman teetering above welfare. "I have failed to contact Gordon," he wrote, "because I am so embarrassed I can't face him….As you know the television business is about as secure as playing the races…."

Another man, an ex-African-mercenary-turned-wild-animal-trafficker-turned-TV-producer, had delinquent bills for his completely forgettable nature show. The man—we'll call him Sam—was a brilliant, violent guy who had killed natives in the Congo and sat in pits swarming with 250 rattlesnakes. When my uncle demanded he pay, there was no baser insult.

"Sam, you owe me. My accountant is busting my chops about it."

"You're gonna get your money. Just edit these last couple shows and I'll tell you what. I'll throw in a $100 bonus."

"A whole $100! The answer is no."

"Listen, if I were you, I'd be grateful I had any business."

"Okay, Sam, I'll bite. Why's that?"

"Don't play stupid, Zahler. We both know that if the bleeding hearts around town didn't feel so sorry for you, you'd be out on the boulevard with a tin cup."

"Gee, I'm sorry you had to stoop so low to come to me at all."

"One last chance. Edit these shows and you'll get your money."

"Sorry. You're credit's no good here."

The veins in Sam's neck dilated. "Okay, if that's the way you want to play it. I'll get you your money next week. But a gimp thinking he's going to intimidate me." Sam grabbed his valise. "What a joke you are."

Later in the day an editor asked what to do if Sam returned.

"Give him the bum's rush," Gordon said.

He could afford to be glib, some anyway. His share of music publishing royalties arrived regularly with the name ASCAP embossed across the crown of every check. When the secretaries held them up so he could view the amount, it was nearly a religious moment. Gordon considered himself a member of a moneymaking priesthood the Hollywood cognoscenti barely knew existed. The priesthood was lorded over by the American Society of Composers, Authors and Publishers (ASCAP), the world's premier licensing agency. ASCAP music, once copy-written and owned, collected a few cents here, a dollar there, from primetime in the states to one a.m. Brazilian TV. If it played, he got paid (actually, he and the composer). By the early 1960s, he had learned what Abe had beaten into him: music is immortal. It's a commodity. "There's big money in background music," Gordon would exalt in later times. "In thirty years, the royalties will still be paying my relatives." He was right.

All it took was moving recorded original music onto radio, TV or through private music systems anywhere in the world. Simpler still was selling songs in bulk to competitors of background-music titan Muzak, which filled the nation's offices, elevators, supermarkets and shops with lachrymose pop standards, or that soulless champagne music Lawrence Welk floated on Saturday nights. Atmosphere songs like *Beautiful Dreamer* were everywhere in America's consumer Valhalla. The sociologists who theorized it was subliminal mind control knew their stuff. Gum-snapping, background music stimulated workers' brains to fend off sleep as they pushed their paper. It nudged diners to wolf their food to make way for the next party. Moving "product," Gordon spouted, was easy cash if you knew a copyright from a mechanical right and had an ear for what sold.

Agreement by agreement, he cultivated a shrewd side-business feeding the mood-music stampede. He'd hired Walter Greene partly for that reason, and kept several other composers (Tim Spencer and Earle Hagen) around to write songs he could record with foreign orchestras. Partnerships were fashioned with sub-publishers across Europe to get Lantz Music Co. and his own music companies airplay that would bring liras, pounds, deutsche marks and francs into his pocket. He cozied up to ASCAP, which took its own share, and won posthumous membership for his dad's music.

Signing Hans Salter, the versatile Austrian, might have been Gordon's niftiest maneuver. Over forty years of composing and conducting at Universal Pictures, years that earned him multiple Oscar nominations, Salter wrote music for *Dracula*, *Frankenstein*, *Sherlock Holmes* and *Abbot and Costello* to name a few. His résumé just didn't buy him plush retirement. Salter by the mid-1960s was just another forgotten, émigré composer. Introduced through Abe, Gordon tried to sway Salter about doing business together, but the old man was skeptical his creations could live another day in sitcoms and foreign radio. "You sure I'll make money from this, Mr. Zahler?" "You betcha," said Gordon. Out of nothing, Salza Music (Salter and Zahler) was born, another unlikely partnership.

Success cramped him. General Music now vibrated with such hectic activity on so many shows and side-projects that Gordon wanted an office in line with his cachet. Through connections he tracked something down at Sam Goldwyn Studios, another Hollywood-area mainstay at Formosa Avenue and Sunset. The space was a straw-colored, corrugated-metal prop warehouse converted for postproduction. Studio wags called it "the barn" on account of the drafty, twenty-five-foot-high ceiling, where crap-happy pigeons roosted under the eaves. Inside were a bank of large offices and a row of cubicles. In the far back was a scene dock. The barn matched Gordon's needs. There was elbowroom here and a decent place to park; the labs and recording houses were blocks away. Having an address on a bustling movie studio didn't hurt, either.

It was such a find, so affordable and modular, that Burt Lancaster inquired about renting it for his own production outfit. Lancaster had his eye on the barn for some time, probably figuring it was his to lose. Not only did he have more pizzazz than some sound-editing house, but his company was already based at Goldwyn. Naturally, Gordon heard about the actor's posturing within the week. After verifying it with his advisers, he railed about getting screwed. He imagined Lancaster waging a charm offensive with studio managers to weasel into the space he had dibs on first. "Who the hell does he think he is?" Gordon snorted at a meeting with Abe and Jack. "The guy's a great actor and everything, but he's got some big ones doing this. I thought he was such a gentleman." The three brainstormed. Abe even may have contemplated phoning Lancaster's attorneys to ask how a virile, broad-shouldered movie star could exploit someone like Gordon. How would that play in *Variety*?

In the end, General Music was able to keep its rental claws on the barn, but the Lancaster affair failed to prepare anyone for their moving day debacle. A ruddy-faced union man with his arms across his chest blocked their entrance into the studio when Gordon and crew pulled up in a rented truck and two cars early one Saturday morning. The teamster asked who was in charge and everyone pointed at Gordon. "Have you read the friggin' rules, Mr. Zahler?" the man asked in a Brooklyn accent, leaning on the passenger side of the Cad. "I'd advise you to do that, cuz you ain't coming in like this, not on my watch." No one had seen Gordon so tongue-tied before. In assigning his own workers to move instead of unionized ones, he'd apparently breached the studio's collective bargaining agreement. Only teamsters were allowed to lift things over a certain weight on studio grounds. Gordon got fifteen more minutes of dressing-down before the gates swung open. For my overachieving uncle, all that mattered was that they did.

As much as Gordon relished his new office, Europe was his choice destination. So while the Beatles played Ed Sullivan, he set off to show Judy every gothic capital he could afford.

Gordon's man in London was Danny O'Brien. He'd first met Danny in New York City in 1954 while shopping the sewing program. Danny was an independent music publisher in his forties with kind, fleshy jowls, a barrel chest, loads of contacts and a bedrock faith in God-and-Queen. He met my jetlagged uncle's party at Heathrow International. A few nights later Gordon, Jimmy and Judy were at Danny's house for a proper English meal cooked by his wife, Mabel. From England the four of them flew to Stuttgart to record with the civic orchestra. Next it was on to Austria with plans for Switzerland from there.

They had intended to load their rental car, an Opel sedan, on a special car-train for overnight passage into Geneva, until they arrived late and found the train was gone. While everyone else stewed, Gordon got his dangerous smile. He was reconnoitering. "Hey," he said. "Let's cross the Alps ourselves. We can do it." Danny quickly shook his jowls. "Daft idea. We don't know the roads. What if we get stuck?" Gordon was adamant they try. "Don't be such a pantywaist, Danny," he said. "It'll be an adventure." It was 9:30 p.m. when they departed. Jimmy wound the Opel along a sloping mountain road that skied 7,000 feet above sea level with vast sheets of snow one side and a lethal drop on the other. The road was so narrow that when another car's headlights beamed at them, Jimmy had to back up a sweaty quarter mile to let the other vehicle pass on the shoulder. He remembered being so high up they were "looking down on the stars." He was afraid to clutch the Opel out of second gear. Everybody was pissed at Gordon for suggesting this route while he sat up in the front wishing it would never end. About five a.m. they made it down the Alps with popping eardrums. The manager at the

Geneva hotel they had reservations at called them stupid for attempting that drive at night. Then he informed them they were too early to check in. Gordon shot him his pitiful-cripple look and the manager at least arranged their breakfast.

The final leg was a plane flight to Rome. Gordon had already swallowed hard and agreed to meet with his Italian publisher on another trip so he could play tourist with Judy. She was dying to hit the museums and Gucci. An excursion to St. Peter's Basilica and a chance to be blessed by Pope John XXIII was penciled in for the end of their stay. Again, their timing flagged. It was the high tourist season, and 10,000 perspiring Christians were already lined up in a controlled mob for their turn into the baroque dome. "Ah, bloody hell," Danny said seeing the crowd. "Maybe we should call it a day. Let's get a Coke." Gordon again had other ideas. He had Jimmy push him over to a Papal Swiss Guard, and tried once more for pity. The guard, who was dressed akin to a beefeater in a tunic and helmet, was a sucker for it.

He waved the four of them through a door at the side of the basilica, and they followed him into the darkness. Down a ramp they went, past cubbyhole offices, under an arch, through damp hallways and by a sweeping, illuminated brick wall they didn't recognize initially. What they saw few tourists had. Bodies of dead popes dating back centuries were catacombed in the grotto walls. Each was preserved in his own sarcophagus with a thick, crystal-like bubble over him. Our travelers were cutting through the storm cellar of the Holy Ghost. After walking awhile, the guard gestured them up a ramp close to the stage where the Pope sat regally in a red, crushed velvet chair. The four somberly shuffled to him, butting ahead of the throng for their blessing. Pope John took extra seconds with Gordon, uttering something in Latin about the sufferings of Jesus.

That night Judy did some talking to him.

Jimmy was snoring in his hotel room when his phone rang at three a.m. "Come over right now," Judy said frantically. "Something's wrong with Gordon." "What?" he asked. "I don't know," she said. "I think it was those awful clams we had at dinner.

Hurry!" The hotel doctor knocked on the door after Jimmy got there. My uncle told him the last he felt this way he was in the hospital. He had been vomiting and had a 104-degree fever. The doctor, who spoke clipped English, immediately suspected food poisoning. There had been an outbreak of salmonella-tainted shellfish knocking tourists off their feet. Could be serious for someone with Gordon's digestion, the doctor volunteered. "We must take precaution." Wary of his patient's unusual body, the doctor rolled him tenderly onto his left side to examine his lungs and heart. In doing so, Gordon's eyes spun up like gyros into his head. His head slumped forward. He wasn't breathing.

The once-placid house doctor went pasty. Judy cried, "What's wrong with him?" but the doctor had never seen this reaction in all his years. He diddled with his stethoscope weighing whether to begin mouth-to-mouth resuscitation. He obviously wasn't hearing Jimmy until Jimmy said, "Put him flat." "What?" the doctor said. "Flat!" Jimmy repeated. "All the way flat." The doctor reluctantly rocked Gordon onto his back. He expected to try more drastic measures in about five seconds. What could this little Negro possibly know about respiratory shock? He, Jimmy and Judy watched for movement, anything.

When Gordon's chest finally shuddered, Judy hurried toward the bed intoning, "Oh thank God, thank God!" Gordon hacked a few times, took a deep breath and coughed some more. In five minutes he was conversant, albeit dizzy. "I'm better, honey, really." Judy didn't believe him until the doctor checked his vital signs and said he seemed fine. Afterwards, Jimmy gave his homespun explanation. "If you twist him hard on his left side, his breathing stops. It's like the On/Off switch on the Movieola. Something about lying down all those year twisted his insides." (Point of fact: some quadriplegics rotated too sharply to one side can develop a circulatory condition called autonomic dsyreflexia that can trigger dangerously high blood pressure and respiratory arrest. Jimmy didn't know the lingo, only the result.) Gordon's On/Off switch had been tripped a couple of times with him, Jimmy said, lighting a cigarette. "Don't worry about it," he told Judy. "He always gets over it." In a few days, with some antibiotics to handle the clams, he did.

It'd taken a while, but Gordon's pragmatism had made up ground on his competitiveness. When Goldwyn Studios' property manager wrote my uncle he had decided against renewing General Music's two-year lease, Gordon accepted it without contention. He realized he had lost this round to Burt Lancaster. If there were any doubt, Lancaster showed up in person that week, asking to speak privately with Gordon about a favor.

A few Mondays later at 8:30 a.m. sharp, Gertrude DuCrest, General Music's longtime secretary, swept her chiffon dress beneath her and sat down at her neatly arranged desk. She was the first one in as usual. Gordon had hired Gertrude because she was a former librarian at RKO who had promised to be fanatical about maintaining the files that were his lifeblood. Her eccentricity was extra. Gertrude ate her lunch almost every day in the front seat of her white Corvair with the windows rolled up regardless of the season. She would chomp her lo-cal meal as the fellas passing by pointed her out like a landmark. Her fashion choices also were original. Gertrude wore flowing outfits that she accessorized with pillbox hats, long white gloves, pastel scarves or some retina-burning combination. But on this Monday morning she was scared. There was a squeaky, persistent racket emanating from the rear of the building and no machinery switched on. Being the only one there, she walked back to investigate trembling a little, wondering if someone might be pilfering Gordon's beloved equipment.

The noise was actually old Burt Lancaster. He was in his workout skivvies whipping around a gymnast's high bar set up in the corner of the barn. It took about five revolutions before he noticed he had an audience. He dismounted, and Gertrude eyeballed his beefcake chest while he walked over moping his face with a towel.

"Geez," Lancaster said, "I hope I didn't alarm you. Gordon told me it was okay to bring my exercise equipment in here early," explaining he was preparing for a role.

Gertrude, now beet red, groped for words. "Gordon must've forgot to tell me. I'm his secretary, by the way."

Lancaster smiled at her. "I figured."

Then, without asking, he caressed the shoulder of her tapered white dress with the back of his hand. "You're so beautiful in that outfit," he said. "Like a perfect milk bottle. I hope you don't mind me saying that."

"Mind?" she said. "I'm never washing this dress."

Reminded of the incident years later, Gordon said Burt wasn't merely exercising. He was homesteading for his lease. Gordon had no qualms with it anymore. Walter Lantz had already offered him better space in his office building: 3,000-square-feet, $870 per month plus utilities. It was the prime suite he had always dreamed about and the last he would ever have.

In May 1965, when General Music relocated into the Lantz building, America's crew-cut era had hit the skids. The economy drooped. G.I.s engaged the Viet Cong in open firefights. Space walks had gotten to be ho-hum; skirt lengths and hippies hadn't. Close to Jimmy's house in Watts, meanwhile, race riots that had convulsed the South had migrated west, strewing the land of milk and honey with ill will captured on the nightly news. For Gordon, these disturbances, though vexing, were nothing he couldn't look past. He was chockablock in jobs, mistaking the checks he was pulling down as confirmation he'd be a millionaire, rather than the Hollywood boom cycle preceding the bust.

Two floors below Walter Lantz's animators, he split the biggest room in his remodeled digs with his new general manager. Just outside were a series of rooms, and another two down the hall housed the tape library and film transfer operation. Gordon had special plans for the boxiest space: he wanted to create his own mini-recording studio. The building was a beige, two-story edifice that Walt Disney previously owned. It was on the corner of Seward and Willoughby avenues, between Goldwyn Studios where Gordon came from and a dozen blocks from where his dad worked. He had arrived.

And so had his lifestyle appetite. Gordon saw how the Lantz's and other notables lived, then schlepped home to his stucco quarters on Shoreham. It chafed him. He wanted someplace extraordinary. He wanted a place that said him—a doer. Against Jack's advice, he talked up his vision with Judy, who embraced it immediately, and they hired a real estate agent to comb the steeps hills north of Sunset for a new house. What they toured, though, was all junk, dated Mediterraneans and Tudors. After a few months of searching, my uncle told Judy they should forget buying and consider building their own. Scratch that, he said, he wanted to design his own.

"You're kidding," she said. "You're already swamped at work."

"If you want special, you don't look to anyone else."

"Well, dear, shouldn't we wait until Jack gives his blessing? We could hold off a year."

"Jesus H. Christ, Judy. Where does waiting get ya?"

He chose a spit of land up against the hillside on a half-developed street about five minutes north of Shoreham. The neighborhood was just off the Strip, due west of Mel's Drive-in and the old Marlboro Man sign, where Sunset bends decadently into the cradle of the snootiest fashion boutiques this side of Bel Air. To get to Blue Jay Way you dipped in and out of wormy roads like Rising Glen Road and Thrasher Way, toward hills that would be speckled with vain, post-modern houses by the early 1970s. Nonetheless, you could live majestically in the Beverly Glen unless the heights bothered you. When the smog dissipated, there was a spyglass view of L.A.'s entire floor-bed.

Gordon, stubborn as he was about his ideas, recognized he was incapable of completing this one alone. So he resorted to an old trick in selecting his architect. He approached a legend near retirement age and badgered him for a discount. Paul R. Williams was his man. Having designed dozens of celebrity houses and public structures, LAX's tripod-legged restaurant and the Ambassador Hotel among them, Williams was arguably America's preeminent black architect, at a time when it was illegal for him to stay in many of the edifices his imagination had given form. "Dreams," Williams once wrote, "couldn't alter facts." Gordon, I imagine, flew at him with an unusual proposition. Erect him the first house ever designed for a quadriplegic. Make it his capstone. Williams was tired but not too tired for a challenge. After he agreed to design the house, Gordon said, "Reach in my breast pocket. I have a few ideas about how we should do things."

CHAPTER NINETEEN
Border Menace

The men of General Music Corp. could nurture their career ambitions with time as an ally. Not Gordon. He was positive time would shortchange him, so he recruited talented help via promises and smooth talk, Louis Mayer take note.

Bob Glenn, son of a machinist, was a handsome, brown-haired young man, the serious one. He had graduated from electronics school after a stint with the U.S. Navy underwater demolition team during the Korean War. Mining his education, in 1958 he opened a TV/radio-repair shop in Studio City next to Republic Studios. If he needed comfort it was limelight location, he didn't need it long: John Wayne was his first customer. Though actors—Clint Eastwood, Peter Lorrie—were always breezing into his store with fried gizmos to fix, Bob's own curiosity about Hollywood took awhile to germinate. When it arrived, it spun desires in him that transistors never had. He enrolled in acting courses and earned a running part on a detective show set in Miami Beach. Moviemaking interested him, too, and he tried his hand at producing a small film; Gordon covered the postproduction for it cheap. After Bob had a row with the director, my uncle courted him much as he did Joe von Stroheim. Come aboard, he said. We're a perfect match, brains and skilled hands.

Norm Pringle was a gap-toothed disc jockey/newsman from Vancouver who had traveled to California with his wife and young son in the late 1950s. Friends had encouraged Norm to head south, predicting he would make a splash in L.A. radio. His friends were wrong. None of the stations bit on Norm's DJ routine, at least before his work visa expired. Hamstrung, he cinched up his trademark suspenders and accepted a job at a Sunset Boulevard recording company. The irony taunted him. As a sound engineer, he taped other people's talents without anyone asking about his. Among Norm's clients were comedian Jack Benny, there as a neurotic violinist, and a chatterbox cripple. His employer was sold a few years later to some Chicagoan who swiftly axed jobs, Norm's one of them. He was about to pack up the family car and retreat to Canada with his excuses rehearsed when Gordon said whoa. General Music needed a part-timer doing film transfers. "Interested?" Not only was he, he would stay with my uncle until the end.

Unlike Joe with his rip-snorting stories and flashy jewelry, Norm was the embodiment of that dutiful, short-sleeve working stiff who filled General Music's payroll. His quest for lunch precisely at noon was a running office joke. What his colleagues didn't see, what Gordon did, was that Norm's vanilla demeanor was surface coating over a quietly digging industriousness. In his off hours, Norm tinkered and experimented, because he wanted his name out in front someday. Towards that, he produced a homemade novelty record, usually of a topical nature (*LSD: The Final Voyage*), every year. My uncle respected that spunk, probably believing he could gravy train off it, though none of Norm's ideas made either man rich.

Horace Jackson was another stray who would find work at General Music. Horace was a fiery, extroverted young black man from Philadelphia. He had come to L.A. to get backing for an autobiographical story he had written about a young man torn between the pulpit and jazz. Horace was more than a gifted pianist with a script: he was perceptive. He immediately assessed Gordon as a sponge for underdog stories. (Someone might have told him Gordon once lent $500 to a stranger with a movie idea.) Horace bleated to Gordon that the studios he had approached about reading his treatment wouldn't give him the time of day. Wouldn't even bother. Gordon offered to read it and decided something afterwards. Horace, this brash, devout kid who wore sunglasses at night, would be his protégé, his star. "I'll help you make your movie," Gordon assured him. He did, low budget all the way. When *Living Between Two Worlds* premiered under the klieg lights at South Central's Balboa Theater, Gordon, Judy and Joe were the only whites invited, "token whites" in Horace's estimation. The movie attracted hundreds, and the association continued. Horace, who disciplined himself to say "motorcycling" instead of motherfucker when he was upset, huffed it constantly after Gordon put him on payroll doing film transfer work next to Norm. Horace was always more musician than techie.

Igo (pronounced ego) Kantor was the fleshy-faced, star music editor from Portugal, the son of a Jewish diplomat. As a kid, Igo had been so entranced with American cinema that he watched starry-eyed at Lisbon's 5,000-seat Coliseum Theater that he got himself hired as a projectionist. He'd set out for L.A. to study foreign affairs in college, but his love for editing overwhelmed academia. Columbia Pictures hired him, and his aptitude for cutting music was evident. He spliced cues into staples like *Hazel* and *Father Knows Best*. At twenty-three, he was anointed head of the music-editorial department. Never short on self-confidence, Igo billed himself as the "fastest editor in the West." Give him scraps and he could make it sing in half the usual time. Hopping between Universal and Columbia, he edited for A-releases like *Bye Bye Birdie*. After his mentor Johnny Green left Columbia Studios, Igo called Gordon, who said, you're hired, my boy.

These four men with little in common personally were professional brothers. They wanted success in their craft but accepted livelihood as the Hollywood equivalent of a drywaller. The studios paid well and there was union protection, yet they could be impersonal employers whose shows were prone to snap cancellation. General Music, now one of the larger independent shops around, was a solid alternative to that corporate enmeshment. Still in their twenties and thirties, Bob, Norm, Igo and Horace knew they could wait for the prime of their careers a few turnpikes ahead. Until then they spliced sound and music. Until then they edited kiddy TV programs (*Mr. Magoo* and *The New Three Stooges*) and rural sitcoms (*Green Acres*). They molded B-sci-fi (*Human Duplicators, Women of the Prehistoric Planet*) and commercials plugging meat, aluminum, aspirin, sink-cleanser and Frisbees. None of it had much substance.

Luckily, once the material was shined up, there was plenty to gossip about.

Gordon, caught in the right mood, could out-jaw practically anybody. Where his legs failed, his electrifying mouth rarely did. He was living the kick-ass adventure his Humpty-Dumpty neck was supposed to deny him, and he was anxious for you to know he'd been in Italy's Blue Grotto at high tide, had broken bread with Sidney Sheldon. Sympathy was for the sickly and the static, which certainly wasn't him. When clients popped in to shoot the shit, he often recited his employees' funniest anecdotes as if they happened to him. He was an avid storyteller about his own past as well, especially his achievements to boyhood hell-raising. Oh, how he tormented those nuns at St. Rita's, who, parenthetically, he stowed a grudging respect. Oh, those jumps he made off bridges, piers, roofs, never specifying the jump he didn't complete. He liked crowing how Monaco secret service agents tailed Hugo when Prince Rainier was in town, because the prince was aware of the ruckus Hugo had raised about his claim to the throne. "You ought to see how Hugo and I ditched them off Mulholland," Gordon would snicker. "Hilarious." Gordon's storytelling voice was sonorous, sort of Harvey Keitel with a bad head cold. Inject some caffeine in him and he was raring to go. It confounded the workers. At ten a.m. they could hear him on his headset saying, "Morning, Sweetie Pie" to the phone company operators he knew by name. Generally, the boss-man had a silky touch with women, even with the secretaries he pestered all day.

Inside the cutting bays with them, the editors agreed Gordon could be as endearing as a rope burn. According to Joe, the energy my uncle lost in his body regrouped in his head. "Where the hell you going?" Gordon would ask the cutters if they had their car keys out before finishing their assignment. "We've got to redo this." His brain micro-processed every cue they spliced. If he detected something slipshod in their work during the playback, he jerked his shoulder to indicate where to revise it. And when he studied the film and said to juxtapose soundtracked clips named with letters within a scene, it was sage not to argue. "Switch G with I, D with B, put A here. Just toss out E. You don't need it, believe me." Played over, his suggestions usually worked seamlessly, and the editors' frustration and admiration for him gurgled up together. If he could dream it, you could do it.

There was a story that he became so adept at tracking he nearly edited himself into a minor scandal. A Hollywood awards group had nominated Walter Greene and him for best original score on a documentary. Big honor, right? Dust off the tuxedo? No. The two had soundtracked the entire program from the Zahler Music Library and waited too long to inform the nomination committee there was nothing original about their effort. By the time the awards presentation rolled around, Walter, a gray-haired, broad-shouldered man with the looks of a British politician, was shaking. Better pray we lose, he said, or we'll be exposed as cheats. Thankfully for them, someone else won the award, Gordon woofing at the ceremony, "Yea, yea, yea. You guys deserve it." Walter, legendary for his drinking, probably ordered a whiskey in relief.

Only one cutter, a testy, interesting guy named Ted Roberts challenged Gordon's melodic judgment. "You know," he'd say, "you can't tell your ass from third base." Privately, Gordon probably agreed he was a dabbler. Ask him to identify a Brahms concerto and might say it was Beethoven. If he spoke into a composer's ear, it often was to suggest he try reversing the notes to an existing song to see if was worth selling as mood music.

Another thing that wasn't so flattering would cost my uncle kinship when it counted. He was a tightwad with salaries, unrepentantly so. Base pay sagged at the low end of the scale. There was no time-and-a-half for overtime at General Music, the Industry standard, or other perks. In Gordon's mind, the wages he offered his editors was a take-it-or-leave it proposition. Labor reps alerted to his practices by malcontents warned him to comply with standards or they would cite him, this being the accepted Industry practice. Gordon slicked his way out of it, that being his practice. Talented scabs were hired for small jobs. Card-carrying editors were promised future raises. Joe was assured he would be a partner. That is who

Gordon was. A twenty-dollar bill was the Christmas bonus. The chief might spring for lunch or offer workers a second chance if they bungled an assignment. People just knew not to expect an extra fifty dollars in their paychecks for a job done well.

Rumors about him sizzled when he was out of the office. Gordon undoubtedly bred some of it by never acknowledging in any substantive way that he was so different from them, the difference being so obvious. The conversations occurred in the shadows.

"I heard he busted his neck on a trampoline," one editor said.

"Wrong," another answered. "It was diving off the Santa Monica Pier. Either that or the monkey bars."

"Well," the first editor said. "Did you know he has a photographic memory? Supposedly memorized every cue in the library."

"I don't care about his recall," the second editor offered. "I know a client, that same guy who did that pro football promotion, who calls Gordon the biggest music hustler around."

"I can beat that," the first editor said. "One of the girls said they overhead him talking to a doctor—now get this—about taking injections so he can get it up for Judy. Makes you want to cross your legs, huh?"

"Oh, please," said Norm. "That's bullcrap. But could you blame him for trying? Just think how you'd act if your johnson didn't work?"

"Okay Normy, since you're defending him, doesn't he get under your skin with his 'do-that-over, it's not right'?" a colleague asked.

"What do you think? My wife says I come home every other night swearing about that 'damn Zahler.'"

Jimmy, Joe and Bob typically weren't part of these discussions. Bob didn't gossip, Jimmy never divulged secrets and Joe wasn't sure who would believe him, anyway. Such was the enigma of working for Gordon. As inspiration who refused to believe he was one, he caressed your heartstrings. As a skinflint employer, he choked your Adam's apple.

~~~

From the curb, the new house was proof of Gordon's Big Life. Up close, the question was whether he could sustain it when the novelty faded. He and Judy switched addresses from Shoreham Drive to upper-crust Blue Jay Way sometime in 1966 after Gordon nailed his biggest TV deal ever. Paul R. Williams and Gordon co-designed the house. A contractor who lived down the street patched their ideas together.

The 1,600-square-foot residence was a sleek, shelfstone-and-wood number done in earth tones. It had a sharply angled roof, a high French front door, two bathrooms, a carport with an entrance into the kitchen, and a curving asphalt driveway. The way the house was seated into the terrain lent it the air of a fortress, which it'd later become.

Just inside the front door was an entryway leading to a parquet-wood hallway. A small living room anchored by a pair of beige, muslin couches that never got broken in was fashioned to the right. Near the living room window were a telescope and a fern. As Gordon plied his business ventures deep into Africa in the coming years, he decorated that room with a hunter's panache. He had the heads of an antelope and gazelle mounted on the living room's southern wall and a Tiger skin rug laid on the floor. For him, they were travel trophies. For me, they were kid-eating carnivores. I used to visualize those three heads reanimating when I was dropped off at his house as a youngster. The beasts would chase me down the hall with snapping, bloodthirsty teeth while my uncle gabbed about a movie deal into his headset phone in the other room.

The furry creatures so engrossed me I never took notice of the wooden contraption next to the telescope. The Hammond pump-action organ that my grandfather played until his death was the soul of that place. Gordon and Bob had recovered the instrument in some studio-executive's garage and had it lovingly sanded and re-laminated. Today I can appreciate why Gordon had a lamp illuminating it so he could spy it from his bed. Without the music that organ produced, he and Rose might never have escaped Sierra Madre.

To the left of the entryway was a spacious kitchen with the latest brushed steel appliances and olive-green, Formica cabinets Judy had embedded with gold sprinkles. Further left was a full-sized bedroom where Judy often slept. A special shower stall customized for Gordon adjoined it, along with the bathroom bidet that surprised the rumps of more than a few exposed guests. Foresight made it work. Every room in the house was framed wide enough for a wheelchair or adjusted for its owner. Gordon may not have been able to stride a foot in his own hallway, but he could billow pride when others did.

Gordon's king-sized, contour bed was 1634 Blue Jay Way's center of gravity. Set in the middle of the house, it functioned as the living room, conference center, captain's bridge, love-nest, dining area, and party spot. Elevated there, Gordon was Caesar. He could watch the twenty-five-inch color television set recessed above the stone fireplace, or entertain his friends in gaudy style. He could follow Wall Street on the stock ticker crawling below the set or gaze out the bay window whose sight lines he had debated with Mr. Williams. Where the window faced the scruffy highlands was a varnished bench that ran the length of the south wall. He enjoyed urging his star guests to examine its construction, to sweep their hands over its lathing. The bench featured twenty types of wood, from teak to birch, some of which he had personally handpicked on a special trip to Mexico.

Realistically, if the action didn't swirl around Gordon's bed in those early years it wouldn't have swirled at all. After he and Judy overspent on blueprints and construction and the small, kidney-shaped swimming pool they added late, there was only enough money leftover for essentials. A year after moving in they didn't have any spare furnishings, knickknacks, assorted housewares, landscaping or what you might term art. Judy laughed if off to her girlfriends as the chic, minimalist look.

~~~

They diagnosed Mama Rose's cancer while the walls were drying on Gordon's house. She had been grappling with stomach pain alone in her apartment until it became so unbearable she decided to call her doctor. He asked her if she felt listless. Had she noticed any weight loss? Tests then were run, x-rays taken. The tumor, a specialist told her, was malignant. The mass, he noted, was inoperable.

If I close my eyes, I can envision her reaction to the news being consistent with her temperament. I can see a pursed smile branch over her creviced face. Granny glasses removed, she massaged the bridge of her nose. The M.D. who issued the diagnosis probably misinterpreted her gesture as shock when it was really the opposite. There was no blubbering from patient R. Zahler when she learned she was dying because now she had her timeline. For years, Mama Rose had assured us that death was the interlude between the semi-consciousness of fickle earth life and the magnificent hereafter in the lap of Jesus. At sixty-six, with Gordon bound to outlive her, there was no point to resist going.

I was a mischievous five-year-old with a short attention span and the best Hot Wheels collection on the block when the tumor was almost done with her. I recall bouncing on her daybed in fall 1966 and her apologizing about being too tired to fetch me Crackerjacks at the market. "Oh, come on, Mama Rose, please. I won't ask you again. Please, please, please!" "I can't today, darling," she said. "Forgive me. How about a cookie instead? Oatmeal raisin."

Grandma made amends on my birthday in October, handing me a gorgeous, red-and-white striped package. I tattered the wrapping paper. Inside was a plastic, kiddy pool table with imitation green felt and two plastic, spring-loaded cues. It was the same model I'd drooled over at Macabob's, Pasadena's best toy store. To my adrenaline wonderment, two heaping boxes of Crackerjacks were taped to the present. I jumped into Mama Rose's arms saying, "Oh, thank you, thank you. Can we open the Crackerjacks right now?"

Mama Rose had been in and out of the hospital, half-numbed with morphine, when I hugged her that day. No one had told me she was on her last rebound. No one even had told me that she was sick. In later weeks, I wanted her to battle me in a scorching game of kiddy pool, and was flustered when my mom sobbed Mama Rose couldn't. Up until then, death was an abstraction to me, something that befell Nazis on TV shows or a friend's pet hamster. As such, Grandma's funeral was sad and scary. In my little kid way, I understood no one had immunity.

She died three weeks after my birthday, in early November 1966. The night she went voters elected her law-and-order hero into the California governor's mansion. Had she not so dreadfully ill, Grandma herself would have stumped for Ronald Reagan around the precincts of the Greater San Gabriel Valley.

You can excuse my mom and Gordon if they weren't tracking the polls that evening. They were in the parking lot of Huntington Hospital embittered by cause-and-effect. At least my mom was. She was screaming into the passenger side window of her brother's newest Cadillac with a fist-shaking, cigarette-breathed tirade that made the car vibrate. Gordon reacted to it by imitating his now-deceased mother: he sat there taking every jab without so much as cocking an eyebrow.

"Don't you have anything to say for yourself? Don't you?" she blasted. "You put her through hell and back, then you kicked her out. It's a miracle Mom lasted this long."

"Mur, I'm not going to fight with you. Definitely not here," Gordon said quietly. Judy was in the back with him. Bob Glenn was behind the wheel. They had been there to say farewell.

"That's too damned bad," she continued. "You're not getting off that easy."

My dad may have tried to lead her away, but Mom could throw an elbow backwards if need be.

"She'd be here right now if you hadn't beaten her down," she continued. "I hope you go to sleep tonight knowing that. Knowing YOU killed Mom as much as the cancer!"

My mom heeled out her cigarette. She then tugged her scarf over her face and was escorted home, presumably toward some Valium.

The soothing of Gordon commenced once the rant was over. Bob guided the Cad out of the parking lot and toward the Pasadena freeway. Judy rubbed Gordon's shoulder in wide, loving circles.

"I'm sure your sister didn't mean that," Bob said. "She's just overwhelmed."

"I guess." Gordon said.

No one spoke for a few blocks. The car seemed to float down the slate roadway.

"Muriel will be better in a few days," Judy said. "Give her time, dear."

"I will. But what she said was still right."

"C'mon," Bob said. "You're being too hard on yourself. People get sick."

Gordon staked his eye out the window. "I'm starting to think its people who give each other diseases." Judy lit him a cigarette. "And if you want to know the truth, I did the same thing to my dad."

Hearing that, Bob pulled over the car to the side of the street near a pharmacy so he could face Gordon. It was dusk on low-slung Fair Oaks Avenue. "Now wait a second," he said. "I remember you telling me your father died of heart disease."

"Officially. But anybody with the real story knew it was a broken heart that killed him. And the cause was yours truly."

"That was, what, almost twenty years ago?"

"Nineteen."

Gordon, as this episode depicts, recognized the never-ending toll from his fateful Tarzan jump. He just couldn't bear to speak much of it. If a stranger asked him how he'd been hurt, he sometimes lied about it. Called it a "diving accident. Nothing more to it." If a woman wanted to shake his hand, upset she couldn't, he'd adjust knowingly, "Oh just bend down and kiss me, honey." These words were his armor, but they only protected so much. It was crushing enough for him to know he'd sent Mama Rose to her maker earlier than she might otherwise has gone. It must've been nearly incapacitating for him to dwell on how he'd made her a throwaway-relic when he would've been one himself had she wanted her own grand life. Loyalty and guilt can be opposite sides of the same family coin.

CHAPTER TWENTY
Circus Shadows

Summer 1967. The guests gripped cocktails in a semi-circle around my uncle's Blue Jay Way bed. They were hearing a classic Gordon adventure tale that had most spellbound, others clucking, "Man, you're bullshitting again." Brassy trumpet music jangled merrily out of the speakers. The flower-power generation could have Jimi Hendrix; this crowd swung to Herb Alpert. Overhead, the aroma of cheesy-vegetable hors d'oeuvres wafted through the party smoke. Just up the street, a dozen groupies loitered outside the house that Beatle George Harrison was renting. And there I was, six years old, under the kitchen counter wishing for once Gordon would give it a rest.

His flapping lips told another Big Life story. It spilled out with inflection and crescendos and a flicking arm for theatrical effect. His house in the hills had been built for these uproarious occasions. Visitors saw Gordon had ornamented his life here with a Ford Mustang convertible in the carport for Judy and a yipping, gunk-eyed poodle on the bed for him. Gordon let this dog lick food morsels directly off his lips—a practice that Judy gasped was "disgusting."

Incidentally, he called the dog "Chip," probably revealing what he thought about me. It went by "Chicken" when my mom was around.

Gordon told his guests he had wanted to relocate his boat from its Orange County slip to a closer, less expensive one near LAX. (Joe had sold Gordon his share of *The Take One* after his divorce.) A relaxing Saturday cruise with Joe and Bob hugging the coast northward was how he set up their near-death-at-sea debacle. If America was at war with itself over Vietnam and civil rights, there was no blowback at them. The three men had ventured out in the early-morning mist expecting to chug into Marina del Rey around one p.m. The wives would be waiting for them at the dock in anticipation of a fresh seafood lunch together.

What the three had not foreseen, Gordon narrated, almost got them drowned. They missed the news reports about the huge swells from a Hawaiian Island storm pounding south-facing beaches. The magnitude of their oversight grabbed them as soon as they sloshed outside the Balboa jetty. Whitecaps frothed 200 yards from shore.

Around the oil derricks of Huntington Beach, roughly one-third of the way, the boat was being shellacked by the waves, set after pounding set, Gordon said. It took them more than two hours to make it that far. Near Long Beach, Joe and Bob huddled to talk. Maybe they should head for calm water inside the harbor to take stock of the situation. Gordon, mounted in his chair, enjoying the pounding like a kid on a carnival ride, asked what the whispering was about. "Nothing," they said. He didn't buy it. Okay, they told him they needed to get out of the chop for a bit. He objected, but they ignored him for a change and motored into the breakwater so they could think without wanting to up-chuck their breakfasts.

In the open ocean north of there half an hour later, the sea heaved as before and the wind howled a shrill tune. It was about then Gordon announced he was starving—"salt air and the stomach, you know." Joe took the wheel so Bob could remove the lid from the cooler. Sitting on top of the Fresca was the ham-and-Swiss sandwich that Judy had prepared with Gordon's favorite deli mustard. Bob started hand-feeding it to his boss, who was happy and sassy in that rollicking ocean. Soon Bob's mind drifted. The beating waves had him anticipating a capsizing scenario: how Gordon would be flipped upside down into the freezing waters buckled into his chair while he and Joe dogpaddled for their lives. As this image bloomed, a wave they didn't expect smashed into port side of the boat, thrusting it sideways. Bob's jostled hand missed Gordon's waiting mouth with the sandwich because of it, and a wedge of food got squished into his ear-hole. He had fancy mustard on his sideburn to boot. "You know what I told, Bob?" The guests leaned forward for the punch line. "Please get lunch out of my head."

Gusts of laughter rained down with his side-story, none louder than Judy's. I myself couldn't see Gordon's performance and didn't need to. His voice undulated clear into the kitchen where I assumed I was safe from him.

Being near him had always injected me with the heebie-jeebies. As a toddler I'd convinced myself he was a spider in disguise working to lure me in close to his wheelchair so he could grab me and gulp me down whole. Later from his words, I concluded my mother's brother considered me too unappetizing to digest. I also knew he and my mother weren't that close as adults, despite the get-togethers and regular phone calls suggesting a warm sibling relationship as they each negotiated the circumstances middle age had thrown at them. To my eyes, the notion they were tight seemed a cover story concocted for their own consumption as much as ours. There was an emotional distance between them that happy talk didn't mask and common history couldn't gulf. Whatever divided them felt unrelated to Grandma or personality differences, and buried too deep in their life journeys for me to decipher.

From my own vantage, Gordon was a strange, voluble little man who dripped in charisma and his own tendency to order people around. Small, hyper children gamboling around his wheelchair annoyed him to no end. Was it his witchy body that made him this way? How his legs canted sideways from his waist; the fingertips he'd nervously bite into bloody nubs; his runt chest; his stick-figure arms? Gordon's silhouette intrigued and horrified me, no matter how nattily Judy outfitted him in cardigans that softened the freakishness. Just as disturbing was how he could be speaking with you civilly when he detected something that irked him and a swipe would rattle out of his lungs. "Judeee!…" Afterwards, he would return to the conversation exactly where he left off. As a teenager I remember thinking he was a monocle short of a Bond villain.

One afternoon a few years after his boat story one of his swipes targeted me. I was dashing off near the front of his bed to splash cannonballs in his eighty-two-degree pool when Gordon told me to freeze where I was. Why, he was curious to learn, was my chest so "underdeveloped? Seems kinda pigeon-chested, if you ask me." He suggested I lift weights to make myself manlier if any punks hassled me. He followed that up by inquiring what I was doing that summer. I said skateboarding and camp and he remarked, "Why don't you build a model and use your brain? I heard you got one…" For him, it was an empirical observation. To me, my defects were tossed shamefully into the open. I hankered to crawl inside my Hang Ten swim trunks with my other insecurities. Unlike Paul, I never got invited up on Gordon's bed to watch a ballgame as his designated little buddy.

What I didn't understand the day of his Big Life tale was my mom's thinking. Her intention had been for me to attend this grownup bash and spend the night with Gordon and Judy. An "overnight adventure," she'd termed it, as if that would be laughs. Mom's plan imploded within three hours. I was homesick. I was the only kid there. The house stunk of booze, cologne and ashtrays. Judy coaxed me to mingle with the adults, but I was merely a shrub inside a moving forest of panty hoses and gray-flannel slacks. Invariably, Gordon's guests would pat me on my head before some witty sendoff. Their words were as mumbled as the cascade of *wa-wa-waahs* Charlie Brown heard from his grownups.

I hated everything. Judy was kind, but consider her spouse. Mostly I hated my parents for banishing me here, so I decided to be invisible. I filched a couple of Oreos from the cookie jar inscribed with "Though-Shall-Not-Steal" on the front, snuck under the counter and hoped Gordon's story would end. I'd plead my case to Judy when it did.

Nobody besides me seemed to mind that his yarn dragged on and on. He only braked for pulls on a cigarette and a straw-fed scotch Judy provided at understood intervals. About three miles away from its destination, he continued, *The Take One* swooshed sideways twice as much as forward, hammered by "five-, no six-foot waves." The boat would be lifted up by one, cresting for a second, before free falling into the blackness of the trough. Riding the pitches in his chair, Gordon said he gained enough altitude to glimpse the houselights of Palos Verdes. Up the coast he tried to make out the beacons at LAX when the boat's Chrysler engine coughed a half-dozen times. Somebody said, "Shit, not now," and the engine died.

None of the three was panicking, but they were getting there. The current in a few minutes time washed them within about 500 yards of the hulking, taupe colored cliffs. Noticing the drift, Bob sprang off his chair. He needed to diagnose what happened with the engine, and there was no time for unlatching Gordon from his perch. He grabbed my uncle from behind and tipped him backwards ninety degrees, which retracted the engine casing and exposed the metal cylinder block. Gordon commented that with the back of his chair parallel to the deck, feet pointed skyward, he probably looked like an astronaut the NASA boys didn't want you to see. More laughing from his audience, which numbered about ten people. Joe would've taken a picture, he said, if their situation weren't so perilous.

The problem that Bob observed was the backwashing seawater. It poured into the engine intake faster than it poured out. Not to fear, Bob sprang again. He began cranking the manual bilge-pump like a human piston while gas fumes from the engine puffed out in acrid plumes. The fumes, which shouldn't have been there, made Gordon and him dopey. Bob pumped anyway. Once the water was bilged, Bob hollered to Joe to start her up. *RRRRRhhhhhh-na-na-na-na.* Success. The spinning propeller ended their drift toward the rocks.

Everything, from the cushions to my uncle, was now drenched in saltwater, meaning Bob and Joe couldn't rest. They scampered around the edge of the boat in soggy deck shoes snapping a blue canvas canopy over the bow. The two brought Gordon's boat chair into an upright position next and panting, agreed they needed a break. Bob palmed his pack of Marlboro's and his friends asked for their own. A few cigarettes later and they had some nicotine sedation.

They just didn't have smooth sailing. Before they could curse this time, the engine died again from the onrushing water. Now the pleasure boat was in genuine danger, only about 150 yards from the cliffs of Playa del Rey. They were so close they could see the contours in the bluff, where the primal ocean had atrophied giant, dagger-shaped shards of rock. The cruelest part was that they were about a mile from the marina.

Bob for one followed his instinct. He scanned the horizon to the west and belly laughed until his ribs hurt. Gordon and Bob frowned at him, but he didn't care. This situation demanded some type of gesture. In all probability, these were everybody's last dry moments, definitely Gordon's. They were going to smash into the cliffs and the hull would disintegrate. So far away from help, they probably would be dead. Why not, Bob reasoned, an irreverent howl for man and maker? He couldn't restrain himself.

Up in the front, Joe looked like he was French-kissing the radio trying to raise the Coast Guard over the ship-to-shore radio. "May Day! May Day!" he said. "Can you hear me, Coast Guard? This is an emergency. MAY DAY!"

Gordon, witnessing his friends' scramble, felt frustrated he couldn't contribute anything besides sarcasm. He hoped they had a better escape plan than Joe shouting S.O.S. into the radio. As the current sucked *The Take One* toward the cliffs looming larger every minute, goose bumps stood attention on his neck. Yet him terrified? Get real.

"Bob, hurry up with the engine," Gordon said.

"Coast Guard, Coast Guard," Joe said. "This is The Take One and we have an emergency. Our engine is dead and we're close to the rocks. We have a quadriplegic on board, too. Repeat, a quadriplegic. May Day!"

"Any time now Bob," Gordon said. He'd been tilted into his astronaut position again so Bob could assess the engine.

"*Ha-Ha-Ha-Ha*," Bob giggled. "Can you imagine what the papers will say?"

"Tell you what, let's think about that later. I'm getting dizzy."

"It's just so silly," Bob said. "Listen to Joe...*Heh-Heh*...thinking they're going to rescue us just...*Heh-Heh*...because you're on board."

"Coast Guard, Coast Guard," Joe continued. "I say our engine is dead. May Day! May Day! The current is pushing us on shore. Our position is..."

Their position was fifty yards from the cliffs.

Last resort arrived, Bob scrounged for help in the ship toolbox. The engine was pumped free of seawater and still wouldn't turn over. Bob found the can of ether he was searching for and shook it hard. He flipped off the plastic cap and sprayed the liquid directly on the head of the carburetor. Ether applied correctly acts as a catalyst to prod fuel and oxygen to combust. Used recklessly and you have a fiery explosion. Bob hoped to resuscitate the engine and steer *The Take One* out in front of the marina, where they could wing it from there. He sprayed once, twice, three times and *nada*. He checked the oil mix and sprayed some more. Still dead. Gordon told him to use "the whole damn thing," and Bob shot-gunned the contents and stood back. Gordon shut his eyes when Joe keyed the ignition.

All praise that ether. It brought the engine to life on the first try and they were moving again. A few minutes later a Harbor Master tugboat was in sight; Joe had contacted them on the ship-to-shore when the compound was being sprayed. Three hours late, the men dragged up the boat ramp like a chain gang. Waiting for them there were their livid spouses. Nobody was in the mood for that seafood meal afterwards.

Hold on, he told his rapt audience, they didn't hear the best part. At 7:30 the next morning he received an urgent call from the Coast Guard. *The Take One*, they said, was leaking gasoline in the slip and they had it towed out to a jetty buoy for precaution. Gordon said he pressured Bob into driving him back to Marina Del Rey to see what's what. After two monotonous hours watching the boat tugged from the buoy and inspected in dry-dock, Bob went over to confer with the repairman. When he walked over to Gordon to explain Bob had a somber mouth.

"What gives?" Gordon said. "How bad is it?"

"Not nearly as bad as it could have been," Bob said. The boat had a clogged air intake that made her stall as well as a more serious problem. "One of the fuel-tank brackets came loose in the chop. You got a punctured tank, my friend. That's why all the fumes. We had a giant leak."

"And?" Gordon said.

"And remember how we pulled the canopy over us and smoked after we got the engine running the first time?

"Yeah."

"Lighting a match in all those fumes should've gotten us blown to kingdom come. The mechanic said there wouldn't have been pieces of us big enough to float."

"You know what I said?" Gordon dragged out the suspense. "I said, 'Relax, Bob. You're going to worry yourself into an early grave.'"

Raucous laughter and backslapping. Soon Judy danced into the kitchen to check on her poppy-seed dinner rolls, and that's when she spotted me under the counter. "My heavens," she said. "What are you doing under there?" I clutched my sleeping bag and blubbered, "I want to go home." Judy dialed away. My mom retrieved me about ninety minutes later, prodding me about what had gone wrong, "Didn't you have a good time?"

All I remember after that was being too ashamed to say goodbye to Gordon. I was afraid he would call me a coward. He was the only relative I had who would be that honest.

If you were a kid, you either dealt with him like a grownup—fearless if his shriveled hands brushed you, poised to recount questions from your latest math test—or you were wasting his valuable time. Aimless youth infuriated him, and that went for hippies. Aimless anything infuriated him. Random silliness was for knuckleheads. "Oh," he would say, "so you think that's important, do you?" He needed to determine that you had the drive to succeed without stopping too long for the tomfoolery that had made him who he was. And who he was, at least sometimes, was a man bitterly, hopelessly envious of your childhood. No overstated boating tale could help him recapture his. And as astute as he was, he never asked what made you happy. I could have told him.

As a kid, I worshipped a University of Southern California football player named Bobby Chandler. Bobby played wide receiver, flanker to be specific, and caught everything tossed his way on teams that racked up conference championships and Rose Bowl victories. A Heisman Trophy-winning tailback (and future murder defendant) named O.J. Simpson was his teammate. I didn't care about bronzed statues, though. I wanted to be all things Bobby C, and for more than his flypaper hands. When we would drive the freeway bisecting his hometown of Whittier, I used to stick my head out the car window hoping to see him. Bobby was handsome in an average-man way. He was, for lack of a better description, ragingly normal: average-bodied, generic-named normal. I desperately wished I were, too, had circumstance allowed it.

For starters, my real name is Millard. (I was named after my father, thus the nickname "Chip" as in off the old block.) Both monikers were red meat for the bullies. My Zahler-inherited ears also stuck out so far that I could've performed "Dumbo" in the class play sans costume, as some peers reminded me. Had they known, I had a worse frailty inside my head. It revolved around Peter.

My problem with him wasn't his specific disability and never was. By the time I was in second grade and could out-read him, I recognized Peter as my strange sibling. Unlike Paul, he didn't drive, date, hide under my bed to scare me or hold a job. An electric razor was about his sole grownup possession. What came across about Peter was his essence, an essence that was as unsophisticated as it was true of heart. Every Christmas Eve, for example, would find him rubbing his five o'clock shadow, jumpy about whether Santa had received his wish list in time. Belch at the breakfast table and he would whoop, later reminding you he had outgrown that trick. Feel like malingering with your chores? Not to worry. He gladly swept the driveway leaves in your place, and would take the fall for your mess-ups. When he came home on vacation, Peter always bore presents, too—usually a calendar from the previous year. "See," he would say, "it's got your favorite color on it."

Visiting Peter at his school in Santa Barbara is what made me want to leap out of my skin. Spending time up there meant hours around a menagerie of decidedly abnormal people I wanted nothing to do with. I dreaded those treks to Devereux School three times a year. I cringed when Peter's schoolmates would swarm my dad's car like extras from *Dawn of the Dead*. The second we crunched the school's gravel driveway in the car and *whamo*, they'd be hanging all over us with their monosyllabic grunts and their shuffling gaits. What did they want from me?

This group, afflicted with Cerebral Palsy, Downs Syndrome, autism and other undeserved conditions, wouldn't harm dirt, of course. Attention is all they wanted. In some recess of myself, I understood that. Yet, I was brusque to Peter's classmates. I saw them as funny-faced crooks out to steal what little ordinariness I'd accumulated. Sometimes I hid from them by sinking low in the leathery confines of my Dad's chocolate-brown Cadillac El Dorado. I fretted that if they touched me or if I ate their bland food I'd be reconstituted into one of "them." Cognizant that Peter and I sprang from the same genetic pool, I wondered if I already was.

By the age of twelve or so my troubles were elsewhere. This was the mid-1970s, and I had grown a tad slump-shouldered. My parents, particularly my mom, had worked themselves into such a state about it they insisted Dr. Risser and only Dr. Risser examine me. To my mother, his legend was up there with Mickey Rooney. Doc had retired from staff at the Orthopedic Hospital of Los Angeles by the point it was my turn for him. At seventy, he was a laureate of his field with a brisk private practice and an orthopedic-casting table he was trying to mass-market. Same as always, Joe Risser practiced medicine with a homey iconoclasm. A rich old lady once came to him complaining of back pain and bunions. To her horror, he cut the toes off her expensive imported shoes with a plaster knife saying, "That should do it." Years earlier he had performed a daring, life-saving operation on the son of Italy's future prime minister, an operation Europe's best surgeons were afraid to touch, and the Italians honored him with a prestigious national medal. Doc was humble about that. On how to live well he was an unapologetic dogmatist. He kept miniature skull-and-crossbones in his home sugar bowl to warn guests of the dangers of sweets.

He developed a list of sayings that became his hallmark, voicing them often. "Sharpen your wits before you sharpen your knife," he advised surgical colleagues. To everybody else: "If you are not punished for your sins, you are surely punished *by* your sins." People listened. His mastery of scoliosis, his reputation as the first to cure a humpback, lured doctors from all the over the globe to study his technique in the brown air of Pasadena.

For all our ties, and the fact he lived directly across the street, I knew virtually nothing about the geezer with liver spots when my mom herded me into his office. Doc took measurements of my spine with an orthopedic protractor. He told my mom in his calm, don't-fret-it tone I had a mild form of scoliosis that a lightweight brace worn at night should reverse. But before he handed me over to a junior associate to do additional measurements, he and my mother double-teamed me.

"You know, Chip," she said, "Dr. Risser was the one who first took care of Gordon."

"That's right," he added. "I've known him almost since he was your age."

"What do you mean?" I asked.

"I treated him immediately after his accident, and for a long time after. He and I have quite a history. Didn't your parents fill you in about it?"

"No," I said. "I would've remembered that."

"Then I bet you didn't know I stunted one of Peter's legs when we found the other one was too short."

I shook my head and felt as if I might pass out on the doctor's carpet. Gordon was our family's headlining freak. And now we were brethren? If we shared doctors, I assumed, we must share the same weirdo category. It seemed to compute. Dabble in my unspoken fear that I might not be so different from Peter and you can see why Dr. Risser was a name I wanted wiped from my vocabulary. And why I loathed that brace even if it held the promise of restoring normal posture.

Truth is I didn't remember Joe Risser, who died in 1982, until I began this book, because I'd repressed it. Truth is, I was skittish around people in wheelchairs, including a paralyzed college buddy who could've used my company.

As a kid I knew my curse. I hadn't been born Bobby Chandler. I wasn't running post patterns against the reviled Irish of Notre Dame with cool, black shoe-polish under my eyes to deflect the glare. I wasn't out on the turf of the Los Angeles Memorial Coliseum with my eminently average Bobby-C face aglow from the winning touchdown I'd hauled in for my Trojans. No, dreaming about it in my room where the freaks weren't welcome was the most I could manufacture.

In my freakless haven, my ears weren't NORAD tracking radar, my posture was perfect, my name common and my relatives as normal as bread. The idea that outwardly abnormal people like Gordon could be so firmly confident was confusing. I hadn't experienced the power you garner from taking a wicked blow only to get up laughing. Not until I chased Gordon's story as an adult would I see it liberates you to try anything.

CHAPTER TWENTY-ONE
King of the Wild

Year after year, Gordon's get-rich-quick schemes dissolved one into the other. The mini-record player you wore on your wrist gave way to Bibleland, which segued to the Hollywood Entertainment Museum, which led to the "microphonograph," a pocket-size tape recorder for tourists that never came close to mass production. It was the same old, same old. While his core editing and music businesses flourished, his every bid to branch out, either by himself or on somebody's coattails were perennial dogs.

There were glitches securing investors or with suppliers or patent issues or convincing folks who wouldn't say it to his face that he didn't fit their image of the next Ron Popeil, let alone George Westinghouse II. It wasn't until the mid 1960s that a revolutionary new product about to debut in U.S. electronics stores that my uncle was hopeful that his perseverance would be rewarded with a mound of minty $100 bills. He had partnered with a New York company that claimed the inside track with this auditory sensation—a way for the public to transport their favorite music wherever they went.

The idea was the cassette-tape player.

And Gordon and company never stood a chance. The record companies were already miles ahead of them, and easily monopolized the market. By 1970 they had pocketed millions off America's love affair with smaller and better. Bashing around in this field, Gordon was able to sell canned music to a Van Nuys company that had patented a continuous-loop tape system. Nevertheless, the money he earned felt like the prize for honorable mention. History did repeat. His instincts were unrivaled but his execution stank.

A producer named Ivan Tors would be the one who would free Gordon to scheme more wisely. Always hesitant about overspending at work, he was glad to pocket Ivan's cash.

Tors was a brainy, middle-aged Hungarian expatriate who had converted his schoolboy zeal for biology and space exploration into a succession of better-paying Hollywood screenwriting gigs, then producing. To take in his trimmed gray beard and erudite face, to notice his chronic absent-mindedness and ruffled shirts, was to guess Harvard anthropology professor, which he easily could have been. Ivan had forged a niche for himself as a science-fiction producer serious about his science. His underwater series, *Sea Hunt*, had been the smash he had waited for, because he used it as a fulcrum to promote the other ideas that clanged off his typewriter. Then in 1961, Ivan's candor nearly leveled his career. Called before a Senate subcommittee, he did the unthinkable: he told the truth. He testified that NBC programmers had leaned on him to knit sex and violence into his family-oriented *The Man and the Challenge*. The network waited a respectable time after Ivan's testimony before canceling the show. But Ivan won his revenge, literally on the back of a sea mammal. He created the wildly popular *Flipper* series, which led to follow-up deals, plump bank balances and offices in L.A. and Miami. Flipper's network: NBC.

Ivan was a wealthy, Renaissance man living in a company town he ridiculed for sliminess when he intersected with my uncle. Some thought him pompous, others brilliant. Trendy Holmby Hills was his neighborhood. He probably would've swapped it for the Outback. Jetting off to Bangkok on short notice relaxed him. So did punching up a script with a boa constrictor coiled at his feet. Friends wisely knew never to rib Ivan about his zoological convictions. He preached that animals were man's ethical superiors, and didn't need a whip to be trained. To prove it, he co-owned a one-of-its-kind spread north of Los Angeles where 600 lions, bears, snakes, cheetahs, elephants, hippos, zebras and assorted varmints used in his shows lived and roamed like communal hippies under an "affection-training" regime. The commune's name was "Africa-U.S.A." Ivan didn't much believe in cages there. He believed in feeding tranquilizers to the fish. He believed dogs were psychic and in the primacy of nature's gene pool. His wife, Constance, was a stunning, ex-actress who sired him three sons—boys Ivan hoped would bolt hedonistic L.A. someday. To drive with him, meantime, was to appreciate life insurance. He was so immersed talking to Gordon once that he steered the wrong way over a set of metal parking lot spikes at the Lantz Building, blowing out all four tires on his luxury Mercedes. Eclectic Ivan also was devoted to his own voice. Once it got sailing under one of his famous anecdotes—how, for instance, two lions had stalked him on the Serengeti Plain until they started going at it doggy style—you'd better find a chair.

My uncle had Ivan's drive, albeit none of his academic refinement, and went in guns blazing to win Tors's business. In memos and meetings he vowed quality work. He pledged cost-cutting efficiency. Harsh deadlines? Gordon said they brushed their teeth with them after cutting tape for network shows since the 1950s. For added sweetener, he even trumpeted having more production capacity than General Music possessed. My uncle calculated that he had to embellish. Ivan had commitments for three, count 'em three, primetime network shows.

What Gordon might not have seized on was how much Ivan needed *him*, especially his low-cost creed. Ivan was a creative pro, a whiz packaging network shows, too, and simultaneously a serial budget-buster who couldn't say "no" to demanding stars or crews who ate well—thousands of dollars of French pastries well in the case of *Gentle Ben*—on his inattention to detail. Once he hired you, you were initiated as a member of Ivan's Hollywood family. Short of some egregious act, your job security was indestructible.

His programs were feel-good, family TV about wholesome folk in unforgiving lands stretching from the Florida Everglades to equatorial Africa. Lantern-jawed actors like Chuck Connors and Dennis Weaver played the leads as outdoorsmen who were self-reliant and vice-resistant—sort of the anti-showbiz honcho. These men raised precocious kids always getting a lesson or giving them, usually with the families' sidekicks—lovable dolphins, black bears, monkeys and cross-eyed lions—in tow. His villains tended to be incompetent criminals after these critters or the virgin land. The crooks rarely got away with it because Mother Nature was boss. Ivan's conservation politics spilled all over his plots.

It was over Monte Cristo sandwiches at the MGM commissary where Ivan and his brother, a sharp, chubby accountant named Erwin, congratulated General Music for beating out the competition. Gordon almost levitated out of his wheelchair hearing the news. "Ivan, Ivan that's terrific," he said. "We're going to do some great things together, and not just with your programs."

Ivan held his palm up to temper the celebration. "I appreciate your enthusiasm, but I want you to be realistic," he said. "We have three series going now and all seems right with civilization. Mark my words: we'll all be out of business in five years."

"Five years," Gordon said. "Who cares after that?"

He didn't. He leveraged those future earnings to plank the lifestyle he could suddenly afford, starting with the house on Blue Jay Way. General Music would rake in $3,958 per *Gentle Ben* episode, $6,286 per *Daktari* and $8,298 per *Cowboy in Africa*. Multiplied by the projected number of episodes per season, my uncle would be on the receiving end of $490,008 in gross income annually. Now that was real mullah.

After six months of earning it, he decided he'd burn some abroad. Africa. He had always wanted to journey to the eastern coast of the Dark Continent to see where man began. Had always wanted to saunter into the bush, into the view of the Great Escarpment Mountain Range, since he had read *National Geographic* as a kid in wonderment about Tarzan. Wouldn't even cost that much. He could write it off by stopping in London on business and visiting Laetrec Music in Johannesburg, South Africa, on the way back. CPA-Jack would permit it. They could charter a plane to Nairobi, Kenya, and drive in from there. Bob Glenn had a buddy who would make the arrangements. Bob's friend co-owned the Safariland Club in the Great Rift Valley. The guy's name was Dirk Brink. He was supposedly a high roller.

Johannesburg was a bumpy stop for more personal reasons. South Africa of the late-1960s was a land of untamed savannahs and rising skylines. It also was a place where 3.5 million whites controlled 17.5 million blacks with wall-to-wall segregation laws. Jimmy assumed he would see the injustice firsthand and why not? Over the years he had logged thousands of miles tending Gordon across Europe and the Far East. (My uncle's kowtowing Japanese clients referred to him as "Mr. Jimmy.") He had pushed my uncle through snowstorms and humidity between Canada and South America. With the low wage he brought home, travel was a major chunk of his compensation.

Bob was the first to tell him that maybe it wasn't so smart for him to go. "Jim, they might not let you stay in our hotel. We don't even know about the restaurants. Why subject yourself to that?" Jimmy's style was non-confrontational, but Gordon could read the disappointment in his eyes. "Jimmy," he said, "edit to your heart's delight while I'm gone. Come in at 11:00 if you want. You've earned it." Jimmy said okay though he felt ambushed inside. He hankered to see Africa whatever the risks.

As the 1960s came to a close, while the campuses burned and the longhairs loafed around Sunset, Gordon had achieved enough for two men, and they could lace their own shoes. Look at his thirty-five editors on payroll—so many he had to encourage several to go work for an associate. See how happy he had made Judy. To think about how the St. Rita's nuns predicted he would never amount to more than a degenerate was to bask in his station. If only his mother could've seen the self-made success he'd become, he'd feel better about living with it.

Rose in her final months may well have cautioned him about things that still scalded years later. Dear boy, she might've said, don't steamroll loved ones in pursuit of your goals. Money won't comfort when life turns black, and it always does. But Mom, he might've responded. I have to charge full speed. I have to bulldog those I care about. There's no point in me living from the neck up if I don't sample what's possible. No money, no sampling. Well, she might've rejoined: that was the paradox of being him.

It was a downer that hung in the attic of his soul, but no place else. In 1968-69, the inspirations tumbled so quickly from his mouth the secretaries had trouble capturing them accurately in their steno pads. His latest hook was to blitz the American consumer with music and advertisements everywhere in their daily existence. He would be the middleman here by selling tape-broadcasting equipment to small retailers. They would rely on him for servicing and, cunningly, exclusively licensed General Music Co. tapes. Bothersome details would be addressed later. In Gordon's world, when Joe Q. Public pulled up to a gas pump in the family station wagon a friendly cartoon-type voice would prod him about adding a lube job. When his missus was having her hair tinted at the corner salon, a lilting song would caress her eardrums from the beauty parlor blow dryer. Somber, classic songs would flitter down at them at the funeral home, finger-snapping, up-tempo ditties in their hotel room. Sports stadiums with those captive crowds were luscious possibilities. With Ivan's money, there was no corset on what he could invent.

Gordon was always calling Bob and Harriet, his newest secretary and Joe's second wife, to grab their writing pads and meet him in his office with their thinking caps on.

"What if," he posed, "we sold our system to every gas station in the United States? Multiply 50,000 by our per-unit cost, and you have what, $10 million bucks to divide up among three partners. Not bad, huh?"

"Right," Bob said with a skeptical brow. "And we better assume every one of the oil companies will go along. That's a pretty tall assumption."

"Okay. I'll concede we won't get 100 percent. Let's revise our expectations down to, say, eighty percent. So, it's 40,000 times $200. Eight million works. Bob, stop rolling your eyes."

"Eighty percent?" Bob asked.

"All right, you wet blankets. Let's say we secure forty-five percent of the stations? Type that up in a memo, Harriet."

"Do I have to?" she asked.

"Yes."

"That's it," said Bob, half-smiling. "I'm going to lunch."

"Before you go, how much time do you think people spend in Laundromats? It's an avenue."

Gordon's personal affairs, taboo subjects at the office, moved at a more deliberative clip. Saturday mornings, if he wasn't traveling, on the boat, or inside the office double-checking the tapes they would rush off to Ivan Monday, he spent at home kibitzing with clients over the phone. Sometimes he would tackle house projects, which translated into him sitting in the wheelchair instructing Jimmy how to scoop leaves out of the rain gutter. Weekend afternoons were for relaxing, preferably with a guest or two watching a college football contest or the baseball game of the week on TV. On hot days, he might be out in the pool on a Styrofoam raft lounging for hours. He harbored no fear of slipping off and sinking to the bottom. He feared the impulse to play it safe for the mirage of more time.

Gordon had realized since his early twenties that he would never grow old in a sunset retirement village. Making fifty, if that, was chancing it so why embrace caution? Occasionally, he resorted to gallows humor, telling friends readying for a trip: "Before you go, touch my head for luck. You can't end up any worse than me." Mostly Gordon stowed his cynicism down deep so he could stick outwardly to what he had promised himself. Others with static bodies would be the bed-bound. He had limitations he would trounce by ingenuity, science or sheer balls. Being a role model was drivel. The acquaintances curious how he felt about *Ironside*, the TV show about the paralyzed ex-cop, completely misunderstood his bearing. Sought or accepted, victimhood to him was for wimps. He aimed to water ski.

Accordingly, Gordon studied how to maximize the little physicality he still retained. One possibility was a semi-proven surgery that would cost upwards of $10,000. It was an operation in which his hands would be lopped off at the wrists so they could be replaced with something better.

He explained to Judy, who was dead-set against the idea, and to chosen associates, who were flabbergasted by it, that it would be an amputation for practical purposes. There was nothing grisly about it. Minus his hands, the stubs at the end of his arms could be form-fitted with stainless-steel hooks and, someday, lifelike prosthetic hands. They would act as pincers. The specialists had shown him how the apparatus performed. He would manipulate his hooks by the inward and outward flexing of his shoulders. Sleeve-like covers that used guide wires and hinges to reach the pincer would let him grasp, maneuver and release all sorts of small objects. Think of the independence he would regain, he told Judy—holding his own cigarette, turning pages. "I wouldn't be on you all the time." My brother Paul was one of the few to see a model. An inventor had built Gordon a demo pincer that connected to a shoulder sling. The demo would have been a vision of a robust future, too, if it weren't so worthless in tryouts. Everything he clamped with it slipped out of his hold in a matter of seconds. "Mechanical bug," he'd pooh-pooh. "They'll fix it in production." For years he turned the amputation over in his mind. He was unsentimental about his real hands. The trick was how to convince his insurance company to pay for their replacements.

Having intercourse with Judy was another supercharged desire. Kissing and cunnilingus on her had punctuated their lovemaking for the first few years of their marriage. She was fine with it. He felt inadequate. She said travel was her climax. He asked for how long? Then a truck-dealer pal with a script he was pedaling mentioned to him about some drugs he had read about. Supposedly, he said, paraplegics and quadriplegics have someone inject a chemical into the base of their manhood and with any luck up springs an erection where there had been flaccid hydraulics. Gordon was intrigued if just a shade dubious his wasted genitalia could still function. His method to find out, as it was with his hand replacement, was cold analysis. Detached from so much sensation for so many years, his body became like a machine that you could retrofit with spare parts. So, he perused technical literature. He went to urologists during his lunch hour. Several out on the Westside confirmed there was a class of experimental injection drugs approved by the feds that had achieved results for some spinal-cord patients. The side effects could be revolting—seizures, penile malformation—but the alternatives were a noisy suction pump or chastity. He voted for the injection. A hard-on was worth the puncture.

How many times Judy shot him up and mounted him is a secret gone to the ages. What matters here is that Gordon and Judy, behind shut curtains, against all probability, consummated their bond same as any heavy breathing husband and wife who took their humping for granted.

It's just that neither one of them were prepared for Judy to get pregnant.

They might have been sitting on this news during Christmas 1967, when Gordon toasted associates and worker-bees in uncharacteristic tradition. As rich as he would ever be, he splurged for an expensive holiday party with an open bar, three-course dinner and music in a ballroom at the Beverly Hilton Hotel. Everybody important to him was there gussied up—Walter and Gracie, Ivan and Hugo, Nat, Jack, Abe, Paul Williams, Nathan and sundry movie people. Most of his employees tugged along their wives. The table arrangements alone cost more than their holiday bonuses.

Drinks flowed and personal stories unfurled. Joe might have entertained his table with a story about his daughter Lori, the one in her early twenties who worked as an Africa-USA animal handler. She'd recently come home with a large bandage on her chest. "'Hon,' I asked her, 'what happened?' She said, 'Dad, you won't believe this. I was working with this money and the goddamn thing bit me on the tit. But I'm okay. I took it behind a tree and kicked the shit out of it.'" Across the table, Norm must have been dazed there was festivity at all. It hadn't been six months ago that he had requested to skip out from work a few hours early one afternoon to attend his son's high school graduation in the Valley. Gordon had said no, "A deadline's a deadline." The room went still momentarily. "Gordon, come on," Norm fired back. "Gary will be crushed if I'm not there." Another editor who had heard the exchange raked Gordon under his breath for being so coldhearted. Gordon had waited until the editor went into another room before he told Norm he could go.

Later, somebody noted that Gordon had left the details of this soiree to Dorothy Garner, a vivacious secretary who reveled in spending the boss's money. Supposedly he was so busy with all his programs that he had Dorothy manage the expenses with the Hilton people. The day of the event he finally asked her what the tab was and discovered she had set him back more than $5,000. Dorothy said she'd never seen such a pained look on his face, "sort of constipated."

By nine p.m., in the whirl of the gathering, Gordon had apparently forgotten the $5,000. He looked like a million. Could it have been on account of what Judy was carrying?

CHAPTER TWENTY-TWO
Million Dollar Baby

After a decade behind Gordon's wheelchair, Jimmy paycheck-by-paycheck existence had driven him to his knees. He had been at General Music since it was little more than hustle and bailing wire. He had watched Gordon bulk up from a fast talker that producers felt pity for to a cocksure businessman with the most active postproduction shop in town. Jimmy remembered those early nights at the clubs, where he would have to grab Gordon by the scruff of the neck on the drive home so the boss could puke his liquor out the Cadillac window. He could reminisce about gondola rides in Venice, and that time he had nearly jumped off *The Take One* outside Catalina into a swarm of man-eating blue sharks. A storehouse of memories Jimmy had. A durable bank account should've accompanied it.

Being my uncle's everything man hurt Jimmy as a family man. His twelve-hour days tending Gordon came so frequently he often said goodnight to his kids by phone and plopped down in Gordon's back bedroom. In the morning he'd be taking orders anew, sublimating himself to the boss, repeating, "I'm getting to it as fast as I can." He was Gordon's secret service agent—shielding him from dangers, surveying rooms to anticipate requests before they were made. Jimmy's versatility complicated matters, because he had become a serviceable sound editor himself when he wasn't schlepping Gordon around West L.A. It tore at him. His employer, though generous in spurts, refused to pay half of what Jimmy believed his loyalty already merited him.

By the late-1960s, the glamour on Jimmy's job had surrendered much of its sparkle. If he arrived at Blue Jay Way with Judy in the kitchen not speaking to Gordon because of a barb, he knew Gordon would be nitpicking him later. Jimmy's Hollywood was unlike the others, too. Unionized black editors were almost nonexistent. Most blacks in town were relegated to errand work for executives and their self-absorbed cronies. Jimmy could dig that. When he delivered papers to Ivan's office, the producer sometimes acted more interested in cooing the wild animals near his desk than addressing Jimmy. Or Ivan would be splashing in his pool with his 400-pound, de-fanged, star lion, "Clarence," which made Jimmy want to throw down the papers and sprint for the car.

If you asked Jimmy, which no one did, it almost seemed fitting what happened to Ivan. In 1968, a once-in-a-century rainstorm clobbered Southern California. A rain-swollen dam above Africa-U.S.A. overflowed as a consequence, and it flooded the complex, including the *Daktari* set. Many of the animals, including the 1,000-pound Grizzly that played the lead in *Gentle Ben*, were temporarily unloosed into the local neighborhoods by the storm, prompting residents to lock their children indoors in fright. Housewives fretted: "*Honey, is that a Rhino behind the hedge?*" All in all, it was a million-dollar loss. Jimmy wondered how the beast-loving Mr. Tors liked that.

Jimmy's brushes with the Los Angeles Police Department made him question whether any of it was worth it. He would be driving home in Gordon's car, as my uncle permitted him, when the red-and blue-lights flashed as he approached Sunset. "Get out of the car and tell us where you stole this thing," the officers would demand. Or, "Boy, you realize this ain't Watts? Why aren't you there?" It had happened eight times, maybe nine. They searched the car before they released him. A couple of nights the cops had roughed him up, elbowing him toward the curb while the beautiful people of the Beverly Glen slowed down to gape. Jimmy, who didn't like fusses, got so fed up by the persecution he spilled to Gordon. He in turn called the L.A.P.D.-Wilshire bureau and ripped into the desk sergeant. The sergeant said he would take care of it, but Jimmy would be hassled again.

All this he could have abided as L.A. life if his take-home pay was respectable. He'd never campaigned to be full-time editor despite being able to splice truck backfires or monkey squeals into network shows like everybody else. So what if he didn't always spell the show titles right on the tapes? In a previous life, before he'd met Gordon, Jimmy had been a trash-man with Jerry Lewis on his route. (Jimmy was grateful Jerry hadn't recognized him when Gordon introduced the two years later). Today he was much more. All he wanted was to accrue a decent living. Try supporting a family on $150-week; it was a dishonorable wage. When he toted up his servitude to Gordon, it battered his pride more than the L.A.P.D. had. Why, he asked himself, couldn't the man own up to the resentment his cheapness stirred in his so-called best friends?

The breadth of Jimmy's expenses stretched all over South Central. His marriage to Lovella, his Louisiana sweetheart, had withered after five kids. Jimmy didn't bother with an official divorce. After Lovella, or maybe during the tail end of Lovella, came Florence, with whom Jimmy conceived six children over ten years or so. "Wild things, uncontrollable events," drove them apart, Jimmy said. Florence's successor was an attractive, younger woman named Peaches who Jimmy had picked up on at a bus stop. There would be other pretty women, and more children out of wedlock, with Jimmy sworn to own up to his responsibilities, all nineteen to twenty-seven of them. If only they weren't always outgrowing their sneakers.

Jimmy's zipper damaged him other ways, too. Between Florence and Peaches, there was Clara, my parent's sultry, Costa Rican-born housekeeper. Jimmy got acquainted with her when he would drive Gordon and Judy to Pasadena for dinner at our house, and he and Clara would eat their supper together in the kitchen. Jimmy was smooth. Clara was high-spirited—and probably bi-polar. She swooned for Gordon's man with a pillaging infatuation.

In the spring of either 1967 or 1968, Clara notified my parents she soon would be quitting her job so she could marry Jimmy. This all was news to Jimmy, who'd only consented to shacking up. Still, Clara unpacked her stuff at his place on a Friday. The following Monday, as Jimmy was leaving for Blue Jay Way, Clara claimed she had a "sour stomach" and was calling in sick. Feel better, he told her. Try toast.

Around nine p.m. that evening, with three of his kids behind him, Jimmy slipped the key in the door and stopped in the arch. The house had been cleaned out. "Daddy," one of his children said cutely, "Are we moving?" No, but Clara had. While he had been with Gordon, she and a friend had rented a Beacon's van and removed his refrigerator, his pots and pans, and the $2,000-plus furniture set Jimmy had just purchased on credit from Sears. Even his cufflinks and drapes were gone.

"What the hell did you do that for?" he grumbled over the phone. To bankroll a new life in Costa Rica, she said. According to my mom, Clara was scared out of her fling. Supposedly one of Jimmy's ex-wives showed up at the house with three of her children that Monday, and rapped on the door. Clara answered. "Since you took my husband," the ex-wife reportedly said, "I'm giving you his children." Jimmy denied that happened. Either way, their standoff got nastier. Clara threatened to drench his possessions with gasoline and make a bonfire out of them rather than return them. Jimmy refused to make payments on furniture stolen from his own house.

Neither would relent, and the police were alerted. Sears filed charges against Jimmy for defaulting on his installments and garnished his wages. Gordon finally had to intervene, hiring Abe's law firm to settle the case against Jimmy for $600 while Sears repossessed the furniture. Clara only dodged jail time because my folks paid her fine. When she later moved to Costa Rica, the hubbub died down, except for one thing. Jimmy felt poorer than ever.

~~~

Joe von Stroheim was done complaining about his salary. One Tuesday, he burst into Gordon's office and stood there, arms akimbo.

"Okay," Gordon said, "I'm laying odds you're not here to talk about the Rams."

"Cut the crap," Joe said. "I just got done speaking with Ted and he told me something very, very interesting. He said you're paying him 300 a week. Three hundred. Shit-all-mighty. That's fifty bucks more than me!"

"Oh Joe, come on. You know I negotiate with everyone individually. Besides, that's Ted's business, not yours."

"Bullshit it's not my business. This is a competitive industry. And you're the one who says he values loyalty so much."

"I do. Aren't I always telling you you're my top editor?"

"So pay me like it!"

"I'm really buried right now. Do we have to get into this today?"

"Yeah."

"All right. You've heard me say this before but I'll repeat myself. I have a budget to stick to. I just can't throw it away when somebody decides they deserve more money. It'd be chaos if I did. And do you have any idea of the juggling I do to keep you main guys around when the shooting season is over?"

"Look at the hours we put in."

"Understand where I'm coming from. We'll have to keep you where you are until next season."

"Maybe you've forgotten I was here way before Ted, when all you had was *Bozo the Clown* and a few other chicken-shit projects? I want to be paid what I'm worth."

"You already are."

"Don't be so tight, Gordon. We all know you're making good coin cuz of Ivan."

"Back at you, Joe. Don't be so ungrateful. Think of the peace of mind you've had."

Joe crossed his arms. He paced the room and tapped the filing cabinet. "I really hoped it wouldn't get to this but it obviously has. If you don't raise me up to what Ted is making I'm gone. I won't have any trouble pulling down a lot more at Desilu. They've already offered me. Harriet and I are trying to buy a house. You know that."

Gordon stuck on a poker face before replying. "Well, since you've applied elsewhere, you have to do what you think is best."

"Aren't you going to counter?"

"Why? You said you'd be happier someplace else."

"No I didn't. I said I'd be making a lot more."

Gordon went quiet listening to his office humming with activity. "Then go. I can't stand in a friend's way."

"And that's it?" Joe said. "You won't even sleep on it after everything we've been through?"

"Sorry. I got five companies to manage. I can't overspend."

Joe walked to the side of the bed near the phone lever. "Overspend, huh? You've just made it simple. Consider this my two-week notice."

"Done."

He and Joe glared at each other until Harriet's head popped into the doorway. In a timid voice, she said there was an urgent phone message for Gordon from an overseas supplier.

"Not now, Harriet," Gordon said. "We're in the middle of something."

"Wrong," Joe said. "We're at the end of something."

Joe would make good on his threat. He left for Desilu, where he cut sound effects for *Mission Impossible*, then *Mannix*, then up the chain to *Three Days of the Condor* and *A Star is Born*. In the 1970s, he'd be honored with a couple of Emmy awards. Before all that, his departure from General Music as the senior guy, the funniest, most irreverent of the crew, sucked camaraderie from the office. The secretaries pelted my uncle with *how-could-you* looks for a week.

Call it the triumph of Gordon's survival agenda. Igo Kantor, his quick-gun music editor, had already quit a year earlier to open his own rival postproduction company. That was okay. There were jobs aplenty. What completely blindsided my uncle was when Jimmy said they needed to speak not long after Joe resigned.

They were in the car heading toward Ivan's office; one of Ivan's minions wanted Gordon's input on a $500,000 "Daktari Junction" animal theme park they were contemplating. Jimmy stopped the Cad on the side of the road in Culver City. He had been taciturn all day.

"Why'd you pull over?" Gordon asked. "We're already late."

"I know, boss. I got to talk to you about something first."

"Jimmy, look at me," Gordon commanded. "You're mumbling. "

Jimmy turned to face him. "This is hard to say so I'll just say it. I have to leave. I've gotten a job offer over at Desilu. Going to be an assistant editor on *Mannix* with Joe."

"You are?" Gordon looked bilious.

"Hope you understand. Between Lovella and Florence, I got me eleven children to support. This wage I'm getting ain't nearly enough. Not unless you can get me to $225 a week right away."

"Two-twenty-five. Out of the question, Jimmy. That's way too much. We've discussed this."

"I thought that's what you'd say."

"This isn't about me. Haven't you been saving anything in the bank? You said you were going to."

"I tried. But my family has already spent my paycheck before I earned it."

Neither man said anything over the purring white noise. An ambulance screamed by on Pico.

"I hope you and Joe will be happy out there. Drop me a line so I can let Judy know how you're doing. I'm sure she'll miss you."

"I knew you'd get hot. But you gotta know this ain't personal. You're like…," Jimmy cleared his throat. "A brother to me."

"As in brother can you spare a dime?" Gordon said bitingly. "Some idea of family you have."

"Gordon, you couldn't be expecting me to stay with you forever making what I'm making. It's been ten years. It's embarrassing how little I bring home. Not right."

"Don't be so naïve, Jimmy. If I start doling out raises, everyone will want one. Then I'll be worried about paying my own bills. You ever been on welfare? I have, and it feels fucked. The answer is no. I can't make exceptions, even for you."

Jimmy drew in his lips. He leaned in tight towards Gordon. "Then you can have your job. I'm done with ya."

He was gone two weeks later. Judy and Bob were saddled with the aftermath.

Gordon parceled out his secrets on a need-to-know basis. Jimmy and Bob had gotten a few. Joe heard the whopper. They were the chosen. For everyone else, Gordon maintained a strict firewall between his personal life on Blue Jay Way and his professional one on Willoughby Avenue. The barrier wasn't as much for privacy as for desecrations of this grand life he was pulling off.

He only revealed to one associate I could hunt down the bombshell of Judy's pregnancy. The timing could've been early 1966, while Blue Jay Way was under construction and my grandma was dying, or the year after. Igo recalled it as the happiest he had ever seen my uncle. The conception, Gordon let on, had been a spontaneous event, an unbelievable slice of kismet. He and Judy hadn't thought to worry about birth control. Imagine him, father of a miracle baby.

Jazzed as he was to announce the pregnancy, he decided to keep the news under wraps. When Judy's belly grew big, then they could host a champagne celebration at home and the office. Then they could discuss baby names. It was better for now to avoid that exuberance. For years, his staff had been told not to make his condition a conversation topic around him, but this was a whole new area. The conception would inspire a thousand questions he couldn't blame anyone for posing. How could somebody out of contact with his torso, who couldn't feel his bellybutton if you wailed on it with a crowbar, impregnate anyone? How could he do the deed if his manhood was insensate? How, how, how? Quadriplegics like him, with their so-called "sensory deficits," lose control of their sexual plumbing because blood won't engorge there easily. Assuming they can get aroused, only about one in twenty-five paralyzed men can coax out their seed. The quad that clung to secrets was one of the exceptions. As frustrating as it was not being able to publicize his loin's accomplishment, Gordon realized he had to for now. Keeping certain hopes unspoken was psychological hedge. If things went wrong, the hurt was better insulated.

And things did go wrong. Judy miscarried the child a few weeks into the pregnancy in a bleeding-out that might've happened in the bathroom at Blue Jay Way. The worries about announcing the miracle conception were over. "Gordon was devastated for a month," Igo said. "Just devastated."

Judy herself only confided to one person I know of about the baby, and it was after the fact. She explained to my mother that she was actually relieved about the miscarriage. She said Gordon felt the same. They'd worried that taking care of a child and him would overpower her and crimp their lifestyle. "Muriel, I don't have to tell you how much attention kids need." Judy, who adored children and was adored back, insisted that losing the baby was a blessing in disguise. Really, she and Gordon were okay, no bereavement necessary. It seems Judy had picked up some acting as a Hollywood wife.

CHAPTER TWENTY-THREE
The Vanishing Legion

The delectable beaches and hotel-casinos that ensconced Cuba as a Caribbean Las Vegas for American jetsetters was Gordon's kind of resort. Shame, he thought, those shaggy-bearded Marxists had to ruin it. My uncle apparently had had the superb bad timing to be zipping around Havana when revolution came calling there in 1959. The regime change caught many Americans off guard, none more than former TV cowboy Russell "Hopalong Cassidy" Hayden.

Now a producer, Hayden had whistled Gordon down there to discuss either a TV series based out of Cuba or a feature film. Game, my dateline-hopping uncle and Jimmy boarded the first plane available. Hayden's assignment to them was legwork under the tropical sun: rustling up Cuban musicians who'd toot their trumpets and bang their drum for U.S. scale. Insurgency bushwhacked their plan to scout postproduction houses.

Fires started raging, buildings closing up. Gordon, Jimmy and Hayden, having been there a week, skittishly knew what the arrival of the Castro brothers meant for them. They had to get their asses off the island before martial law was imposed. According to Jimmy, Gordon had him make a mad dash to the central airport. With messily packed suitcases and passports firmly gripped, they got away.

The two couldn't wait to have a celebratory drink in the comfort of U.S. airspace. I couldn't wait to discover why it was Jimmy—and not my mom—who clued me in on Gordon's Cuban misadventure, among a hodgepodge of other revelations about him. I'd been dredging Gordon's life for several years by then because my mom had persistently wound me up to dredge it. Make it yours, she'd say, but do it for others. At family get-togethers and odd moments, in the years after she'd let on about her trip to San Francisco, she preached the gospel of Muriel. Her brother's life-story was inspiration ripe for the plucking. Motivational caffeine, if you will. The handicapped, she believed, could borrow his creed of scheming and frolicking with as few assisting fingers as possible if only they knew they had a hero to emulate. It still bewildered her that Gordon, often referenced as the "most fascinating man on the lot" by some sitcom stars he knew, was not a household name. To her, he had conquered more and suffered greater than Christopher Reeve. I also suspected *she* wanted the exposure, because writing about him was in a sense the same as writing about her.

Whatever her reasons, she been pulling her punches of late in my interviews with her. Or rather, pulling her recollections, saying she didn't remember events she couldn't possibly have forgotten. A resentful volt infused the curt responses she answered about names and dates. The Gordon I was collecting material about seemingly wasn't the marvel sibling in adult-diapers she recognized.

Gradually, she told me less and less, knowing she was my chief pipeline to the past. Between answers, she snarled I was chucking bombs at the family's good name. She wanted Gordon presented as a thrill-seeking Lazarus who inspired people wherever he journeyed to stop carping about their own miseries and find a way to matter to the world. I insisted on a warts-and-all profile. Gordon wasn't *my* hero, wasn't my beloved. He was my subject. As these differences foamed with each new fact I pried loose, interview sessions with her that once netted pages of notes barely captured a single important new fact. Our teamwork had disintegrated. She'd become a hostile witness to the biography she'd conceived. I was her betrayer.

There was only a single act I could take to keep the project afloat. I invited myself to Shreveport, Louisiana to drain the memories of a now-old man. I hadn't him seen in twenty-five years.

"Aw sure," Jimmy told me in a croaky voice. "Come on out." He thought it was terrific, me, "little Chipper," doing a book about *his* old employer. "Course I remember Gordon," he said. "Who'd you think were his legs all those years?"

Jimmy's place was a fifteen-minute drive off the interstate in Bossier Parish, Louisiana, where church steeples still outnumber the monster-soda mini-marts. The rolling, phosphorous-green hills are placid America, the countryside studded with forests, bayous, emu farms and lakeside vacation homes. The humidity there during the summer months bathes you in a roaring sweat. That was my first surprise. The second was that Jimmy's house was hardly the manicured country estate I expected after my mother's depiction of "all the money Gordon paid him." A huge dirt square with a gloomy, 1970's-era sedan at one end and a garbage heap at the other constituted his front lawn. Behind it sat a mobile home set up on blocks with rust stains along the lip of the roof and a fading Jesus statue near the steps. Welcome to Jimmy's retirement pad.

As soon as I opened my rental car door, a crimson-breasted rooster jumped in and began pecking my shins. I should've guessed Jimmy wouldn't answer his front door after that omen. I walked around the side and he wasn't there, either. I went out back and saw fifty hogs in a pen ringed by eerie dead trees but no Jimmy. A half hour went by. Maybe he'd forgotten about me and gone into town? An hour passed. Did I botch the date? I perspired some more and kicked dirt clods toward the rooster. Exasperated, I walked over to a young man repairing a fence across the road. He identified himself as Jimmy's nephew. Didn't you hear, he said? Jimmy was in the hospital. He'd had a stroke three days ago.

You know that plunging, spiky feeling in the lining of your belly when you realize defeat has you in its clutches? That was my belly out on Jimmy's dirt lawn. He deserved better than this threadbare existence. I wasn't sure, with my gall and naïveté, what I deserved.

Jack Perry had been the first person I'd tried to interview. The years, however, had piled on Jack, and he'd had a stroke, too. Snug in the kitchen of his Redondo Beach home, the man who did Dinah Shore's taxes and pooh-poohed Gordon's cockamamie ideas labored to give me what I wanted. He was in his own wheelchair now. A few of the recollections Jack stuttered were mildly helpful. Mostly, it was watching his mind stumbling around his haywire speech, and his liquid-blue eyes imploring me, "I'm sorry, I can't tell you what I know."

Jack's silence would become a familiar refrain. In the proceeding months, I'd discover that lawyer/confidante Abe Marcus was dead, Walter Greene and Hans Salter, too. Hugo Grimaldi had a terminal illness and Nathan Jones was MIA in Northern California. Twenty others were unreachable. A few washed-up celebrities that Gordon once palled around with didn't have time for me, or in the case of an old TV-clown, demanded money for their memories. Just as bad, Judy bequeathed no diaries or personal records from which to reconstruct her life. A local librarian trying to dig up archived stories about Gordon's accident at Marshall Junior High came back empty-handed. So did the assorted hospitals where I sought medical records.

Inside my rooster-pecked rental car, in the parking lot of Jimmy's hospital, I closed my eyes. Rain from a thunderstorm clinked on the windshield. The reviews were in on my judgment. I'd committed the biggest mistake of my adult life walking away from journalism to chase Gordon's ghost. Everything about him was dead or hurdling there. My managing editor had been right. Only a dope would jump into this breach. I should've listened to him instead of those lessons from the Mesa fire.

Not that Jimmy, a smaller, balder version than I remembered, didn't buck up when he spotted me from his hospital bed. "Chipper, my goodness." Jimmy clasped my hand with a sinewy firmness that he attributed to tending his hogs. We caught up on kids and such for a few minutes, and then he nudged me to crack open my laptop. "Ask whatever you want," he said.

"C'mon," I told him. "I should come back."

He insisted he was okay. "I just had me a little decline," as he called his stroke. In short order, Jimmy recounted some astounding things. He talked about recruiting Cuban musicians in 1959 only to see Fidel's insurgents march in. He slid over to stories about his boss's respiratory blackout in Rome and a couple of boating escapades. He hinted, as had others, that Gordon may have been waylaid in Munich on a 1972 music-recording trip there when Palestinian terrorists seized members of the Israeli Olympic team, and the airport went into emergency shutdown. His memory seemed downright remarkable until I returned to the Cuba story for additional details and Jimmy contradicted what he'd said minutes earlier. "Nah," he said, "we never did make it to Havana. We sure did try." "Jimmy," I said, "let's take it slower, all right? How old are you? Seventy-two? Seventy-four?" He didn't remember.

Vexed at myself for even interviewing him in that state, and just frustrated in general, I returned to Los Angeles in a prodigious snit. Who was going to help me now? My instigator—that's who.

I confronted my mother as she laid reading on her chaise. "Tell me everything," I said angrily. Drop the sugarcoating. The Gordon she'd described so far was a super-human who razzle-dazzled the planet from his chrome-wheeled chariot. And here sat his sister, the one who'd prodded me to chronicle him, still making excuses for him twenty years after his funeral. It'd all been revisionist history to live by.

In the preceding months, she had glossed over her father's affair. She'd skipped Judy and Gordon's lost fetus. She'd ignored Mama Rose's martyrdom, and had never mentioned why Gordon's dearest friends had quit General Music in a huff. Her *coup de grace* was minimizing two family murders that were once the talk of their respective towns. She wanted a canonization of her family because the truth was untidy.

"Sensationalist!" That's how she classified my questions. Her finger stabbed the air back at me as if I was a tabloid dirt-monger wallowing in the salacious past. A sellout.

"Exactly what kind of story are you planning to write?" she asked.

"The real one."

"I'm not hiding anything. You're just focusing on the things that don't matter."

"You mean like your dad's girlfriend—the one he ran off with? She was a Goldwyn dancer, wasn't she Mom?"

"I don't want you to include that," she said, herself bristling mad. "Understand?" She lit a cigarette at the wrong end. She junked it and tried a new one. "I thought this was Gordon's story."

"It is—him and the family."

"I don't care what you call it. All this other stuff is private. That goes for the murders and the (religious) conversions. It's nobody else's business."

"Then you shouldn't have gotten me started on this."

"I'm starting to wish I hadn't."

"If you won't tell me about the killings, I'll fly up and interview Uncle Harold (my mom's uncle). He said he'd set me straight."

"You're going down a dangerous path if you take his word. He's part senile. All he talks about is conspiracies."

"I'll judge for myself."

"So you're going to use all these other subjects, even though you know I'm against it?"

"Yeah. I am."

"I'm warning you that if you do, I won't tell you another word. And then I won't let you use my name. I don't want any of my friends reading this trash."

"Fine," I said.

She took her glare off me. She went back, in fact, to reading her *National Review* like I no longer existed.

The entire story was in shambles. To be honest, I already suspected something besides my mother's denials might be tripping me up. Other doubts, absurd doubts, were poking me. It was a theory I kidded about because I was nervous people would think I was a delusional idiot if they believed I was serious. But could it be that the cosmos wanted this story squelched? That maybe, in the name of keeping things buried that should stay buried, Gordon was interfering, you know, reaching through the dimensions to stymie me. Perhaps he wanted his biography halted because my portrayal of him was too boorish. Or he was upset about how Paul and I had tormented Judy during dinner table conversations after he died. Her vapid remarks about then-President Reagan had inspired us to crown her the "Queen of Inane." *"Oh, sport,"* I could hear him saying, *"you're royally blowing it. That stuff you're chasing about me is a blind alley. Look over here. No, that there! Here. And don't talk to him — that loser doesn't know boo. Here's a flash, Mr. Hotshot Reporter: put yourself in my shoes. Good luck with that one."*

Soon enough, I shook out of that lunacy. I was looking for a scapegoat, which is easier on the eyes than staring in the mirror. Gordon wasn't crossing through the continuum to sabotage me. The departed can't monkey with the living for payback. The Almighty has rules about that. Clearly, my subject remained very much in his coffin.

Even so, my mom was right about me missing the point. It just wasn't the one she voiced about letting family skeletons rest. There was symmetry here. This reassembling of her brother was supposed to be *my* crucible. Nothing ever came gift-wrapped to him when so much had for me. Why should I keep getting the breaks when he'd endured those steely tongs in his head? As I moved further along, I saw it would catch up with me one way or the other. My uncle's legacy, his costly legacy, had reached up and grabbed me with such force I couldn't give up. If I were dissecting his life so righteously, it would mean doing the same to myself.

The only person capable of giving me what my mother refused shuffled his feet around the room in his old-folks home. Ninety-two-year-old Harold Ross scratched a wispy, white hair at the base of his nearly hairless skull. Things, he complained, were easily misplaced here, and now he had lost some papers. You could see why. Behind him was a teetering, floor-to-ceiling agglomeration of clothes, end tables, books, Persian rugs and bric-a-brac transferred here from the splendid San Francisco apartment he and his wife had grown too feeble to manage. It was a terrible commentary on aging.

Harold, however, was a gamer about his new living conditions. He set his mind to editing a tract on his latest faith, a, pantheistic religion called Theosophy, for whom he never said. When he wasn't stooped over his desk, he obeyed the rules of his institution. A few of the blue-haired widows expressed interest in his company, but Harold was very much the distracted old man. The backbone of his being, his wife, Dorothy, commandeered most of his attention. She lay in a nearby convalescent hospital unable to speak because of a progressive brain ailment. Everybody knew what a strong lady Aunt Dorothy had been. How she'd been the grounding to Uncle Harold's quixotic search for why men behaved as they did. He would have given himself a tumor if it had brought him closer to her. Yet he was healthy in his longing, striding briskly in his 6'1" frame while retaining that booming, honey voice.

Uncle Harold and I sat on the lumpy sofa inside his room looking at each other like strangers. We'd seen each other on maybe a dozen occasions, if that. Why had I come here again, he asked in a blink of senility? "I'm Muriel's boy," I said, "remember, the writer? The one interested in your dad and brother." "Oh yes, oh yes," he said. He flicked eye crud out beneath his thick glasses and continued: "Tell me where you want me to start." I explained, and with a minimum of direction out poured family history concealed for fifty years. They were gothic tales about lost people that Harold retold impassively, with no trace of the victim's rage my mom said embittered him most of his life.

It would take digging to recognize later that Harold had juxtaposed his facts and his villains. Calibrating how Gordon fit into this lacerated past was edgier business, but more enlightening. His recovery from that gym class swan dive proved something. You could out-last fate's death-call provided you had loving hands to lift you.

Harold knew. After his father's wealthy relatives turned their back on him for wedding a commoner, Maurice Rossman made a fine Texas life for his family as a junk and commodities merchant. El Paso circa 1915 was a dusty, freewheeling town within shouting distance of the Mexican Revolution where crank-started cars were called "machines" and men combed handlebar mustaches. Maurice's wife and kids had it good, too, with a driver, housing and money. On special nights, if he weren't busy on guerilla raids, rebel honcho Pancho Villa would ride to their house on Montana Street to drink with Maurice, his gringo soul mate. "Honest?" I asked. "The same guy who outran the U.S. Army?" "Yup, " Harold said. "Uncle Pancho."

Harold was a little boy on vacation with his mom in New York City when he heard the six-word telegram he wish he hadn't. "MAURICE KILLED BY FOUL PLAY! STOP." Harold was certain it was Pancho himself who organized the posse that located his dad's corpse on the outskirts of the city. Maurice, apparently, had been forced to dig his own grave before being shot in the rear of the skull execution-style. I pushed hard into the sofa. "Who would do such a thing?" I asked. "A government assassin?" No, Harold said, it was hardly that conspiratorial. It was *his* own uncle, the brother with whom Maurice had entered the trading business. The rumor was that Maurice was schtupping his sister-in-law and the brother killed him, or contracted for it, to obtain his revenge. The idea it had been a violent robbery was baloney spread by the San Francisco Rossmans. The reason for the secrecy was beginning to leach out.

J.E. "Red" Mullen began the family's undertow. The twenty-one-year-old Texan with the black, lifeless eyes murdered my great grandfather; of that there is little doubt. Maurice Rossman's body was uncovered near the banks of the Rio Grande River on February 18, 1915. Ditch workers found the bullet-ridden, mutilated corpse, not Villa's posse. Nearly the entire El Paso police department was assigned to investigate, as it was very unusual for a wealthy merchant to be slain. *The El Paso Morning Times* branded it "one of the most sensational and complex cases ever" seen in those parts.

In the saloons, there was chatter about whether it was violent thievery or a more premeditated crime. The detectives, after all, testified that Mullen had stolen Maurice's diamond-encrusted ring and gold watch while ignoring other valuables. It seemed odd. Police also were troubled why Mullen was bothering with Maurice at all, since Mullen made his living as an arms dealer selling machine guns and other munitions cheap to both sides of the unfolding Mexican Civil War. Villa's security agents, in fact, were tailing Mullen the day he baited my great-grandfather into his car. Maurice still might've been alive then, able to be rescued, but Mullen gave Pancho's men the slip on those unmarked rural roads. After the killing he fled to a Juarez boardinghouse with Mexican authorities hot on his scent. He was arrested a few days later, and within hours of that deported across the border.

El Paso prosecutors described their suspect as "a cold-blooded killer" who'd left three children fatherless. They bragged how airtight their circumstantial case was. Their thorniest problem was finding a jury willing to believe the accused might be innocent. How could they? Two star witnesses who were clerking at Maurice's shop when Mullen sauntered in sealed victory for the district attorney. The most persuasive of the two was a fifteen-year-old girl who sobbed on the witness stand when she saw Mullen at the defendant's table in his blue serge suit. The girl said of the victim: "He left with that man (over there) and I did not see him again until his body was found." The witness was reduced to such a quivering, rubber-legged mass after her court appearance she had to be escorted to another city to regain her sanity.

Another overflow crowd was on hand to hear the jury's verdict, townsfolk chomping to see how the auburn-haired defendant would react. He'd been nonchalant throughout the trial, chewing gum and smoking his briar pipe as if he were being charged with jaywalking. When the jurors returned a guilty verdict, he whipped his leg over a chair for sarcastic effect. On April 1, 1915, he was sentenced to a maximum of thirty-five years in prison for killing Maurice, whom he baited into his car with the promise of selling low-cost hides. Asked if he wanted to appeal,

Mullen said no, cryptically proclaiming he was happy with the outcome he had. "What do you think I am?" he told the court. "A fool?"

After his father's murder, Harold said the family lived hardscrabble in the Brooklyn tenements. His big brother, Nat, was the man of the house now, Harold the bookish tagalong. Nat, with piercing blue eyes and tight black curls, had boy-wonder written all over him. He used his receptionist job with producer Lewis Selznick as a steppingstone to become a film salesman and later manager of the Strand Theater on Fulton Street. At only sixteen he was wooed to Hollywood, where he roomed with his buddy, future studio legend Irving Thalberg. Young Nat Ross so impressed his employer, Universal Pictures, that he was promoted to personal assistant for company president Carl Laemmle.

Before he mastered his filing duties, it struck people the kid was too talented to be a professional lackey. He'd been an amateur moviemaker himself, and Nat talked Laemmle into giving him a directing tryout. One picture led to another and soon he was overseeing screwball comedies and dramas. Cowboy star Hoot Gibson and Tinseltown's "It Girl," Clara Bow, swore by his methods. Producing gigs were offered.

Nat exuded the breezy confidence of someone who resolved his difficulties with clarity and compassion, disinterested in grudges. The trait made him friends around the set and enemies at the office. Some expected him to be appointed one of Universal's managing officers, a post that would've cemented him as one of Hollywood's founding fathers.

Around the family, Nat's ego never outgrew his hat. He moved Dearie from New York, setting her up in a swank apartment on Wilshire Boulevard. He'd "kidnap" Gordon for daylong outings that'd begin at the set and end at fun restaurants. He even gave Harold, who had hitchhiked across the country sleeping in phone booths, bit parts in his films.

In 1936 he wed a sweet actress/dancer named Audrene Brier who he'd met directing. Photographed on their wedding day, they resembled pudgy versions of Gregory Peck and Esther Williams. After Nat resigned from Universal under undisclosed circumstances, he and Audrene moved to London, where he produced for Columbia and MGM. Right before the German Lufwaffe began firebombing the city, they returned to Los Angeles.

Like his father, Nat Ross was tricked into the casket. His undoing began innocently enough when he hired a man with his own father's first name at the downtown L.A. rag-manufacturing plant Nat owned with a cousin. Cotton Products Corp. at Seventh and Broadway had never had it better when Maurice Briggs cashed his first paycheck from Nat. The Navy had awarded the company a contract to furnish rags to clean battleships, and that was before the U.S. fleet was getting grimy in World War II.

With his movie-star looks and wise-guy veneer, Briggs had bigger things in mind than being a model laborer. Around the factory floor, he pursued a lithesome co-worker named Susan and persuaded her to marry him. Whether he confessed to her he was a paroled bank robber is anybody's guess, and probably moot because his temper torpedoed the marriage a few months into it.

One night, after Susan threatened to leave him, Briggs, twenty-five, beat the stuffing out of her and ripped her clothes off. "I'll never let you go," he vowed. They brawled some more, but he did scram when his bride told him she wanted a divorce. Soon after they split, Nat fired Briggs from Cotton Products for an unknown cause. It wouldn't stick. My great-uncle took such pity on him that he rehired him. He then fired him again.

Briggs was rabid with jealousy if he wasn't already mad. (As a kid, he'd torched part of the orphanage where his parents had dumped him.) Even before he'd been canned, he groused to friends that Nat was "chasing around" his wife. He had no proof, only suspicions, and for him that was fine. He stalked Susan. He showed up at the plant one day swearing out loud that Nat was a dead man; police found a pocketknife on him and shooed him off the premises. Evading security the next time, he told Nat to his face that his days were numbered. Nat shrugged it off as an empty threat by a harmless jerk.

Briggs stewed over his next move as he drank himself blotto at the downtown flophouse where he was staying. By the time his unemployment check arrived in a week and a half he had it all mapped out. He went to a pawnshop and purchased a thirty-five-caliber deer rifle and a carton of shells. He returned again to the plant and stashed his merchandise behind an outdoor trashcan. At 10:00 p.m. he knocked on the factory's side door. "Nat around?" he asked courteously. He only needed a minute. Nat, who'd been discussing an order with some employees, sighed loudly. "I wonder what he wants *now*?" he said. "I'll be back, girls." Wrong.

As Nat approached the doorway, Briggs grabbed the rifle and aimed the weapon at Nat's heart. *Kaboom*—he squeezed off a round. Twenty-five women on the late shift, including Brigg's estranged wife, heard the shot that blew Nat backwards. They watched Briggs stand over him and let off a second shot. There was screaming and the clatter of ladies' heels scurrying into the bathroom. A male worker rushed toward Briggs to disarm him, but Briggs waved the rifle at him with a naughty expression. Calm as can be, Briggs walked two blocks to Olive Street and threw the rifle onto somebody's lawn like it were an empty beer bottle. "Why'd you do that?" a passerby asked. "Oh, I just killed a guy," he explained. "You better call the cops."

Once Briggs was in custody, the media circus put down its stakes. The victim had been a journeyman director, an all-around swell guy, with movie people writing condolences and famous columnists interviewing his widow. The defendant, a cigarette dangling from his lips, meantime, reveled in the notoriety. L.A.'s press corp printed every demented word he uttered. Briggs, for instance, was widely quoted discussing his repentance. "Am I sorry I shot him? Yeah!" he said. "I'm sorry I can't do it again."

He maintained his defiance through most of the trial. He refused to testify. He pled not guilty despite his earlier confession. It was only when he realized he might be gassed for his crime that he switched to not guilty by reason of temporary insanity. His new tactic was to make a run for the jury's heartstrings. He testified he had gone berserk after learning that his wife had aborted their child (a so-called "illegal operation" in those days). He so wanted a baby that he'd misdirected his anger on his ex-boss, whom he admitted had done nothing wrong. He was sorry.

Nobody believed him. The jury found him guilty and sentenced him to die in San Quentin. On August 8, 1942, weeks after he won a brief stay from California Gov. Culbert Olson, Briggs entered the gas chamber and gave the official witnesses a mocking up-yours salute. Cyanide pellets killed him in nine minutes.

Gordon, just then about to be discharged from County General as the bony adolescent nobody expected would leave, was probably unaware of the dramatics in San Quentin. Rose, from what I know, quarantined word of the execution like a bad virus she did not want him to catch.

Before I would nail this down, I flew back to L.A. from Harold's, disturbed yet revitalized. Murder. Fraud. Betrayal. Cover up. It rang true. There was context for Pancho Villa, whose name had echoed disjointedly through family myth as proof positive we were somebody. Even so, I was onto something bigger than Pancho. The cause of the undertow was in my grasp. Gordon's spill hadn't unleashed it. Gordon's spill had perpetuated it!

Story-wise, Uncle Harold's words gave me a road map where I'd only had tidbits before. My old journalistic hyperactivity surged. I barged into the library. I mastered the archives. A death certificate mailed to me from Texas had my juices pumping. I couldn't stop reflecting on how my brothers and I would be sucked into fate's undertow. Were one of us in store for a cruel ending? Had Peter's retardation been our sacrifice, or was another male going to take a hit?

Twisted as it may sound, digesting both murders for the senseless acts they were also tranquilized me. In the process of unearthing Maurice and Nat, I'd grown attached to them. I tossed out particulars about them to my friends, who thought me weirdly obsessed. I wanted to believe I'd inherited some of their ingenuity, some of their fortitude.

The idea their sins had killed them, as Uncle Harold postulated, would have destroyed that. Luckily, the facts exonerated them. There wasn't a hint of evidence about Maurice Rossman's alleged tryst or a homicidal sibling, though the police records and most of his kin are gone today. There was nothing to support Harold's theory that Nat had been shot because he had slept with Briggs's wife. Rather, he and his father were simply honorable men with the misfortune of stumbling into homicidal thugs.

One soft, spring afternoon I tugged my evidence pile — the death certificate, the newspaper stories, the police materials — out of a brown Manila envelope and handed it to my mom. After she read it, I intended to concede that she had been correct about Harold, the bearer of our secrets. He had been mixed up about the killings. Blaming them, I suppose, was more comforting than acknowledging the unsettling truth that calamity could repeat itself whenever it damn well wants. Grief is a poor historian. The next time I saw my mom, though, she told me she didn't want the bundle that verified this. "Take it home," she said. "It's awful."

But, I hammered back, this is why Gordon mattered so much. He didn't succumb at his moment to. Mama Rose couldn't let him die short of his dreams or a decent lifespan as almost every other male in her realm had. His survival was triumph — miraculous, compensatory. What more proof did my mom need? Gullibility — simple, lunkheaded gullibility — had killed Maurice *and* his son Nat almost a quarter century apart at the same age on nearly the same day of the year. The parallel was spooky, threatening. Yet Gordon escaped the undertow's most treacherous surge, didn't he? I waved my papers under my mom's nose more forcefully. She shoved them away.

The skeletons were banging into each other now. My mom, I realized, had fully bought into Mama Rose's tautology where you catacomb heartache in letter-filled shoeboxes and photo albums and stupefying silence and reinvent yourself however you like. Sweet old lady, social butterfly: you could be anything if those intolerable flashbacks didn't blow your disguise.

With my rooting around into these murders Mama Rose's most crushing secret unexpectedly came tumbling out. It was there, in a 1915 newspaper article, sad and brave. Remember the teenage girl the El Paso D.A. made his star witness in the prosecution of Red Mullen?

The girl was my future grandmother.

Barely fifteen, her testimony put a killer away. Not one word did she ever expend telling us about it.

One reason she internalized not just that trauma but the entire onslaught that was her life sort of slapped me in the face one day as I was driving by the remnants of her old Sierra Madre apartment. Suddenly, it was as plain as Gordon's devil-may-care smirk. Mama Rose wasn't just suppressing the marauding past. She was protecting us. Ending something. By her epic silence, my grandma had single-handedly tried burying the undertow where it couldn't hurt Gordon or us.

She had buried it in herself.

CHAPTER TWENTY-FOUR
The Worthy Deceiver

Judy heard it from girlfriends like Hank and Frieda. They posed it in hushed voices at weekend get-togethers while the men huddled around Gordon's bed watching sports. "Don't you ever get worn down, honey," they asked, "taking care of him *and* the house?"

Judy, her Benson and Hedges smoldering close by, would shake her bangs. "No dear," she'd say. She didn't fatigue easily, not unless she had the flu. "Well," they pried, female-libbers at heart, "how do you stand it when he rides you for not doing every little thing the exact second he wants it?" My aunt's pat reply: "If there's one thing I've learned is that Gordon has his good days and his bad days. On his bad days I act a little deaf."

For better and for worse, 1968 was a lovely year to be Judy Marie Zahler. Her part of the marriage bargain had been honored. This sequined life Gordon had furnished her was better than she had imagined when they lived on Shoreham Street—more hectic with his unyielding medical demands, but more glamorous, too. Up in the glen, Beverly Hills in sight, there was rhythm to Judy's routine that she never enjoyed as a working girl at Bullocks-Wilshire. She didn't serve customers anymore, quite the opposite.

Once every few weeks, she shopped until her arms tired at Saks, Neiman-Marcus, Bullocks and I. Magnin, where the salesgirls knew her measurements. The Sunset Boulevard boutiques with the European names, the ones west of the bawdy rock clubs Judy never understood, considered her a regular, as did the trendy local cafés. Treating a girlfriend once a month for Chardonnay and sandwiches, at Le Dome perhaps, was a Judy tradition. Thirty bucks plus tip, *magnifique*. Where to start? There was so much to cover—fashion, a novel she'd finished, Billie, the protestors handing out anti-war pamphlets, an upcoming trip. Gordon easily was her number one topic. Her girlfriends were amazed at what a dynamite bridge player he had been at their last party.

Judy was as delighted by his moneymaking plans as she was when she first met him. "I don't know how he thinks them up." Soon enough she moved onto how Gordon had "fixed" the TV the last weekend by having the repairman unscrew the back and lay it on the bed so he could specify which vacuum tube to replace. "He and his gadgets," she would cackle. "You ought see the Nikon he bought." After lunch she was back in her Mustang because dry cleaning had to be picked up or she wanted to visit General Music with Chicken, the dog, for an hour. Dinner took special doing with the freshest ingredients.

To-do list checked off, Judy would prepare for their next trip. This required forethought because of Gordon's special needs and the fact that they were venturing beyond the tourist traps most Americans flocked to on vacation. They were worldwide citizens, Gordon and she: Ensenada, Rio, Buenos Aires, Lisbon, Hamburg, Beirut, Bangkok, Capetown. Gordon was in music publishing with the most enchanting foreigners, Judy would write, men who would invite them into their homes for exotic local dishes and insider tours of the city.

It was one spectacle after another once they cleared customs. In Hong Kong they stayed at a hotel with a postcard view of Kowloon Harbor. In Thailand they lowered Gordon's chair into a boat to see a floating market, and a native boy on the riverbank flashed his privates at Judy. No place was too remote for hubby. He was out to visit every continent besides Antarctica, maybe that too.

So Judy packed the bags. It was "God's Country," she said, seeing the swaying grasslands of Africa from the window of a chauffeured jeep. Same for the terrace of the Kenyan game reserve, where they ate croissants fifty feet from a herd of milling elephants. None of these month-plus excursions would be possible if they had children, Judy reminded intimates. It was stressful enough boarding their poodle.

Show business by association was a separate thrill. Five years into the marriage, Judy still got a head rush talking about hobnobbing with the celebrities drawn into her doings. Her cocktail parties were never so animated as when Sidney Sheldon, Ivan, Jerry Lewis, Sam Fuller or other A-list names made the rounds. "Is that," she'd ask, "Larry Hagman over there?"

They were very different people off camera. In Judy's head, the men who visited Gordon, be it right-wing newscaster George Putnam or Nat King Cole, saw something extraordinary about her spouse. Mel Blanc and John Banner (*Hogan Heroes'* "Sgt. Schultz") did, too. It was prestigious to have their home numbers in her phone book. And the fun, well, there was plenty of that watching Gracie Lantz, her professed "gal pal," dub *Woody Woodpecker's* voice in Gordon's very own studio. Not a bad life for a girl from Long Beach.

And yes, there were minor dust-ups with mother. Still, she had fulfilled her pledge to Billie, marrying up like this, and Billie was justifiably proud. Billie would have spent every minute with her daughter if Judy had obliged. Judy also could have done without the quarrels with her niece, Janice-Lynn, Anna Katherine's girl. To be candid, Janice-Lynn embarrassed she and Billie now that they'd broken into the mink-stole circuit.

Feisty, pretty in that blue-collar way, Janice-Lynn represented where the Wetzels had been, not their glamorous future. She had been backsliding for a while. After a divorce, she'd become a Ralph's Supermarket checker until she was stricken with an acute case of colitis. When she recovered, Gordon hired her as a secretary at General Music. It was there she put in her hours between Gordon's impatience to get things done and his compassion to force-feed self-esteem into her. Judy assisted her niece more remotely. She doted on Janice-Lynn's three kids with Westside shopping trips and Saturday matinees that made *her* feel maternal for the day.

It wasn't as if she had it soft. Judy worked her fanny off being a style maven that my uncle depended on to project him as the suave, successful dynamo comfortable with his immobility. Gordon needed her sartorial flair, and she attired him impeccably in suits that gave his puny shoulders respectable width. Her dinner parties were just as painstaking. Impressions mattered down to the creaminess of the salmon mousse or the tinsel wrapping on somebody's birthday present. Those men who pigeonholed Judy as a ditzy blond with a serving tray, and there were some, underestimated her.

Gordon's zingers also were part of the bargain. The "Judy, you shouldn't have done that. Were you blind?" burned. She tried ignoring his jabs, usually by letting his words float into the rafters. If he became too caustic, if he said, "Oh, pipe down" around company, she might walk into the kitchen for a smoke. She recognized he didn't mean it, just as Mama Rose recognized it when he had flamed her. Truly loving Gordon required thick skin and a philosophy, so Judy reminded herself that weathering his digs reflected *her* strength of character.

None of her contemporaries were responsible for the care-giving load of such a vulnerable, multifaceted man. Anyone could see he needed a steam vent. During the TV filming season, he had thirty-five editors on three primetime shows and two cartoons to worry about. Once filming was over he had Ivan's movies to do, plus the documentaries and commercials, and those music libraries to manage. People who judged him harshly should try maneuvering all that without being able to lift a pencil for their own cause.

And, Judy always could resort to an old trick Jimmy had taught her if Gordon snapped at her in a way she couldn't ignore. She would feed him a sifter or two of Benedictine brandy and he'd nod off like clockwork. Though she wouldn't admit it to Hank and Frieda, Judy wished gimmicks like that were unnecessary.

With Jimmy gone, it was the era of Bob. Bob Glenn, General Music's straight-arrow general manager, could handle Gordon while permitting himself to be handled by him. Gordon trusted Bob to be the other brain of his operation in a fashion never bestowed on anyone else. In the busy season they split the supervision workload, passing the other in the hallway and rendezvousing on sedate weekends to review the week. My uncle squeezed the counterbalance for all it was worth. Where he would be too aggressive in negotiations or apt to suck up to a big name, Bob would steady the conversation or modulate him. Bob was more deal-minded than the other fellas, more crusading too. Bob, born-again Christian, sometimes ticked off colleagues by casually asking them how close they were to Jesus. Piety notwithstanding, nobody on payroll got along as smoothly with Gordon as Bob. They lived a life together around the Movieola studying film, disclosing bite-size parts of themselves when the chance presented itself.

In the mornings, Bob would wheel my uncle down the linoleum and the lion roars and chimpanzee squeals emerging underneath the editing-room doors were the *cha-ching* of Gordon's green being produced. "You know, Bob," he would say grinning, "it's getting interesting." When business was good, Gordon loosened up about micromanaging the editors. As long as their deadlines were met, he didn't mind if they made private gag reels inserting vulgar words into *Gentle Ben's* mouth. He'd have done it if he could.

Bob exerted his own will amid the pressure. He learned on the job, slowly undoing the impression of him among some as Gordon's "hay boy." He massaged blown deadlines with producers. He goaded veteran editors who thought they knew everything to do glossier work. He certainly made an impression with one of the attendants who had replaced Jimmy. The man, a 6'3", 230-pound ex-jock, had concocted his own response to Gordon's imperiousness.

One afternoon the attendant pledged: "The next time Gordon bugs me, no matter where we are, I'm going to grab him out of his chair and slam him into the ground." Bob sauntered over hearing that, flexing more bravado than sinew. "Oh yeah?" he said. "Then you'll have to do it through me." The attendant was fired the next week.

Bob's chivalry evolved from kinship as much as sympathy. For him, there was nothing disabled about my uncle, not unless you saw him shirtless looking like an Auschwitz survivor. The dynamic was unlike that with Jimmy. Where he had served with quiet bondage, Bob relied on intellect and attitude. If Gordon wilted at seven p.m.

saying, "Take me home, I'm beat," Bob often refused. He would inject him with a shot of B-12, or threaten to, because the vitamin acted like cocaine that'd kept Gordon up half the night. It would be Bob giving him a sip of tea after Gordon sorted out a set of tangled cues. He would be there on wearying transcontinental flights from London to Johannesburg. When Gordon would ask the maitre d' at a dressy restaurant with a long wait out the door, "Sir, could we please have a table?" in his Tiny Tim falsetto, it was Bob clenching his teeth alongside.

Why Bob's dedication? Why endure the drudgery when he would rather have been doing major motion pictures? Easy. Being in Gordon's contrails was a kick in the pants. There Gordon would be in the mornings, in a crisp suit Judy picked out, with a *let's-get-after-it* expression over his aftershave. Hang around enough and it was infectious. Gordon had reconfigured what was expected to be an invalid's lifestyle into one extended joyride. That's why he relished the contract haggling. That's why he insisted on driving with the top down. It was the sanctity of being in the thick of it.

The reactions he spawned were priceless. The contradiction of him being both the lamest member of his species and the most extroverted guy in the room gave new acquaintances either a nervous tick or the desire to befriend him. Some compared him to an old-fashioned liquid-fueled rocket. He would either blast into fame as cripple in orbit or combust on the launch pad spewing fireballs into the night. Whatever happened, it was a beguiling show, and Bob had box seats.

The pace of new ventures that Gordon walled off from his rank-and-file workers definitely made Bob's days zesty. Two months before NBC erased *Flipper* from the Saturday-night lineup, Gordon held a series of meetings at Blue Jay Way with Lou Scheimer and Norm Prescott, the men of Filmation. Filmation was an upstart cartoon company in the western valley challenging venerable Hanna-Barbera for the kiddy-TV audience. Its specialty was knocking out cartoons based on old superhero series. Gordon's vision was to create a music company publishing songs from Filmation shows, and gearing them toward the surging teenybopper market. (General Music already had added the music and effects to Filmation cartoons like *Superman* and *Batman*.) The corporate superstructure was all arranged for the new company. They'd baptize it "Chipper Music," inspired by the poodle, not by me.

If that wasn't promising enough, Gordon finagled a sit-down in New York City with promoter Don Kirshner, the brains behind *The Monkees* records. Gordon wanted Kirshner's company to showcase Ivan's music around the world using Kirshner's formidable marketing connections.

Inside Kirshner's Madison Avenue office, Bob watched Gordon jut his head forward in sales-attack posture. "Don, picture this. The animals from Ivan's shows—you know Gentle Ben, Clarence—are led out on stage, while a live orchestra strikes up the TV theme songs. *Da, da, da daaaah.* Everything is choreographed. Dramatic lights. Poses. You wouldn't believe the tricks Ivan's animals do. And we'll call it—prepare yourself—an African Rodeo! Brilliant, don't you think? Ringling Brothers is going to be crapping their pants, they'll be so jealous."

Returning to L.A., Gordon found Kirshner wanted half the profits to be involved. Gordon's lawyer told him that was "unconscionable" but Gordon hungered to have his name next to Kirschner's. It wouldn't matter. For three months Kirschner gave Gordon the long-distance brush off. The bigwig New Yorker wouldn't return his dozen calls or his fawning letters. Ivan's personal appeals failed to change his mind, too. He simply lost interest, or didn't like the pitch-man, and the plan to take Ivan Tors Music global pretty much fizzled right there.

It would take a more resounding thud for Gordon to realize he was on the down-slope of a losing streak that might never release him. After nine profitable years, each one better than the last, his rut started with one pigheaded move.

Before they got Chipper Music rolling, Gordon wanted Lou and Norm to clear the books. They had promised to send Judy and him on a trip worth $2,750 as repayment for postproduction work on an old Filmation cartoon. Gordon told Norm he would just as soon get the debt retired. In the broad scheme of founding a new enterprise, it was one of those minor annoyances that should have been papered over. But after Norm, the taskmaster of the two Filmation partners, checked the ledger, he said his company didn't owe nearly that much. Gordon, a little more rancorously this time, said check again. Norm countered they would shell out for a trip to Hawaii, grudgingly at that. Gordon answered that Hawaii wouldn't do; a European trip with return passage through Tokyo would fulfill his requirements.

The annoyance got personal. Norm and Gordon swapped letters accusing the other of phony integrity. They brought in their lawyers to war over technicalities. As the dispute festered, Gordon's advisors privately urged him to split the difference. Chipper Music, they said, held the potential to make him rich. Gordon plugged his big ears.

At skin level, money was his issue. Just below it, his sense of vulnerability ruled the day. The instincts that had once piqued his interest in video-tape recorders and cable television before they meant anything to the world had been hogtied by the insecurity of being him. Fact was Lou and Norm had recently brought in-house some of the editing work that General Music used to do, and Gordon felt snubbed. He wanted what was owed him. Relent on a small debt, he feared, and clients might view him as a creampuff in a wheelchair they could flatten next time.

Eager to be done with the disagreement, Norm wrote Gordon a $2,300 check and negotiations for Chipper Music Co. were terminated. Lou and Norm simply put their heads down and incorporated themselves. They were counting their money the very next year when the song *Sugar, Sugar* from their latest cartoon, *The Archie Show*, sold two million records. Their follow-up show was *Fat Albert and the Cosby Kids*. With a little less pride, Gordon could've been splitting that fortune.

In defeat, the indefatigable optimist Gordon channeled his mind onto the next hot trend. When someone in the Tors camp

recommended they record an album of original music sung by the
cast of *Gentle Ben* he consented to executive produce. Cross
merchandising: that's what they would do. They would use the show
to hawk the record and vice versa. He lined up English composer Joe
Lubin to write the songs and smoothed out the contractual kinks. In
the middle of it all, a kidney infection grounded him, but he'd
learned to shake them quickly and returned to the office in under a
week.

While he was out, one of the editors was busted smoking pot
and strumming Bob Dylan songs on a guitar in his cubicle. Things
happen. So Dennis Weaver's TV wife couldn't carry a note during the
recording sessions. So Capitol and Columbia Records rejected *The
Bear Facts* album. Gordon signed a contract with a tiny label in
Century City instead and it pressed dippy songs like *Don't Cry Little
Gator* onto vinyl. In the summer of '68, you could never be sure
where the money would gush.

There was always that intriguing prospect in sub-Sahara Africa.
Perhaps, my uncle mused, that's where his gusher hid. He had heard
it through his business sources that the stodgy South Africans had
finally bowed to pressure.

After years of political jousting about the subject, the
government had decided to introduce television to the populace.
Even the *über*-conservative, ruling Afrikaners who'd demonized TV
"as the destroyer of once-mighty empires" realized they couldn't
hold out any longer. It was the last industrialized nation to resist the
tube, a situation that forced many citizens to rent 16-mm movies for
their weekend entertainment while scratching their heads about
exactly what it was the government was so afraid of them seeing.
Programming was to be eased in by 1969 or the early 1970s if the
nonexistent infrastructure could be established. The state-run South
African Broadcasting Corp. was oblivious to the engineering
requirements.

It was Dirk Brink, Bob's friend, who flattered my uncle into
believing he might be their answer. Dirk had invited them for a few
vacation days at the Safariland Club in southwestern Kenya. The

resort, nestled inside an enormous valley of deep-water lakes and marshes, pulsed with horned, furry wildlife. Teddy Roosevelt had once trekked here for its big-game hunting. After Gordon notched the first of what would be numerous safaris there, they chartered a small plane to Johannesburg, where Dirk outlined his plan over drinks in the hotel lobby. "Gordon, with your years of know-how, you could be...the wizard of TV here. The South Africans are all thumbs with this technical stuff. Make a deal with them." Gordon asked Dirk how he knew so much, and Dirk said he had his sources.

Dirk was a trim, sandy-haired smoothie, roughly Gordon's age, with a high-octane zeal to try new things, though the fatalistic side of him suspected the good things couldn't last. As a former POW held by the Japanese in Malaysia, he had his wounds. He moved money as a Hong Kong-based financier for his livelihood. Away from work, Dirk had an impressive stash of his own. He held an interest in the Safariland Club as well as property in rural South Africa, a place he hailed as "the greatest country around despite what the bleeding hearts said."

Dirk ran in different circles than the insular Hollywood types with which Gordon and Bob were accustomed. That first morning in Nairobi, Dirk's face appeared on Kenya's main newspaper with a headline saying he was wanted for currency violations. No worries, Dirk reassured his unnerved travel-mates; he'd iron out the misunderstanding with the local authorities. As my uncle would find out, Dirk was a player.

A few months after the Johannesburg meeting, Dirk showed how adamant he was about inserting Gordon into the foundations of South African TV. He jetted over from the Far East to Hollywood with an insider connection, Zachariah Swanapoel, "Swanee" for short. Swanee worked in the Hong Kong office of the South African trade department for a good reason. His uncle was South Africa's trade minister.

Swanee said he was dying to tell what he knew, which was considerable, but for him it was pleasure before business. He wanted a full-blown day at Disneyland. Gordon was afraid that was coming.

Most of the out-of-towners visiting him asked to be chaperoned there. Must-see, they said — The Matterhorn, Pirates of the Caribbean. Whatever. After a dozen trips handholding clients there, Gordon and Bob renamed the Happiest Place on Earth "their mutual suffering." They hated the park, hated sandwiching Gordon into that nauseating teacup ride, but admitted it was a good for business.

Later in the week Swanee opened up. He confirmed that the government was starved for expertise. It had budgeted $70 million in TV startup costs and was poised to hire contractors. Blueprints called for a studio transmission-production complex to rise on the fringes of Johannesburg. That's where Gordon fit in. Swanee believed Gordon should bid to supervise all postproduction. Swanee said he could set up introductory meetings with the proper contacts. Somebody experienced was going to land the job, Swanee deduced, so why not a veteran TV-man from the land that invented the medium?

Swanee added there was something else, something Dirk had mentioned before about how South Africa was a country with twenty-seven separate dialects, and how that was as another opportunity on which to pounce. Even if the South Africans rotated programming on the same channel at first in the two "white languages," Afrikaans and English, they would eventually need simultaneous transmissions to the entire countryside. How would you do that? How would you transmit a program on the same channel in native languages of the whites and those spoken, by say, the ancient Zulus?

It was a question Gordon had apparently been pondering for awhile. He, in fact, had discussed it at length with John Hall, a lanky local engineer who served as Gordon's technical answer man. "It has to be possible, right?" Gordon asked. John mulled it over. After sketching it out, he answered yes, there were multiple approaches and he picked the best. John said you could re-synch dialogue in whatever dialect was needed, then broadcast separate audio feeds with powerful transmitters. Custom-manufactured TVs could have a switch on the receiver allowing the viewer to select the language track he understood. It would be labor intensive translating and re-dubbing, but it was technically viable to transmit four separate languages all together for the same show. Multiplexing: that's how John Hall phrased it. "You multiplex it." Pretending he'd known all along, Gordon conveyed this to Swanee, and Dirk hooted it was cocktails on him. All they had to do now was bag an investor.

Gordon, fresh off the Chipper Music fiasco, reminded himself not to get too enthusiastic this time. Yeah, piece of cake.

These strange gentlemen were tempting him with his one great thing. He could oversee postproduction and never worry about another pencil-neck network executive again. Handled right, he would be a multi-millionaire, which would rocket him toward a mansion, hand surgery, flying lessons, who knew what else. Africa could be his independence. Though a year or more off, Swanee's proposition was his chance to be extraordinary. When my uncle described it to friends, Dirk's words about being a "TV wizard" did half gainers off his tongue.

Chuck Connors, the gravel-voiced leading man, had Ivan Tors right where he wanted him. Before ABC had approved the show, the network had informed Ivan that without the Chuckster as the main character, *Cowboy in Africa* wouldn't fly. Connors had been the star in the film (*Africa Texas Style*) that inspired the series, so advertisers felt confident he would attract viewers.

Ivan, a softy anyway when it came to confrontations, agreed to the network's stipulation. He believed in the show. Spreading its ecological message was gospel for him. Nobody who'd worked with Connors from *The Rifleman* series on up was surprised he would exploit it. Connors could light up the camera with his roughneck sensitivity, but when the director called it a day, watch out. He was a viper toward the crew and a glutton about his needs. For starters, the cowboy made $25,000 per episode, a record amount for the era. To go with it he snatched up control over show merchandising, a luxury limo, a fully equipped trailer, the ability to fire guest stars whenever he chose, and other accommodations.

By the end of the first season, Ivan's brother, Erwin, wanted the star tossed off the lot. Connors was making so much there was little left over for the rest of them. They were losing thousands every month, especially with the one-sided contracts the network insisted on.

Erwin argued there had to be something better to produce; they did have two other network shows going and a steady raft of films. Ivan remained wishy-washy about the situation, so Erwin reminded him of more Connors's horror stories. Among others, he'd accidentally sideswiped a crewmember with his dune buggy, and physically threatened Erwin over a dozen pair of underwear the actor expected to be comped for after a stunt. Okay, okay, Ivan said, he would reconsider.

After some time passed he did what he'd never dreamed. Without informing Connors, he met with ABC and asked the suits to cancel his show for financial cause. By September of '68 it was off the air.

But in doing so, Ivan must have incensed the TV gods. The next year the roof fell in on his empire, and Gordon's by extension. *Daktari*, the show about an Africa-based veterinarian, was shut down by CBS in January. Later that summer, CBS executives did it again. They abruptly ended *Gentle Ben*'s three-year run despite solid ratings. The CBS people explained to Ivan that "outdoor-adventure" programs were on the outs. Advertisers coveted hipper material like *The Mod Squad* and *The Dating Game* to tickle younger audiences; that's what sold. It was the age of the new demographics.

According to the story that later filtered to Ivan's camp, the actual reason for the last cancellation was less scientific than Nielsen's ratings. Apparently, a network executive's wife with sway over her husband had harped on him relentlessly to kill *Gentle Ben*. In her esteemed opinion, it was too "cutesy" for primetime and should be squeezed in between the Saturday morning children's shows or no place at all. The woman won her argument and unemployment for the show's cast and crew. Her identity remained secret.

To finish off Ivan's tailspin year, his wife, Constance, dropped dead of a heart attack at forty-nine. With her went Ivan's interest in permanent L.A. residency. He wanted to move to peaceful Palm Springs, or out of the country altogether.

Gordon, who had outlasted up-down cycles before, took this one in the belly. He sweated through his pajamas several times. He couldn't eat. Just like that, ninety percent of his cash flow had gone *poof*. For nearly three shooting seasons, Ivan's shows had grossed $20,000 per week for him. For almost three seasons, Gordon prestige-wise was greater than the sum of his parts.

Depressing him even more were the gloomy soundings of recession ahead, and the prediction that Hollywood production would stagnate until the economy shook out. At their regular Monday morning appointment, Jack Perry made Gordon understand it was time to dig in. Instead of nicely chiding Gordon about why he'd purchased a new Cadillac without checking with him first or was dabbling in another money-losing gizmo, Jack was intense. Through closed teeth he told Gordon to lay off the majority of his editors as fast as possible. That endearing thing Jack used to say— "Oh Gordon, why'd you do that?—was never repeated.

Gordon sure wished Jack would tell him what he was supposed to do with the 2,000 *Gentle Ben* albums he would soon have stacked in a warehouse. Who would want a relic like that now that the TV program had been cancelled?

South Africa here he comes.

He might've been prattling on about the editor he'd hired for *The Pink Panther Show* pilot, the one Bob had discovered passed-out drunk on the cutting room floor Monday morning without having done a lick of work. Or maybe it was about that conman distributor who had fooled Gordon into meeting him on the Strip. The man had cleverly swiped Gordon's Carte Blanche credit card, run up an $839 bill and deserted him on the street until the police came. Whatever tale Uncle Gordon was regaling my folks with at our dinner table that evening, my company wasn't required and I was better off for it.

I was nine and reasonably happy. The friends and toys I'd acquired buffered most of the emptiness of being the only child in a cavernous house. But bona fide control? You have none as a kid. You don't handpick your circumstance. You don't select the geometry of your face or the school where you've been trotted off. You certainly don't choose which relatives come and go, and that goes double for big brothers you idolize.

In 1968-69 mine had been stolen from me twice. First, Paul had fallen for a Mormon girl with a Twiggy haircut, marrying her as a twenty-one-year-old college senior at USC. (I am the kid holding his nose as I kiss the bride in their wedding photos.) The Army drafted him after graduation.

Initially I assumed Paul had lucked out because he could be a commando with his hands around a real M-16; the one I played with was a plastic, battery-operated job. Later I came to realize that Vietnam terrified the bejesus out of him and my folks. They wouldn't specifically say the word "Vietnam" anymore as much as bicker over phrases like "going to Canada on a motorcycle," whatever that meant. No one asked my opinion. As a kid, you swap lack of responsibility for having no say in things.

I realized this: Paul's military training removed him from the special occasions that brought guests to our door. "*Hello, hello,*" I could hear Judy say singsong on our stone portico that rainy night. If Judy was out there, you could bet she was with Billie, who I regarded as a wrinkly, surrogate grandma spritzed in peach perfume. And if Judy and Billie were there, a black man was behind them, craning Gordon from the front seat of his Cadillac and aligning him in his wheelchair.

Jimmy! It was sweet Jimmy who was wheeling Gordon that night. The report we later heard was that Jimmy had been laid off from Desilu during summer hiatus and that when my uncle found out, he'd waited about five seconds before offering him his old job back with a handsome raise. (Jimmy's first act was to retrieve the boss's Cad from the house of the attendant he was replacing. The attendant was so enamored with convertibles he decided to keep Gordon's.) It was a blast seeing Jimmy. He'd always shadow box with me if he had a second.

Still, why'd they have to bring that damned dog, whatever name she went by—"Chip," "Chicken," "Chicken Liver?" That thing was twelve pounds of white-fluffed, neurotic trouble. Somewhere in the reincarnation chain, I imagined a prissy French royal lynched by a mob had returned as this furball. Immediately I was ordered to lock my dog in the back porch, next to the dryer, because Chicken was finicky about the other canines she was quartered around. After supper, after I was excused early from the table to play with some spinning tops near my room, another insult flung my direction. Aunt Judy walked toward me with Chicken under her arm. "I hope you don't mind," she said benignly. "She'll be good." Judy lowered Chicken onto the floor. Next she closed the hallway door, presumably so her dog's yip wouldn't disrupt the grownups' conversation.

Her poodle had some nerve treating me like the unwanted guest. Chicken circled, growling that *I'm-queen-bitch-here* yap. Within minutes she'd marked her territory with a lift of the leg, whizzing methodically across the floor and snapping at thin air. She wasn't done intimidating, either. Hearing paws click behind her, she wrenched around her diva neck and nipped my dog, which I'd taken the liberty of releasing from its cell. Her teeth scraped Beulah's left foreleg. Biting my dog—a kid has his limits! I backhanded Chicken out of the way and galloped into the dining room to snitch on what she'd done. Maybe Judy would lock her in the car with the windows rolled up.

When I found the adults, they couldn't have cared less. Gordon was deep into last weekend's adventure, and the spotlight was his. It seems Bob and Jimmy had been helping him inventory the apartment of an elderly cousin who'd just died when two cops tipped off to intruders appeared. "L.A.P.D. Stay Where You Are!"

one said. Gordon, Jimmy and Bob were detained for ninety minutes, Gordon occasionally piping up, "Excuse me officer, but do I look like a burglar?" My mom signaled that "not now, kid" look when I tried to interrupt Gordon's finale. So I stood there and stood there until I had my own glint of genius.

I had a surprise for precious Chicken. Gordon fussed over that dog. He pampered it as if she were human, so I'd decided I would show them both. I walked from the living room into the kitchen, where Jimmy was flirting with our latest housekeeper with his elbows on the counter. The tray of appetizers I wanted—shrimp gooped with pulpy orange marmalade—was on the top shelf of the fridge. No one noticed me sneaking it into my room. I'd already stashed my dog, the multi-talented super-beagle, "Beulah," in there. Chicken protested me rounding her up, nipping my hand when I grabbed her and dashed into my room. "Too late for you," I mouthed, locking the door.

Inside, I fed Beulah the shrimp, except for one. Kneeling down, I then cornered Chicken, who seemed to suspect foul play. I trapped her between my beanbag and my red modular bookshelf, the one with the L.A. Dodger cups on top. Holding her neck, I rubbed the last shrimp on her back, getting the fur good and gooey with the sauce. Lastly I tucked the shrimp under her collar.

My idea was to make Chicken the appetizer.

"Here Beulah," I called, "here, girl. Fo-od." Beulah's paws tread lightly on the beige shag. Nose to nose with my beagle, Chicken exposed her immaculate, white choppers. She snarled again and that was her mistake. I released her neck and grabbed her snout. "Have at it, girl," I told Beulah, prodding her toward Chicken's neck. "Bite her. Get the shrimp." Beulah was neutral. "Come on," I pleaded. "Attack! She's your enemy." Beulah sniffed and looked at me vacantly. "Remember what she did to you in the hall? GO!" More tail wagging. In a last-ditch effort, I clamped Beulah's jaw over Chicken's ear and tried forcing her to bite down. "Do something." Beulah was indifferent. Stupid dog. Ungrateful dog. Where was the loyalty? I released both animals stymied again.

Everything considered, it was better there was no poodle carnage in my room that day. Gordon would have ripped into me for my plot, even in front of my parents. Me going after his defenseless *"wittle baby, poor Chicken.* What were you thinking? Tell me!" My explanation would have sounded thin. "Uncle Gordon, she bit me and Beulah. She peed on the floor." "So? So? How'd you like somebody harassing you, huh, Chip?" Actually, he never caught on. Once liberated from my room, Chicken found her master and leapt into his lap looking for protection and crumbs. I imagine Judy was perplexed on the drive home, asking Jimmy if he knew how Chicken got into the shrimp sauce.

These thirty-plus years later, I can write off this episode as something nobler than inept animal cruelty. What I wanted by taking Chicken hostage was Gordon's respect. As much as he punctured me with comments about my development, I harbored this inexplicable desire for him to take notice of me. If you could get past his gruffness, you could detect the original soul in him. You could see he had stories. Hell, he knew Gentle Ben on a first name basis. I wanted him to appreciate I wasn't so petrified of him anymore now that my brother was training for Vietnam. Wasn't I more deserving of a second chance than that spoiled terror in his lap? You betcha.

CHAPTER TWENTY-FIVE
Kid 'N' Africa

Spring 1971. Gordon had been searching for a benefactor like Nicholas Deak his entire career. Somebody with brains. Somebody with vision. Someone with the guts to lend him a few million dollars and stand back, because it was the concept that mattered, not whether its creator could clasp hands on the deal. Nicholas L. Deak was one of America's richest men. Unbelievably, he was Dirk Brink's boss, so access to him was possible.

Nicholas was a silver-haired gentleman of about seventy, strict about regular exercise and his vegetarian diet, dignified in dress and manner. During the war he had done a little spying. Later he had erected a $400-million multinational banking empire based in New York City with foreign-exchange shops around the world and a knack for trafficking profitably in risky currencies few others dared. For an L.A. businessman out for greatness in South Africa, Deak was precisely the type of gutsy financier my uncle needed to turn pipe dreams to done deals.

Dirk smoothed the introductions. A get-together was arranged. Gordon, accompanied by Bob Glenn, met Nicholas and his main lieutenant, Otto Rothenmound, in Deak-Perera's tower at 29 Broadway, where hundreds worked the phones moving money across international lines. None of those traders could've predicted that Nicholas and Gordon would have such chemistry between them. Nicholas was a native Hungarian, Gordon a boisterous second generation. Nicholas was an urbane moneyman, Gordon a can-do quadriplegic. After a couple of meetings, Nicholas invited him to upstate New York where he lived for an afternoon at the Westchester Country Club. Social talk over club sandwiches then turned to business, which drifted to South Africa, a land Nicholas intoned he knew well. (He had a house there.) Nudged by that cue, Gordon sketched his intentions, trying not to seem too desperate for Nicholas's wallet.

Gordon outlined how he was hoping to build a horseshoe-shaped, postproduction facility in Johannesburg, something in the mold of a scaled-down Universal Studios, with theaters and a performing arts center ringing the editorial facilities. He was negotiating with South African film companies about co-financing the construction if the government there promised him adequate work. He also was fine-tuning a technique where countries with polyglot populations could enjoy the same TV show simultaneously. Maybe Nicholas's holding company, Deak-Perrera, would like to be dealt in? If the mulitplexer was rejected in Johannesburg, imagine the demand in the sectarian Third World?

Nicholas listened. He lobbed a few questions. He rubbed his distinguished chin and said he would have to consult with a few people. When he called Gordon in L.A, Nicholas came right out and stated the company would have to pass on the opportunity. It just wasn't the right million-dollar investment for his bank to subsidize. He and Otto would dispense corporate advice and some personal funds, because they believed the idea had legs, but that was the extent of it. "I hope you're not too disappointed, Gordon." He answered, "Of course not, Nick," and pummeled himself for days afterwards. How many swings do you get with—and he read this in *Forbes*—one of the world's wealthiest, most influential financiers?

Weeks went by and as his dejection lifted, Gordon realized it wasn't a total write off. Nicholas Deak's name would carry weight with other investors. Nicholas laughed when Gordon, back in New York on business months later, vowed he would strong arm him for a seven-figure investment someday.

In the meantime it was default to Plan B. Through Swanee's connections, my uncle and Bob slipped into Johannesburg in June 1969 for another meeting with a heavyset executive and his top underling. Servaas Hofmeyr and Wim DeVilliers operated Sanlam Ltd., South Africa's most venerable insurance company. Sanlam, like any number of connected firms, was positioning itself for the coming of television. Gordon did his dog-and-pony show on the multiplexer for the two men. Why, he posed, let the government own what you can profit off yourself? All he was seeking was a few million in seed money. The Sanlam men smiled at each other, nodding their agreement. They were so smitten with Gordon's idea they said they intended to zoom it to their board of directors for approval.

Some definition of zooming they had. In the eighteen months before the Sanlam board took up the proposal, the world turned manically. A reform-minded Kenyan politician that Bob and Gordon chatted up at an African game resort was gunned down three days later outside a Nairobi drugstore; some people didn't want the popular Tom Mboya running for president. In the eighteen months Sanlam required, Neil Armstrong walked on the moon and Charles Manson's acolytes carried out chilling murders in the hills near Gordon and Judy's street.

But why dwell, Gordon thought? That was then. This was South Africa. It was a reason to smirk. Judy, Bob and he were on a Pan-Am-747 gliding into Johannesburg and he felt invigorated. He remembered the letters he had dictated to his music agent in England and he asked Bob for a puff off his cigarette. Brace yourself, he'd warned Danny O'Brien before he had departed for this trip. The rumblings were true. He was closing his business, within the year if he could manage it. As the jumbo jet's wheels skidded onto the tarmac, Gordon wished his L.A. captivity were already over.

Danny had received the capsule summary. General Music had been bleeding money in the two-year production bust along with the other firms. Few movies were being shot, same for TV. All you had to do was scan *Daily Variety* or drive along Santa Monica Boulevard to tally the postproduction shops with CLOSED signs hung crooked in the windows. Rest assured, Gordon said, he would survive. Adapting was his edge. After fifteen years, he was retiring from the scoring business. Mood music was his future (or one of them). He'd been dabbling in it for years and could see, having thoroughly analyzed the market, that its potential was "truly astronomical."

Danny, he wrote, secure every bit of passable European atmosphere-music you can. Together with his new distribution partners, he was on the cusp of a coast-to-coast sales effort sure to rake it in. They would package his music library—3,000 songs constantly updated, Rogers and Hammerstein to The Rolling Stones—with a state-of-the-art, eight-track tape playback system. The "Globemaster," $345 out the door, was his baby. They would sell units to the Bank of Americas and the J.C. Penneys, to Shakey's Pizza Parlors and experimental Community Access TV, a.k.a. cable television. Muzak, the behemoth of the elevator-music industry, was never more susceptible to competition. Had he mentioned this was a national effort?

The other news: next time this year he hoped to be a citizen of the beautiful Republic of South Africa. Keep that under your hat, Danny.

Judy, seated in the airplane seat next to him, would rather have been in Beverly Hills. She applied her pre-landing lipstick upset about how swiftly events were circling her. The only reason she was here was because South Africa was the second stop of a much broader trip that would droop south to Italy. But residency in South Africa as an expatriated American? Oh no thank you. She hadn't signed up for that. She chain-smoked at the mere thought she might have to swap her Blue Jay Way routine for a pastoral African one.

It had been worth raising a stink about with Gordon, a rarity for her. During one testy weekend before they'd left, she'd clarified her opposition. Just because Dirk was equating his move to South Africa as his personal salvation didn't mean they needed to emulate him. Had he thought deeply about this, about everything they would forfeit biding adieu to the States? My uncle said he had no choice. Economics, honey. He'd only been hanging on doing *Woody Woodpecker* and *Pink Panther* cartoons. As it was, he'd gutted his workforce from thirty-five to about seven, relying on temporary editors if a large job graced them.

She was aware wasn't she that he might have to sell one of his companies to prop up his other flagging operations? Judy answered of course she knew that. She appreciated they sold the old house on Shoreham, instead of continuing to rent it, to cover once-easily covered costs. "You'll soldier through," she added. "You always have before." For Pete's sake, though, what about the safety of living in the sub-Sahara? This wasn't like relocating to Montreal. She reminded him of that scene, what, nine months ago, in the backyard of Gordon's South African producer-pal.

The strapping Boet (pronounced boot) Troskie owned a blue-sky ranch in Bloemfontein, halfway between Pretoria and Capetown. Gordon was arguing with Boet in his friendly, squash-you-manner that there would be a gory uprising if the whites refused to loosen their chokehold on the black majority. "Let's see about that," said Boet. He whistled over his longtime Bantu servant and gave him a scenario. If revolution came, Boet inquired, would he slaughter his family? "Oh no," the Bantu said, anguished, upset. "I'd never do that." He thought for a minute. Then he pointed to some other Bantus servicing a farmhouse down the road and expounded, "But they would."

"Didn't that register with you?" Judy asked him. "It sure frightened me. Besides, I'm not an outdoors type of girl."

This jet ride in March 1971 was the culmination of eighteen months of baby steps. Gordon was thankful to see the Johannesburg skyline expand in the taxicab window. Someday, he bet Judy would be grateful, too. By milking Swanee's connections and being uncharacteristically patient, he had won an audience with none other than South African Prime Minister John Vorster, the leader of the government. If Vorster endorsed Gordon's invention, Sanlam would finance the deal for the multiplexer with a domino effect for the postproduction complex. He then could go house shopping in Johannesburg's modish suburbs at his own leisure. *And people said he couldn't move.*

Judy stayed behind when the taxi driver came to the lobby of the Rand International Hotel to ferry the men to their meeting. They had been rehearsing in L.A. for weeks. It would be Bob, Gordon and John Hall in the bowels of a government building demonstrating the TV-technology Gordon prayed the South African people couldn't live without.

Visualize the tautness of the scene. The government screening room was empty except for select VIPs. The hiss of machinery on standby crackled from wall-mounted speakers. Smoke from fine local cigars coiled in the projector's hot beam. Up front, plopped down in a chair with his aides, was a pudgy, bald, colorless man with bushy eyebrows and a legendary scowl.

He was a man in endless meetings, a man whose fellow Afrikaners expected him to preserve their God-sanctified white way. The United Nations had labeled his party's apartheid policies as racist and slapped trade sanctions on the country. In response, John Vorster decided to outsmart those U.N. weaklings. He would convince the international community that he was slowly liberalizing relations with the natives when in reality he would marginalize them in forced homelands. In doing that, he would honor the blood sacrifice of the ancestral Boers. He would stamp out the black terrorists in the African National Congress, too. "Jolly John" Vorster, his critics believed, was a ruler literally incapable of smiling.

The question for my uncle was whether he could be sold. A few rows behind Vorster, Gordon perspired sweat-moons into his best Oxford button-down. He was here as a salesman with a crisp presentation before packing it up. Ten minutes was all he was being allotted; Vorster's aides had briefed the Americans that the prime minister had more pressing matters of state with which to attend. They would air a three-minute clip from a recent South African movie in three different languages (Afrikaans, English and Zulu), answering questions afterwards if necessary. Protocol called for no small-talk first.

Up at the base of the room John Hall's sheet-pale face was better left unseen. The engineer stared at the black metal control box that powered the multiplexer as if staring would repair it. Here South African's big cheese was in place, and the device supposed to wow him—this black, shoebox-sized device with bristling dials and cords—was on the fritz. When my uncle nodded at John to start, John stuttered, "Give me a sec, okay?" not specifying the routing glitch bedeviling his machine. He'd never needed an extra second in rehearsals. As the minutes stretched out like an hour, Gordon licked the bile in his mouth. *Jesus, he thought. John will die a painful death if this flops. I'll do it myself.*

There was a sudden banging sound, the hollow noise of John's palm slamming the mulitplexer casing, and Vorster looked around. It was a pinching moment in a series of pinching Gordon moments. John then said confidently, "Okay, ready to go." He signaled the projectionist to roll the clips. The floor lights were cut and up on the screen it aired flawlessly: three different audio tracks, the same visual action. It was smart to show it in Afrikaans first. Delivering TV signals to the natives was what Vorster's regime wanted least.

The lights flickered on, and Vorster slowly rose from his chair. He adjusted his jacket and one of his aides gestured at my uncle. The prime minister approached. Smiling. Jolly John was smiling. *Stay calm, Zahler. Know when to shut up this time.* "Anything we can answer for you, Mr. Prime Minister?" Gordon asked. Vorster ignored the question. He cupped his meaty left hand on Gordon's shoulder, towering over him to speak. "Listen my good fellow. When we have TV, this is the system we'll use. Congratulations. Now if you'll excuse me."

In April, two months after the successful demo, Vorster publicly announced that South African TV would be operational in 1974 as part of his "outward policies" to remake his country. Sanlam, as a result, signaled their preliminary approval to Gordon's enterprise. After he worked the champagne from his system, my uncle wrote to Ivan in Europe: "1971 is going to be our turnaround year. I can feel it."

CHAPTER TWENTY-SIX
Tars and Stripes

Impatient, yes, deflated, no. As the defeats of the early 1970s pierced my uncle, the smirk never faded, though his hairline had. He was positive South Africa was his destiny, even if the *bon voyage* date was fuzzy. Up at Blue Jay Way, guests sat through his Africa slideshow giggling at the shots of the tame monkeys of Nazima Springs, Kenya, crouching on his shoulders. When the last slide clicked through, Gordon keenly reminded everyone that by stretching his money right he was picking up for South Africa. "You gotta make it over there. We'll bop up to Kenya for safari." He actually was never more Gordonesque than when he was out on his pool deck entertaining friends, flashy in red plaid trousers, twitching his shoulders, swaggering and cigarette smoking, selling Africa as his antidote for the rat race.

The rough idea was for him to reside half the year in Johannesburg, where he would split time supervising postproduction for South African TV while co-producing shows for it with Ivan. (Ivan had his own deal with the Sanlam boys and Nick Deak.) The rest of the year Gordon would be traveling, most of it

spent in California on music business. And please, no hand wringing
for Judy. She would be well taken care of in Johannesburg. She'd be
in a house better than Blue Jay Way. There'd be a new Benz for her,
and more spending money than she could count. Billie would be
flown over for the sunny season.

Those two deserved it. Lord knows his spoils were overdue.
Will had fortified him long enough. For twenty years he had waited
for something indisputably his in Hollywood. Call it sour grapes, but
he was disgusted with the shallowness of waiting for that anymore,
and increasingly leery of the grand prize if his number was picked.

He'd watched too many bright minds have their talent
compromised because they confused notoriety for achievement. The
sanest ones on the lot tended to be those farthest away from the stage.
Better late than never, he would heed his father's advice and leave
the Industry to ply his luck elsewhere. How much satisfaction could
he have accessorizing other people's stories with the same songs in
the hopes that someday, just maybe, he might produce a feature film
himself that would probably fly in and out of the theaters? Oh, but on
another continent he could reinvent himself. In a new land, he could
have control that had been so slippery.

In Africa, perhaps with his language box, perhaps with an
offshoot, he would be a pioneer. Fast as he could, he would reacquire
a grand lifestyle. His whole life had pointed to this latitude. As an
African VIP, he might finally decode the riddle of why he'd survived
his accident. Until then it was more waiting. Until then he existed
between two continents.

Naturally, people he cared about would be hurt when he jetted
off —his sister, cronies like Hugo Grimaldi and Nathan Jones. If
nothing else, they had means. He would be sending devoted
employees like Norm Pringle and Harriet von Stroheim job-hunting
in the main act of an oil-embargoed U.S. recession. Thankfully for
Harriet, she had Joe's studio salary behind her. Gordon had done
what he could for Norm. He had retained him on payroll part-time
when there was almost nothing for him to do, and applied creative
bookkeeping so he received state benefits as well. (At the Hollywood

unemployment office where Norm filed his paperwork, some applicants showed up in cowboy chaps or cancan outfits to prove they were hunting for work. A few arrived in limos.) It was Jimmy who my uncle felt guiltiest about ending things. Jimmy had left Desilu Studios as one of the first blacks in the editor's guild. Gordon's present to him, for tending him on a second go-round, would amount to offering to sell him the Cad dirt-cheap.

What else could he offer? Gordon realized that he was as disposable as any of the others. The old-time producers he'd partnered with in the 1960s were dinosaurs next to the brash generation, the Robert Evans's and Warren Beatty's in charge now. Walter Lantz, who Gordon wished would've thrown him more business, protested it was too expensive for him to produce new cartoons. Ivan was even more cynical, spending much of his time in Germany. Fare like *Midnight Cowboy*, he sermonized in a letter, was Hollywood committing "moral treason" against the planet. Definitely an upended world, all right. Richard Nixon toasting Mao Tse Tung in Peking; Gordon of Hollywood boarding up General Music.

It was best to entrench in the day-to-day, and that's what he did. As much he wanted his plane ticket to South Africa, he knew he was powerless to bend the government there to his timetable. Sanlam, his financier, was the same. The Johannesburg lawyer his partners had hired to represent them, Angus McNair, assured them the picture was rosy as ever for postproduction and the language box. There was some talk about the television start date being delayed to 1976, nothing serious.

The buzz over television had leapfrogged Afrikaner ideology about TV stealing their cultural purity, and burrowed straight into free-market greed: which companies were licensed to make the sets; who would grab a piece of the $330-million, five-year start-up funds. Stay alert, Swanee advised my uncle. The big day for General Motivations Corp., the name of their South Africa-licensed company, was nearing.

Never doubting that, he made the money he could. He cut for *Mr. Kingstreet's War*, a violent film about African poachers starring

John Saxon, and committed to two additional South African movies. Next he held auditions to find English voices for the U.S. dub of *Pippi Longstocking*, a movie about a precocious German orphan-girl you wanted to string up by her ponytails by your second viewing. Hundreds of children and their parents, many of them practicing squeaky stage voices, jammed the parking lot of the Lantz Building for the *Pippi* cattle call. That, at least, was good for a giggle on the drive home with Jimmy. Like old times, whatever job he could hustle he hustled, be it Sunsweet Prune commercials or more *Bozo the Clown* cartoons.

At their regular Monday meeting, Jack admonished him to take every scrap offered. As his accountant, Jack had seen "the document." Gordon had first read it that foggy morning when he had reached his office-bed and there, propped on his metal reading stand, was the certified letter from the state tax board. The California Board of Equalization was accusing him of cheating. They claimed he had neglected to pay taxes on $250,000 worth of payroll stemming from Ivan's shows. Translation: he was on the hook for $70,000 he didn't have.

No problem, he thought. He downed a steak sandwich at Nicodell's the day of the tax letter to remind himself this financial mess would be a hiccup next time this year. South African consular officials were flying down from San Francisco at the end of the week for a firsthand briefing on his intentions. The week after that Boet Troskie and his director, the talented, withdrawn Jamie Uys (pronounced ace), were arriving in town. They would expect him to show off his homeland as they had shown off theirs for him. Gordon resolved that's where his head should be, impressing his guests, not biting his fingers over a tax dispute Jack would wrestle down.

From the open air of his convertible sedan, my uncle introduced his South Africans to early 1970s Southern California they would brand later as enchanting and immoral. Freeways, Hells Angels, hot pants, pot smoke, airport Hare Krishnas, Rodeo Drive: the people who met Gordon's foreigners said the L.A. sensory overload gave them perpetually blank faces. Equally discombobulating was their host. They speculated about him over brandies at the hotel bar. How was it this man who came up to their beltline could get them waved onto the Paramount Pictures lot to observe filming of a multimillion-dollar movie so out of their own league? How was it he always picked up the dinner tab? They reasoned a cripple could do anything in America, just as a black man was allowed to hold hands with a white girl in public. That touching was forbidden where they came from. There would no race riots, either, not with *their* police. Otherwise delightful sorts, the South Africans grimaced at integrated California such as it was. They fidgeted when left alone in the same room with Jimmy. Asked about apartheid, one of them lectured that the real difference between their two lands was that "they hadn't killed their Indians." (South African "Indians" were the blacks.)

After his guests flew home, Gordon parroted their line about how different things were racially in their country compared to America. The few full-timers he employed rolled their eyes and turned back to their machines. Let them, he decided. He'd already predicted to his Afrikaner chums that apartheid was a dead-end: "Just remember I told you if I'm not around."

It was one of those limbo days between Christmas 1972 and New Years 1973, before anyone had heard of the Watergate hotel, when it all blew up. A neighbor kid named Greg Wright had accused me of one spectacularly unfunny prank. His father, an M.D., phoned my dad early in the aftermath to encourage him to dole out a lasting punishment to me because "somebody might've been hurt."

I don't remember the specifics of my allegedly dastardly deed, though it seemed to bear some relationship to Greg's bike or the Wright-family garage. Porous as my recall is about that, I'm as sure of my innocence today as I was then. The accusation was unfair, I implored my folks, whatever my track record for mischief might indicate. Greg was lying, or framing me, or put up to it by Karen, his zit-faced sister who was always trying to kiss me at the school bus stop. "I didn't do it," I said. "Believe me." The rub? Mom was skeptical. Dad took my word.

They quarreled mildly in front of me about which kid's story was accurate until the fight reverted to their relationship. Seeing me, their eleven-year-old, glued to the action, they transferred their argument to their remodeled bedroom suite at the rear of the house. A sliding wood door was shut, which made my eavesdropping imprecise.

Voices attacked. Objects were hurled onto marble counters. There would be a hint of calm, which made me think they'd made up, and then there'd be yelling again in accusatory bursts lasting twenty seconds or more. It was a curious volley, my father being a distinct non-yeller. Nonetheless, my folks had been wrangling a lot in recent months, tossing grenades at each other's motives. They explained it to me by noting every couple had their friction. True, but the squabble over Greg vs. Me went on for about forty-five minutes with no winner declared.

The frost that blew through their union afterwards is what stuck. You could detect it by the stiffness in they how spoke to the other about the toast having popped and their jerky, paranoid movements around the house. Until that day, I'd never realized how much scar tissue my parents had between them.

A few days later, on the morning of January 2, 1973, the radio announced USC was college football's national champs. The team had annihilated Ohio State in the Rose Bowl 42-17 the day before. Tailback Anthony Davis was my idol right behind Bobby Chandler. It was sacred to be a Trojan swathed in cardinal and gold. That afternoon my parents asked me to come into the living room for their own announcement.

My rump was barely down on the ottoman before they said as unpleasant as their news sounded it was all for the better. "Chip, this has nothing to do with you..." The spongy part of me knew the hammer was falling. My folks tried rationalizing their decision to separate, bumbling and stumbling, a sniffle here and there, a broken couple aiming for that old soft landing. They positioned they were "taking a vacation from the other" but I recognized the permanence of what was occurring. My dad's suitcase, upright in the hallway, meant divorce. This meant I'd be one of those zombie-eyed kids handed back and forth on the weekends. It was so long family, nice knowing ya. This had a lot to do with me.

Guess what? Your mind's eye can surprise you with the angles it can take. In my own moment of numbness I floated on the ceiling, like Charlie in *Willie Wonka and the Chocolate Factory*, with an overhead view of our living room. I could watch my dad rub his temples, my mom practically eat her cigarette, both good souls with incompatible temperaments suffocating on the modern furniture they'd picked out together.

Even stranger, I could observe myself tumble off the ottoman in my faded-blue shirt and saffron cords as I rolled on the carpeting in hysterics where the white-flocked Christmas tree had just been. There I go, between the fireplace hearth and the overstuffed chair, sobbing. Sobbing, "No, no, no, no. Anything but this, please." I'd roll to the right, up to the feet of one of them, then to the other, as timber might in a wild river. "Dad, don't leave. Daaaaaaaad." This being out-of-body, I admit, was a nifty effect. Too bad it was powerless to alter the outcome of my national-championship Tuesday.

Two weeks later my dad was gone and the hits kept sheeting down. Beulah, my droopy-faced beagle, vanished mysteriously. This wasn't one of those times she saw the back door cracked open and made her break to sift through the neighbors' trashcans for vittles. She'd been gone two full days without even a distant howl to indicate she was in the vicinity. Why now, I asked myself? Why'd she have to abandon me now? She was the only family member I trusted anymore. "Fluffy," a gray-striped tiger cat demoted in the attention chain when we got Beulah, also was missing. Both animals had disappeared on the same morning with their food untouched. It was as if they'd been abducted as part of a joke on me. I suspected that snitching Greg Wright.

Yet a happy face was expected. Mom and I were obliged to entertain a houseguest, the son of Gordon's director-friend, South African Jamie Uys. Jamie's boy's name was pronounced "Why-nan." He was probably fourteen, which put him a few years older and a

couple inches taller than me. He was an intelligent, sunny kid with a
gargling Afrikaans accent, the worst bowl haircut I'd ever seen and
an affinity for navy-blue knee pants regardless of weather. Judy had
said I would love him. He had starred in one of his dad's movies (one
I'd later find out involved him as a plane-wreck survivor tricked into
eating his own dog). Obviously, you didn't meet kids like Why-nan
on the playground every day. Neither do you lose your dad on-site
and your dog in the same month. The missing is what mattered to
me, not the foreign kid in our guestroom. Leave it to Uncle Gordon to
muddy the issue.

While Why-nan stayed behind, my mom and I drove to five
animal shelters looking deep into the filthy concrete stalls for what
was ours. We tacked up "Pet Missing" fliers, usually over someone
else's, on every greasy telephone pole around. On day four, the
County Animal Control, which collects dead animals in bulky, white
trucks, told us to stop pestering them, they would call us. They never
did. No one was searching for our pets except for us, which was bad
news for the animals.

For the first time, my mom and I were conscripted into service
together. We'd always had a flammable relationship. There was a
well-established history of us getting along silky smooth until I'd
crossed a threshold misbehaving or defying her. Then beware.
Mom's anger, the one she'd inherited from her Old World dad, took
possession of her. I'd inherited some of that temper, too. Instead of
discussing why I'd erred, we would square off like an old married
couple, mostly in front of her bathroom sink, to rocket hurtful
accusations at each other. This would be followed by three or four
days of strenuous, silly, not-speaking to the other. Could we break
that pattern with two small lives on the line? We had to. It was up to
us, deprived of my dad's Socratic logic, to retrieve the family we still
had.

Meanwhile, it was somebody's brainstorm, probably Judy's, for
my mom and I to show Jamie's kid around. If memory serves, we
took a drive along Pacific Coast Highway in Malibu, circled the Rose
Bowl, wasted time at a Disney movie and spent an afternoon at a

second-rate theme park, Knott's Berry Farm. In me, Why-nan discovered a sullen host indifferent about these trips or driveway soccer games. Every hour spent with him was an hour less for dwelling on Beulah. When Judy came to pick him up, it was see you later, bye, door slammed. I could pity myself properly now. The odds of my dog magically pawing at the screen door seemed infinitesimal. She'd been missing a week.

The day after Why-nan left I spent moping in front of the TV watching *Gilligan's Island* reruns. Around mid-afternoon, my mom ordered me to flick off the set. She decided there was an old lamp in the boathouse she needed. It couldn't wait, she said, and she drafted me to carry it up the hill for her. *Zippity do-dah,* I thought, *a Christmas vacation for the ages.* I followed her as she half-walked, half-skidded down the weedy embankment leading toward the structure that almost twenty years later, wildfire would reduce to charred slag. Asphalt pebbles crunched as we walked up to the barn-like door. It was colder down here, shadowy.

Talking to herself, my mom swore. "Oh, which key is it, damn it?" You could see she was trying to keep herself intact; this was dad's territory. She jammed a couple wrong candidates into the lock and stomped her foot. She located the right key on the wood-block key chain, a minor triumph in itself, and strained turning it in the rusty lock. Her hand yanked down on the mechanism. There was a shuffling inside the boathouse, too. *Pfffft.* It went *Pfffft.* The lock plopped opened. Just as it did, a rivulet of yellow liquid seeped under the door. *Fluid? Why would there be fluid?*

I grabbed the metal handle and threw open the door. Who should poke her head into the afternoon chill that mid-January day but one dehydrated, emaciated, panting, blinking, half-dead, best-friend beagle? She had peed when she heard us outside. For seven days and six nights, she had survived the musty, dark environment with no food and barely a drop of water. Beulah wobbled over to me and fell into my arms, shivering wildly, and it was the most alive I'd ever felt.

Five cans of Alpo and a quart of milk later, Beulah had her legs under her and I was a new boy. It was then my mom rapped her own forehead and hurried toward our backyard. She said she had to check the bomb shelter, a narrow, two-room concrete space my dad had constructed under our lanai after the Cuban Missile Crisis. No longer worried about Armageddon, we stored our inflatable pool toys there, not post-nuclear rations. When mom returned from downstairs, she cradled a zonked Fluffy cat under her arm.

Mom admitted that afternoon the lost pets had been her doing. It was totally her fault. Though I was furious with her then, it took bravery to concede that. She didn't loft the obvious excuse—that her husband of thirty years had left her and she was a bad hair day away from a nervous breakdown. She just said "how dumb" she was for not thinking of it days ago. She had been rummaging in the bomb shelter and the boathouse a week earlier and unbeknownst to her the animals must have blithely padded in behind her. When she'd locked the door, they'd been locked in. There you have it: we had hunted for the animals across the metropolitan grid while the whole time they were within the sound of our voices.

I wish I could say the moral of Beulah and Fluffy's survival inspired me to ride out my parent's marital problems with a valor I carried into adolescence. I wish I could say it prodded me toward Uncle Gordon, who might've soldered perspective into me about mining the courage to eat like a pig at the opportunity trough while pitying the squares worried about you getting stomach aches. I wish I could say I sought advice from his own hurt, but I can't. Nuzzling up to him was the last avenue I sought.

I was so traumatized by sick irony that once the euphoria of Beulah's return passed I retreated into myself in destructive new manners. Bullies I should've hauled off and punched back went unpunished. Report cards that should've shined, and later did, languished, while my knack for getting in trouble multiplied. In our coming visits to Blue Jay Way, where Gordon would exhort my mom that she was stronger than her separation, I faked interest in his telescope in the living room to avoid self-expression. Fate had shown me who was boss. It had knocked me on my can. My dad walking out on the Trojans' big day. My dog almost starving to death yards from my room. This stuff wasn't make-believe.

Judy was in deep. As the years lapsed, and as Gordon's business frustrations warped what remained of his mojo, he had become more cantankerous toward her. He might ask her to dial the number of an associate he needed to catch and if she hadn't done it by the third request, he would go volcanic. "*Ju-dee.* Christ, all mighty. Do it, already!" His tantrums usually sprang from missed phone conversations, over-tipping and car repairs, inconsequential issues out of the moment.

Unlike their earlier era, when his charisma and remarkable will softened his despotic growls, the latest Gordon had a brutish dimension. While he loved Judy madly, doleful she had to scurry for his basic needs, he also seemed to license himself to bully her, particularly when it involved him waiting. It was as if he gauged his life fuel was low, and assumed she would forgive him for his barrages once he was gone. People noticed. Bob Glenn rapped him, as did my father, for his sulfuric meltdowns. Gordon responded he had to raise his voice as a "wakeup" to her because when Judy bumbled a request, he'd bumbled, too.

Some of Judy's girlfriends encouraged her to retaliate to the browbeating, but she was only interested in classifying it. Surliness enflamed by a bout of poor health or office stresses she accepted and always had. It was his resistance to ease off his gratuitous demeaning of her around company that bruised her cheery view of their life together. "Hurry it up with that drink, will ya?" She hated thinking of herself as his doormat after the almost two to three hours of nursemaiding his body required *every day.* She battled her imagination not to dwell on what she had relinquished in marrying him. Sometimes it soothed her hearing he had been churlish around the office. Even so, she had to live with it.

By the early 1970s, Gordon pushed Judy to limited acts of revenge—the periodic cold shoulder, the intentionally scorched roast.

When he lit into her at a Christmas bash at an editor's house over a road map error, Judy did what nobody thought she would. She shoved his wheelchair into the corner while Perry Como blared from the hi-fi and left him for fifteen minutes of isolation until he apologized sheep-faced for being a prick. Judy didn't attempt more. She loved him too much and relied on his money and brains too greatly to consider a formal ultimatum. It was the uncertainty within her that was her x-factor. Would her mental capacity to withstand his cruel streak simply flicker out one day? Flicker out so she had no choice except separation?

The thing was, just when Judy was raw he softened the damage with a gold tennis bracelet or another timely surprise. On a business swing through Europe, he veered off to the French Riviera because Judy always had wanted to see Cannes and stroll along the Promenade des Anglais like a continent-hopping sophisticate.

He hired a driver and they toured Pablo Picasso's village. That night he dined her at a famous, brick restaurant where they ate a table away from Natalie Wood and Robert Wagner. They drained a $200 bottle of Chardonnay, yeah $200, tightwad's heresy. Later on the trip, after a glorious day of sightseeing with him, Judy nodded her head in their Florence hotel room listening to him wax forth about one of his German music deals. It was there, she told girlfriends, that she fell in love all over again with her little hero.

And, she could see, her hero needed compassion. The good fortune that aligned itself with him in the sixties had torn away from its moorings. A lowlife editor who hid in the office until everyone went home for the night popped the trunk to his car and stole $30,000 worth of General Music's best editing gear. Two brothers from the mega-wealthy J. Paul Getty family who met with him about producing a movie had no access to the family's millions. During the next few years, while he rummaged for a winner at home or overseas, that's how it went: whiff. Sometimes this whiffing was so ludicrously all-pervading you had to watch where you walked. Dorothy Garner, Gordon's fun-loving secretary, fell prey to it when she stopped by the *Gentle Ben* set in Florida on vacation only to have part of the bear's metal cage conk her in the head while workers dismantled it. Slightly hurt, she threatened to sue Ivan's insurer until someone paid her off to make the incident go away.

Worse, Gordon's own half-baked ideas eclipsed his potential breakthroughs like never before. There was the newfangled surveillance camera he intended to mass produce, the *Dr. Dolittle* cartoon he would make, the pop records he wanted to record, and then the album to teach the English Las Vegas-style Roulette. Trying to spark something, he, Hugo and one of Ivan's producers approached Sonny Bono at his house about starring in a feature film about a peasant and a Texas oilman. Sonny said no to the part in *Antonio*. Trini Lopez said yes.

It might have been when Gordon persuaded New York comedienne Joan Rivers into taping a series of radio comedy bits that Judy grasped there was more than bad luck at work here. Long before she was an awards-show fashion goddess, Rivers was a hard-working stand-up happy to lampoon her own horsy face and yenta travails if it got her bookings. Her years in the Borscht Belt nightclubs and Greenwich Village cabarets seasoned her so well she wisecracked her way into being Johnny Carson's regular fill-in.

My uncle's flash was to package and sell her routines as a new concept for drive-time radio. Stuck in traffic, urban commuters could be treated to five-minute comedy shows, and the radio stations would bookend advertising around it. For a month, Rivers and Edgar, her stolid husband/manager, came to General's Music no-frills studio for the recordings, which were done in a "Dear Abby" format. Gordon pumped everybody up about selling the concept at an upcoming radio convention at the Beverly Hills Hilton.

He intended to rent a hotel room, where syndicators would make their pitch to outbid one and other for the rights to my uncle's latest can't-miss scheme. Millions of American drivers squished in gridlock to him translated into hundreds of millions of dollars in ad revenues. He was so cocksure that he had his winner with his radio comedy that he occasionally tried instructing Rivers how to deliver her punch lines. The real yucks was in how Rivers accepted it. "Get him (Gordon) the hell out of here," she'd order Jimmy. "Let me work with Norm."

Rivers's material for the pilot welded G-rated raunchiness with middle class uneasiness about the shifting times. She'd say of course "little Johnny" couldn't read; he was dropping his chalk all day to look up the dress of his panty-less teacher. In her mind, feminists who burned their bras during the sexual revolution were extremists, and that's why she only burned one cup.

But as with everything then, Gordon misfired because he'd focused too hard on the sizzle and not enough on the steak. The syndicators wanted 200 bits already taped, plus other provisions he hadn't contemplated. Gordon, they concluded, was nowhere close to delivering a finished product. He and Rivers parted sour on the other with nobody chuckling "oh well."

Worse, his shotgun approach to projects also diverted attention from what might've been his most original creation yet. The application was so ahead of its time it probably came across as whacko novelty to the orthodox corporations of the 1970s.

The sizeable idea came to him visiting a store. His plan required him to hire a stable of classically trained actors, preferably ones with baritone voices. An actor pal of his, Harlen Carraher of *The Ghost and Mrs. Muir,* had agreed to lend his throat to the venture. Working with the publishing houses, Gordon would select a few best-selling books, scour them for their most riveting passages and rehearse the actors until they could dramatically narrate the excerpts in his studio. Swooping in for the sale would be a cinch. The big bookstores could use the excerpts (provided they bought his Globemaster tape player to broadcast them on) as three-and-a-half-minute, in-store promotions. *Tada*: customers would be able to get the flavor of a novel without turning a page! Or the bookstores could purchase thirty-second clips for radio ads. Airlines could contract for longer versions for in-flight entertainment. Sooner or later he would have entire books narrated and take it retail.

What he had stumbled upon then is the backbone of the multimillion-dollar books-on-tape industry today. In 1972 Gordon had nibbles from Dayton Hudson Booksellers, Pan Am, American Airlines and a couple of publishing houses. Bristol Meyers and U. S. Steel expressed interest in sponsoring it. So where did this all lead, this hard sell of his "Book Mark" project? It led to enthusiastic promises by many of the corporations that they would evaluate it in-depth because they had never heard of such a concept.

They just needed time he couldn't afford. Judy finally appreciated how crazed Gordon was for money that evening in late 1972. Jimmy wheeled him in through the kitchen door, past the brushed-steel appliances, and my uncle looked vanquished with his tie unknotted. He'd gone through with it, he acknowledged. Jack had forced him.

They had gone over the profit and loss statement that morning, and he'd signed the paperwork at a "horrible" meeting that very afternoon. Judy fixed him a scotch while he emceed his capitulation. He hadn't expected to do this, he kept saying. Then again, he'd never anticipated the South Africans would string out the approvals this long.

If he ever hoped to make money off his Book Mark idea or his tape player, he needed up-front cash to market them. Consequently, he'd surrendered half the future profits on his best moneymaker, Globe Music Corp., plus an option to sell the company in exchange for a $200,000-loan and an employment contract for himself.

The buyer was a closed circuit TV outfit called Project-7 Inc. A domineering old New Yorker named Bernhard was the admiral. A son Gordon labeled a "competent sharpie" was president. They wanted their mitts on Globe's 5,550-song catalogue because the background music business was exploding and if they took their company public it would help jack up the stock price, among other benefits. Essentially, Gordon explained, he was corporate prey. His financial distress had gotten around.

"Want to know the insult to injury?" he asked Judy.

"The way you've described it, I can't imagine there is one."

"There is. At the end of the meeting Bernhard's kid came around the conference table and kissed me smack on the forehead.

He did it in front of the lawyers and everything."

"That's strange."

"No, it was humiliating. It was his way of saying, 'I feel for ya, buddy.'"

Sad-sack tales like this persuaded Judy she could never leave him, even if she romanticized about it after a bad day.

CHAPTER TWENTY-SEVEN
Fire Trap

My timing had a leg up on Gordon's. In June 1995, while O.J. Simpson's murder trial was bobbing towards celebrity acquittal, I was recruited by the region's second largest paper to be an investigative reporter. At first blush, the *Daily News of Los Angeles* and I were meant to be. *The Los Angeles Times* bureau where I'd been freelancing was being eliminated. Kate also was pregnant with the second daughter we later almost lost, meaning I needed healthcare and a paycheck. I'm in, I told them: I'd take the job.

Reporter-friends were unsure whether to congratulate me or marshal their sympathies. The *Daily News* had a reputation for chasing subjects *The Times* wouldn't touch, and with bulldog verve. Headlines skewering numbskull bureaucrats and union avarice made its copy read like blood sport. You want liberal highbrow? Buy the *New Yorker*. The *Daily News* catered to beer-swilling suburbanites who liked their taxes low.

Its newsroom was a vast, windowless expanse where you couldn't see the back wall and the air conditioning never stopped blowing frost. Editors inside this squat, mirrored building on the western edge of the San Fernando Valley were notorious for playing head games with their scribes. Blow a deadline or worse—get scooped—and they'd be on you like crows picking off field mice. The weak rarely lasted. There was something about being the stepchild to the patrician *Times* that liberated *Daily Newsites* to shuck off pretense and be their feral selves. Pounce or be pounced.

I couldn't wait to start. This big paper was after me—me: the smart-ass son of a self-made man who viewed newspaper writing as a grubby profession but buoyed me when he could; me: the one who avoided the family business that had gold-plated my way because real estate felt too provincial as my way to matter. Like Gordon, I'd wandered and dabbled as a late bloomer searching for my own moonlit heather. Now I knew. Journalism engrossed me the way hard-nosed land negotiations grabbed my father. Proving oneself begins in the chest. I had to play to my nature.

The *Daily News* was freighted with characters that tested it. I befriended a hectoring police reporter in blue jeans named Jaxon and answered to an editor whose eye twitched metrically when you had a hot lead. The paper showcased your material if you could support it, too. Yes, there was pressure. Sure, I thought my stories should have been published without a copy-editor pawing them first. But seeing your name on top of the front page, telling yourself you'd stopped something shady, was narcotizing. It was a vanity rush. I wrote about corruption and stupidity on L.A.'s billion-dollar subway and about a deadly, sham experiment by honest-to-God rocket scientists. I did a long piece on the latest Hollywood Entertainment Museum, which prompted a state attorney investigation, and about the misleading loan practices of the city's redevelopment agency — stories the mayor trumpeted.

It was after a year on the job that the *Daily News* meat grinder sucked me into its blades. Our veteran city editor was deposed in a shakeup of the entire metro desk and suddenly nobody knew who held the power. Nobody knew who the new darlings were. My own editor, who had professed such fondness for me, was demoted, and I felt she double-crossed me by aligning herself with a talented female reporter.

In lieu of playing the game smarter, I moped like a wounded Boy Scout. I told myself it was the stories that mattered, not alliances. Behind glass doors, there were whispers about me being a primadonna who took too long on stories. Most definitely I was out as the flavor of the month.

Like my grandma would when life rabbit-punched her, I clean obsessively when down. My older brother Paul calls it "going Hazel." It's the family defense mechanism. Someone gets hurt. Something gets polished. One evening, needing a diversion from the paper, I was attacking my home filing cabinet when my fingers pinched a hard object in a slim plastic baggie. Curious, I fished it out of the drawer. I twirled it in the artificial light. This black object had the size and consistency of a spent charcoal briquette. The boathouse's last remain weighed almost nothing. Everything else had been carted away. I'd stuffed the lump of charred wood in my Levi's the night of the fire and had forgotten about it going on three years. Now I shook it out of the baggie. It still smelled of mesquite and destruction. How I made the connection I'm not sure, but I knew my mom needed to see what I'd dug up. I reckoned it would do her good. Maybe she would believe it'd come from her dad's piano, a souvenir worth caressing.

On my next visit to the Mesa she examined the remnant with a tired wistfulness, eyeing it like an old friend's obituary. She was done sentimentalizing the piano, and wanted me to know it. She popped out of her orange desk chair, an apricot-shaped seat from which she'd paid bills for twenty years but done little else. "Follow me," she called. "I want to show you something."

For a seventy-six-year-old woman with failing hips, she walked briskly toward the guestroom closet. She pointed up at the shelf to a cardboard box stuffed with letters and keepsakes I never knew existed. She had me take it down and lay it on the rug. Her wrinkled fingers strummed through the box until they flitted over a yellowing manila envelope marked "Dad" on front. She removed a dozen 8"x 10" black-and-white photos, stacking them on the box's edge. "Here," she said, "you might be interested in these." Then she left.

Glossy black-and-white pictures of my grandfather at work in 1930s Hollywood stared back at me. Studio photographers had snapped them for posterity and publicity. In each shot, Lee Zahler is seated behind the wood-scuffed instrument that had been the family's mint. In one frame, taken years before Gordon's accident, Lee's intensity jumps off the sheet. He is rehearsing four costumed actors in a faux prison cell, the quartet singing as a burglar, an undershirt-clad crook, a fatso lawyer in a bowtie and an Irish bowery cop. Their arms are slung over each other's in hambone unison.

These men are sweating for harmony to please my grandpa, and his eyes are pale-blue lasers monitoring their effort. Lee's passion to get perfect a movie song nobody would ever hum riveted me. I wanted to get a closer look at it, and I peeled up the shot from the photo album careful about not tearing history.

When the picture gave way, I discovered something tucked underneath an adjacent still. It was a small, personal photograph that must've been mistakenly mixed up with the studio shots. The picture showed my dome-headed grandfather in white duck pants with his arm looped around his son. It was a Gordon I'd never seen before.

My uncle probably was about eleven then, and nearly as tall as his dad. You can see in his impish face, beneath his unruly bangs, adolescence preparing to sweep in. In absorbing how Gordon might've looked had he not been hurt, I felt a dumbfounding current spread through me. It was in Gordon's cowlick and the way he smiled crookedly with the sun blistering into his face. It was how he leaned. Then I knew. If you swapped my picture with his, it could've been me standing next to Lee Zahler in that shot. Our appearances were almost identical at that same age. When my mom returned, I mentioned the resemblance, and she remarked how lucky it was the pictures hadn't been in the boathouse on the terrible day it went up.

Not long after those pictures rooted into me, I was reeling one in for the *Daily News*. I'd received a tip about a local politician who'd allegedly swapped public funds to pull himself out of hock. It reeked. This assemblyman had received a sizable personal loan from an underling whose salary had miraculously tripled while the state oozed red ink. Coincidence? Bill Hoge, then up for re-election, was a fire-breathing conservative who sat on a couple of key committees. The $10,000-plus-loan he took from his aide was doubly spicy because Hoge had a reputed history of gambling problems. I pushed full bore on the story, finishing it quickly, because two other papers were chasing it. I expected a page one story. I'd gotten them with less.

The article that appeared made my ears burn red. Without my consent, the paper's chief editors had twisted what I'd written into election-time mudslinging over Hoge's conduct. The brass delayed the story as well, costing me a scoop, burying it on page four when it did run. Why they would hurt themselves like that I'll never understand. Maybe it was because Hoge backed what the newspaper desired most—for its zone of influence, the San Fernando Valley, to secede from the city of Los Angeles, so the *Daily News* would be top dog journalistically. Maybe it was something else, something personal.

Whatever their motive, I used it to box in my future. I called a contact at *The L.A. Times* and inquired about any openings. Serendipity must've owed me, because there was a vacancy right in my wheelhouse: investigative reporter for their Valley operation. The man I spoke to scheduled my interview at an area rib joint. He stressed the meeting had to be hastened, as I was a late applicant within a heap of competition, including a Pulitzer Prize winner from Florida. Hearing I had a chance, I had to bite my tongue from shouting yahoo. I didn't want to telegraph my delirium to any colleagues I might leave behind.

On interview day, I arrived at the restaurant a half-hour early aiming to rope a nice booth where I could dazzle *The Times'* guys about what a gem I was. Kid Unstoppable—that's me. What I lacked in pedigree I'd offset with chutzpah and craft. How people loved telling me their secrets. Sitting in my car I daydreamed my entire past was a crescendo to this lunch. Anybody with smarts and hustle can be a reporter.

Only *The Times* welcomes the elite. I wanted to be one of them, if not for the status of being big-time then for the vindication that my blossoming was worth the wait. I wanted to be the straying-son-done-good, rather than the one who weaseled out of advanced high school chemistry for fear of blowing it. My dad's sharp-eyed view had never known what to make of me, and the older I got the more a direct reaction to him I became. He analyzed tasks painstakingly before he acted. I yelled "Geronimo" and leapt. I needed *The Times* job so he'd see what I'd become from uncertain ingredients. I craved that feeling, soaked in its radiance, me busting into the majors with only a handful of years in the business. What stories would I tackle first? — Russian submarines off the California coast, the dirt LAPD had on local bigwigs. *The Times'* gray-marble headquarters is where my own one great thing awaited.

Basking about it overran my days. I obsessed over it so much that I could barely focus on who did what in the stories I was doing for the *Daily News*, or the daily happenings with my little one at home. This was the largest metropolitan paper west of the Mississippi, and my competitive ache to prove I belonged there felt like fever in my bone marrow.

Next to *The Times'* gig, writing about Gordon and my grandfather's intrigues only could be my consolation prize, the complimentary blender. And that's the deal I squared with myself. If *The Times* rejected me, I would throw myself at my family's saga, because there was undoubtedly more in there than my mother let on. Even so, my reverie to have my first choice win out was so consuming that when I snapped out of it I noticed my car windows were rolled up in stupefying heat and the car radio was on a Mexican sports station. Wanting something desperately weaves you into a cocoon. As I walked across the parking lot, the earth felt as though it was spinning half-speed under my shoes.

Inside the Northridge Tony Roma's, I sat with the men from *The Times*, both of whom were named John. I listened to their presentation and mouthed my own while we downed enough greasy ribs and onion rings to flat-line an elephant. The meeting climaxed with the top-John saying my clips impressed and that he wanted me to speak ASAP with the paper's editor-in-chief downtown. He said I was a top candidate. "Congratulations…Eat up!"

Every time my phone would ring afterwards I hoped it would be John No. 1. He was a bear of a man my instincts told me I could trust. When it wasn't him calling, I mentally cursed whoever had. Two weeks stretched out and I'd heard nothing about scheduling my second interview. I decided I'd show them how badly how I wanted it. I started phoning John No. 1 every few days to update him about my schedule or another bravura story idea. Just before we hung up,

I'd coyly ask about the status of the job he knew was the sole purpose for our conversation. Cool your jets, he'd remind me. These things take time. The paper's elders had to be consulted. A manic feeling creased into my chest. I conjured silly what-ifs. I imagined how sticky sweet the ink on my new business card would smell. Later in bed, I tried shushing the pesky voice calling me an opposite direction to plumb family mysteries. I pretended I couldn't hear it.

When another scorching October arrived, warm Santa Anas gusts blew on schedule. Paranoia rode the updrafts. As sure as those once-blackened hillsides, locals know that a spark from a lawnmower or lightning strike could ignite a wind-driven brushfire that destroys for days. L.A.'s fringe crowd swears its worse. It believes the Santa Anas carry a kind of malevolent electricity that murmurs to serial killers and child molesters, if not the general populace. To me, the winds ruffle another message: everything is flammable. So when my *Daily News* boss told me to run over to the TV, I knew the circle was complete. It'd been exactly three years since Altadena had burned.

This new blaze had begun in the unpopulated grasslands around the Santa Monica Mountains before exploding into Malibu Canyon on a flickering-orange conga dance toward the ocean. Chaparral roasted, not panic. The old-timers inured to fires and mudslides in these plunging hills acted inconvenienced by the ruckus. They knew this bastard would be contained before it got to their steps. Unlike the last big fire, authorities were throwing everything at it. As for me, I just didn't care. This disaster wasn't personal. I watched fire-fighting planes scoop ocean water into their potbellied hulls. I talked to smokejumpers asleep on their feet. It was an exciting diversion from waiting for *The Times*.

Once the firebreaks were in place, I was assigned to visit a twisting residential street ringed with celebrity showplaces high up in the Malibu hills. Capture the "incident," my editors told me. A TV news van was leaving as I pulled up. Mouth-breathing tourists clicked pictures as if it were Disneyland, because news had been made here. A day earlier, four firefighters had been badly singed defending estates they'd never be able to afford themselves. They'd been manning hoses around one house, an exquisite glass-framed mansion protruding over the cliff, as hotspots crackled in the gorges. The men had trained incessantly for heat, wind and fire. Yet when the Santa Anas blasted Coral Canyon with hellish velocity in an afternoon gust, the flames rode the wind and scalded the men before they could find shelter. They were supposed to know better than stand uphill of a brushfire. One of them clung to life in a local burn unit with cadaver skin dressing his wounds.

A few days later, the suspense about my future was too much to wait on. I drove to the flatlands and found a payphone in a throwaway building near Pacific Coast Highway. I called *The Times* and asked for John No. 1. I was nervous Nellie during the five-minute eternity it took to get him on the horn. I decided whoever invented Muzak should have his gene pool eradicated. Other people started waiting to use the phone, and one of them was a construction redneck sneering at me for how long I was taking. *Tick-tock.*

Finally, John came on. His manner was stiffly functionary, none of that garrulous good-timer he'd been at the rib joint. If his day was bad before, it was getting no better now. My call required him to mix in bad tidings with boilerplate loser-phrases about "stiff competition" and how they'd keep "watching me." The Pulitzer guy from Florida had been selected.

I placed the receiver into its cradle, and slumped against the wall. I would be canceling plans to sashay into my father's office to brag. Part of me wanted to confront the redneck. All those other life defeats I'd shrugged off before as bum luck or poor timing now formed a clear mosaic of who I was. Losing *The Times* job had positioned me indelibly on the talent pool. I was good, just not good enough.

I waited for the ego crash in the days that followed and wondered if I was just numb when despair merely hovered on my margins. Was this my psyche's gift—sparing me from the truth about myself? Each time I felt like crawling into a dark room and not coming out, my mind wouldn't let me. It kept transporting me someplace far afield of my self-doubt. It took me to those cliffs over Malibu.

Standing where blood had spilled from those firemen, I had watched the sun glint regally off the Pacific. Hawks dipped back into the canyons squealing they were home. It was up there that a serenity I'd never known had warmed my nerve endings. What had been ineffable so long became crisply plain. It was only now that I deciphered it. If logic mattered, if physics counted, this should've have been the third anniversary of my death on that Pasadena hillside under my father's oaks. I'd been in the crosshairs of that billowy orange curtain with no place to run. People who loved me would've been getting on with their lives by now, my obituary notice buried under that day's junk mail.

But there had been no funeral. No, the universe had brought me here to Malibu to remind me it had let me live. The invisible hand had shown up again. This is why I hadn't gone to *The Times*. I had to lose that dream job to make a more enduring one come alive. The exhilaration of accepting the calling I'd tried so long to ignore, the excavation of one Gordon Zahler, made my old career pangs seem like scrap metal.

In late October 1996, I walked into the managing editor's office at the *Daily News* and told him I was leaving to write my book about Gordon. I'd only been his reporter for eighteen months. Ron Kaye, who'd always reminded me of a mad scientist being slowly poisoned by his own experiments, removed his dark bifocals. A wall-mounted picture of one of his icons, Marlon Brando, glowered at me. So did Mr. Kaye. "I'm sorry to hear that," he said of my departure. "There was still a lot for us to teach you."

CHAPTER TWENTY-EIGHT
The Lost Jungle

It was his best performance to date, Oscar-caliber really. Gordon was $35,000 in debt and potentially ten times that amount. From San Francisco to Stuttgart, partners he'd fostered a robust camaraderie with over the years insisted he repay them, to hell with the excuses. The California tax board towed the same line. Every week came barbed letters where the money he owed was underlined came, and every week the wheeler-dealer acted unfazed. Perhaps he evoked his old hospital scares to view this situation as transitory, because his optimism overshadowed the invoices. Associates he confided in were in disbelief how he could go on about the primo, Rams-49ers tickets he'd cajoled from a friend when multiple lawsuits were being threatened against him. Wasn't he nervous about going bankrupt, they asked? Of course not, he said; he would finesse his way out. If he had to, he could sidle up to back channels. He was a lot of things, but he was no flake and certainly no quitter. Besides, the Rams game was Sunday. Someone had given him a sideline pass, and he was hoping to the see the 49ers' quarterback get walloped up close.

They came at him from all directions. Thanks to his and Jack's lobbying, the California Board of Equalization had agreed to shave his bill for delinquent taxes from $70,000 to $14,000. Some comfort. When Gordon offered Ivan's financiers to waive his interest in Ivan's music company if they handled the fourteen grand, they told him no dice. He cut music and effects for Jamie Uys breakthrough movie, an offbeat animal documentary called *Animals Are Beautiful People*, but had trouble getting paid because of South African currency restrictions. This made him fall behind repaying the loan to the company that bought the stock option in Globe Music. Not only was Project-7 moving in on ideas, they flipped around and charged he was "defaulting" on his loan. Defaulting, he knew, was sue-you-to-the-stone-ages lingo. Even close friends like Leo de gar Kulka, his Bay area music supplier, were pressuring him, and that stung. The respect of his client-friends went right to his core. In letters Leo said:

> *Over a year has passed and we have not received a single statement and not one red cent!!! Ad nauseum. I am being accused of having sold the music and pocketing the money. Two (musicians) are threatening me with their lawyers…The time for nice promises is past, Gordon, and we have to put up or shut up…I will have to cancel all rights given to you in the past (unless)…*

All Gordon could do was dogpaddle for time. He wrote Leo he'd been selling slabs of his music catalogue to 3M, a powerhouse conglomerate out of St. Paul, Minnesota, and its bureaucracy was slow sending him royalties. He mailed an apology to a Tokyo customer who had received badly scratched tapes, blaming it on a crooked contractor in Haiti. Danny and others were ordered with no explanation to locate any foreign film distributors they could. Ivan was one of the few who heard it straight: if this continued, he might have to sell everything and beg Nick Deak for a job.

Meantime, office events that would've been forgotten in an hour during his heyday now became the most memorable part of the workweek. One Friday this was furnished when a lazy, pothead editor we'll call Robbie dared Norm five dollars to make a copy of his

ass on Gordon's brand new Xerox copier. Norm, no longer weighed
down with much transfer work, said sure and upped the ante. Let's
make it ten dollars for a photocopy of your johnson. Feeling brave,
Robbie unbuckled his pants and hit the start button. The button hit
back. The machine wouldn't stop at one photocopy. It wouldn't stop
at fifty. Dozens of silhouettes of his pickle shot from the hopper.
Robbie scrambled to flush as many as he could down the toilet, and
Norm went to a secretary. Could she turn the damn machine off?
When Norm confessed what he'd done, Gordon was three shades of
mad. In another time my uncle would have bust a gut laughing. Now
he threatened Norm with "grounds for dismissal. Understand?"
Norm hung his head for a month.

With prospects barren at home, Gordon flew with Judy and Bob
to Europe, where he looked for any deals he could find, and then on
to Africa, where he stretched for answers. Jimmy stayed behind
answering phones, wishing he could go, wondering if he ever would;
South African blacks had begun rising up in townships like Soweto.

In Johannesburg, Gordon met with his people about his
multiplexer and postproduction plans. Both concepts were four years
old and looming more speculative to everyone except him. Swanee
and Nicholas Deak's aide bitched that nothing was happening. All
they had accomplished with their South African enterprise were
debts, including a large one to their lawyer. Gordon masked his
temper, because he needed these cohorts. Everybody, he said, should
be thrilled about the situation. The South African Broadcasting Corp.
still intended on farming out work to contractors like them, because
the politicians were more worried about censoring news footage of
police skirmishes with black militants. Patience, fellas, he counseled.
Patience.

From segregated Johannesburg they drove via jeep eleven hours
to Dirk's spread in White River, a banana-avocado farm town in the
boonies of northwestern South Africa. Here, Dirk opined, life
sparkled again after a morbid few years. His ex-wife recently had
been killed in a horse riding accident and he himself had taken ill.
Before that, a lion at the Hong Kong city zoo nearly had ripped his

son's arm out of its socket when the boy had stuck it in the cage. Dirk
sued the zoo, claiming negligence, and moved here. Gordon, Judy,
and Bob, who teamed with Gordon only on a project basis now,
spent Easter weekend with Dirk in White River soaking up his
newfound serenity. Gordon yakked on the patio about how he
wanted to be Dirk's neighbor while Judy bet herself it would never
happen.

It might have been that excursion when Gordon, Bob and Dirk
traveled north to Kenya on safari for the last time. It could've been
then that Gordon overhead a game ranger, a native Brit, complaining
about a rogue leopard slaughtering the livestock of nearby cattle
farmers. The game ranger said he had baited a trap by hanging big-
cat entrees—bloody chicken carcasses—from the branches of a tree.

He was about to check on whether the leopard had been
apprehended when Gordon flailed an arm, blurting: "Mind if I join
you? I'd love to see that leopard." The only one he'd ever been
around was a tame cat that lived at Africa-USA; Ivan claimed the
animal had a thing for blonde women.

"I don't think that's wise, Mr. Zahler," the game ranger replied.
"It's right risky out in the open." Leopards are not only fast; their
bites can be poisonous from eating rancid prey. "Furthermore," the
ranger added, "your chair would be hell to push in the terrain. It'll
bog."

"That's okay," Gordon chirped. "Bob can do it, can't you Bob?"
He was always saying that. Knowing it was futile trying to dissuade
him, Bob said he'd go under one condition: if they see the leopard
roaming, they're ditching Gordon's treasured Everest and Jennings to
run for the jeep. The only reason Bob agreed at all was that the ranger
had a pistol.

The men walked and rolled along the banks of a riverbed with
the tawny countryside fanning out before them and low, misty-green
mountains in the background. Stands of unevenly spaced papyrus
trees were rooted into one side of the ravine, exposing a primordial
marsh to the west. With every step the sapphire African sky seemed
more infinite. Gordon was in such heaven on the excursion that he

barely minded that half the spokes of his chair were blowing out in metallic pings because of the sand. At the tree where the leopard was supposed to be swinging upside down in a trap, dejection swamped him. All that was there were dead chickens with their intestines swaying in the breeze. On the way back to the Land Rover, he empathized with the bait.

Jimmy quit not long after they returned to California. Jimmy's father, Toby Gillard, had an ailing heart and probably Alzheimer's disease and could not care for himself anymore. After raising that family solo, Mr. Gillard had some tenderness coming. When his brothers squabbled over the responsibility, Jimmy volunteered happily. L.A. had gotten too crowded, too pricey for him, anyhow. This time, Gordon offered no resistance to Jimmy's exit. He told Jimmy to leave, do right by his father.

They said their goodbyes with little sentiment and never saw the other again. It was one flat finale. Gordon and Jimmy had been a thirteen-year partnership that defied glib descriptions about a white alpha male and his deferential black attendant. They saw the continents together. They saw Hollywood's underbelly, then their own. They guarded each other and tolerated each other. What love they couldn't verbalize because macho pride bottlenecked it they displayed in winks and small favors only two guys who smelled each other's breath everyday could appreciate. Neither was as good apart as they were together. Gordon employed other attendants before and after Jimmy—professional chauffeur-types and the college-age sons of friends. None of them ever were as dexterous as the man from Bossier Parish, Louisiana.

My uncle didn't have much luck without Jimmy. Weeks after he quit, Gordon hired a replacement, possibly a handsome, aspiring black actor named Lloyd. One afternoon, Gordon was late for a meeting when he directed Lloyd to take a shortcut through a Hollywood-area cemetery near Paramount Pictures. They spun around a bend in the road at maybe twenty mph when the Cad clipped a speed bump Lloyd didn't anticipate. *Clank.* Gordon was jettisoned from the front seat like he was part of a magic show. Now you see him, now you don't. Unlike his Palm Springs accident, this time my uncle thumped uninjured on the asphalt. When he lifted up his head to check his whereabouts, he noticed he was feet away from the headstone of a silent-picture star. Somewhere that day a sad laugh rang out.

Gordon had enjoyed better summers. Old mates like Hugo Grimaldi and Nat Winecoff were rarely seen. Nathan Jones, who shared Gordon's passions for Nikons and wild boating, spent many weekends holed up in hotel rooms on drunken benders. Jack and Abe were knee-deep in their own business troubles. With too much space and not enough business, Gordon had already asked Walter Lantz if he could shrink General Music's office because he needed the savings to pay his tax bill. In phone conversations, a subtle urgency crept into his tone about "really needing" this or that.

Back home, he delayed informing Judy about the house a month longer than he should have. Blue Jay Way was her trophy as much as his. Jack finally scolded him he didn't dare put it off any longer: she had to know they needed to sell the place and soon.

Gordon waited for the right moment after a nice Sunday dinner. He tried assuaging her that it was only temporary and that they would find a better house once he got his business dealings off the schneid. To his surprise, Judy accepted the news impassively. By then, she was such a pro at disguising her confusion about their general descent that saying, "We'll manage, dear," was her habitual response.

Gordon was on a trip through Europe to sell his music catalogue to anyone who was buying when there appeared a kernel of hope Judy might be right. He was on a jumbo jet from Monaco to London when he locked himself into an animated conversation with a passenger seated next to him. Gordon impressed the man, probably by name-dropping moneyed associates like Nick Deak, and the passenger requested his card.

The stranger later revealed who he was in a series of transatlantic phone calls. In cryptic language, he said he represented "tremendous sums of money in Kuwait," a tiny, oil-rich Islamic country on the shores of the Persian Gulf that Saddam Hussein's Iraq would invade in 1989. The Kuwaiti investors wanted to acquire a controlling interest in an established European food or beverage company with a $75 million-$100 million stake hold. If my uncle could introduce them to a buyer through his connections, his commission would be $500,000 cash. Nail it, Gordon realized, and his losing streak would be over.

But this is what it had come down to: an iffy proposition sheathed in half information. Gordon was instructed by the Kuwaiti's emissary not to reveal to anyone except the most trusted contacts about the proposed acquisition. If he did, he'd disqualify himself from the deal. So, he phoned Leslie Stinton, a savvy English music guy, and asked him if any of the accountants he knew in London could sniff out prospective companies for sale. The Kuwaitis were only interested in a company that grew, packaged and distributed its food with no middlemen involved. The rationale went unexplained. A Monte Carlo resident named Roman T., among other secretive men, fronted for the Arabs. They would decide based on the candidate companies winnowed down if there would be a meeting with the principals. Gordon smiled cheesy confessing to Stinton that was all he knew.

The Golden Globe for best picture that year went to Roman Polanski's *Chinatown*. Newspaper columnists covering the awards show not only rubbed elbows with Jack Nicholson. They were titillated by Raquel Welch's clingy red dress and gaped at the standing ovation for Fred Astaire.

Starstruck, they mentioned nothing whatsoever of my uncle. Mentioned nothing about the perspiring quadriplegic in a rented tuxedo pushed up to the dais to accept an award on behalf of South African director Jamie Uys. Uys was in Africa and Gordon wasn't when *Beautiful People* won the 1974 Golden Globe for best documentary at the Beverly Hills ceremony.

As postproduction supervisor for the film, my uncle was the obvious choice to accept the statuette that day in January 1975. Uys had camped out at General Music for months obsessing over the final music cut. It was fortunate Uys was abroad. For the first time in ages, Gordon had a pretext to gloat.

Still, pretext wasn't what it used to be. Where he previously would've met somebody like Joe von Stroheim at Pink's Hot Dogs to relive the ceremony in "what-a-riot" detail, he was too embarrassed now. Joe undoubtedly would have gotten around to asking about the South Africa venture and the truth about it couldn't be whitewashed any longer. Fact was my uncle's one great thing had atrophied into nothings half a world away. It had slowly unraveled in unreturned phone calls and blown deadlines, and finished off by un-kept promises from South African apparatchiks.

The stagnation was deepening, and his partners acted by recommending they disband the company. General Motivations, Swanee wrote, was "dead and useless." He and Otto, Nick Deak's aide, said Gordon should either assume responsibility for the whole shebang, financial obligations included, or they would "put it to sleep." Gordon himself probably felt euthanized hearing that. There was no point advertising it to old friends.

Given the culture he was trying to get wealthy in, my uncle should have recognized his language machine as the long shot it was all along. The Nationalist Party that controlled South Africa for thirty years with brute force wasn't serious about disseminating television to the whole countryside. The public relations capital from teasing that possibility was their goal. TV, after all, had come to ex-colonies in black-run Uganda and the Congo. It had facilitated a military coup in Nigeria, and the last white regime left standing on the Africa subcontinent was anything but suicidal.

The Afrikaners worried how average blacks would react when they switched on their set after a day sweating in the goldmines or the factories, assuming they could ever afford a set. The populace had already built up an ocean of resentment working for the whites. With TV magnifying the consequences of being the wrong color, what new demands would boil up in them—due process, decent sanitation? Gordon's multiplexer, with its ability to beam audio waves in different native tongues, must've been regarded as especially sinister technology. If the prime minister drew any lesson from the demonstration of its capabilities, it might've been to stall the little American marketing it with false promises.

Not surprisingly, when regular TV service debuted in January 1976 there was one channel—for the whites. The blacks were notified they would have to wait for the eighties, if then, for their own station.

The film companies and others interested in seeding Gordon's multimillion-dollar postproduction complex dropped their interest about the same time, although it's less apparent why. One year the investors were enthused, the next under-whelmed. This much, however, can be gleaned. My uncle was gullible, the same defect handed down through his family. A tight-ass about office cash flow, he subscribed to fairytales when he dreamed of being South Africa's TV wizard.

Among Gordon's pals, there is a split over how he handled the withering away of his African dream. Bob Glenn argued it was just another project and when it flubbed he latched onto something else. People who'd known him longer believe it nicked his last vein of optimism. Beneath his capitalist veneer, they said, Gordon had quixotic notions about how TV would gradually equalize the races. The Afrikaners "gave him a lot of promises, a lot of horseshit," recalled Danny O'Brien. "He was furious. We all knew what Vorster was like. He was a rat. Sanlam and the South Africans (just) wanted Gordon's ideas." That's why "they buttered him up...I saw him a few months (later). He was very disillusioned. He kept using the phrase, 'Danny, I was robbed.' "

CHAPTER TWENTY-NINE
The Black Arrow

He was practically broke when the letter was mailed out. In April '75, Gordon wrote his British associate Leslie Stinton to drop all inquiries. The Kuwaitis' mystery man had phoned my uncle earlier to say they no longer required his services. They would locate their food company by other means. If the Arabs passed along explanations for their change of heart, Gordon was too miserable to elaborate. In his letter to Stinton, the death of his commission— bailout money that might have spared him from selling the house— commanded all of two sentences. He marched forward as usual, writing that his idea to produce a how-to-play-Roulette album would do gangbusters in England. For once, the person he was doing the sales job on was himself.

Workers said Gordon did a lot of staring into space after the Kuwaiti deal fizzled. His shoulders slumped forward like the handicapped you saw on Jerry Lewis telethons. His face was thinner near the cheekbones, too, which gave his head a light bulb-like form instead of its former aerodynamic contour. Increasingly, he asked his secretary to close his door for long durations so he could have private conversations on his headset. Sometimes he piped up about how much he wanted to water ski in the middle of unrelated topics.

The one area he could make money in when everything else tanked was recording music. He was no different in this aspect than his father, who clawed up against bankruptcy near the same gulch in his life. So when Gordon first started feeling ill, intractably ill, he cleared off his light schedule to record new tracks. His voiceover man, Bob Gillies, knew some people.

There was the jaunty pianist Page Cavanaugh, who had started off with Frank Sinatra, and studio musician Bob Jung, who had just recorded with Earth, Wind and Fire. Page and Bob hired four other musicians who sat for thirty sessions when everybody was free. Among them they had a guitarist, a trombonist, a bassist, a drummer, a pianist and a combination violin/clarinet/flute player. They laid down hundreds of songs, mostly instrumentals, in Gordon's four-track studio on Willoughby Avenue over six months, maybe longer.

Before each session, Gordon would outline "the product" he needed from them: so many hours of Dixieland, this many of jazz, and so forth for cocktail and Mexican mariachi. By the way, he queried, can you do country-western? They hated country-western. Jazz was their passion. No song was to exceed two minutes. Gordon promised them he'd sell their creations as mood-music to franchises like Shakey's Pizza and Farrell's ice cream parlors. (Years later Page heard one of the songs playing in a Toronto mall.) He was shooting for familiar-sounding melodies just different enough from the originals not to get anyone in hot water with the copyright lawyers. Done right, he estimated they could be dividing $10,000 per month among them. In actuality, the largest check they ever split was for a $1,000.

Mostly, Gordon sat in the recording booth looking out the glass window, swaying his head to and fro to the backbeat. Sometimes he wasn't there. The musicians with a leering contempt for producers were surprised when he did offer opinions. He understood key changes. He encouraged them to go out and jam, "I'll worry about the rest." If he felt that a certain chord progression sounded awkward, the musicians replayed what they'd done and they tended to agree.

Page and the boys worked up a lather for him recording up-tempo, anonymous ditties. During breaks, many of the session players expressed what, in his prime, was the conventional wisdom about Gordon: his persona obscured the hoax for a body it was entombed in. Their primary grievance was about the shabby studio piano, which Page joked had been around since "Christ was a corporal." To achieve the fashionably out-of-tune sound he dug, he had the others lift it up and slam it on the floor. The musicians came week in, week out.

One morning, Bob Jung and the others popped by General Music in a vivacious mood. They were going for a wet lunch at the Tower Bar at Sunset and Vine and wanted to drag Gordon along. "Sorry guys," he said. "Too much paperwork." Four hours later, plastered to the gills, barely able to stand, they made a return visit to the office. Gordon looked at them wryly and shook his said. "Geez," he said. "I should've gone with you."

When they didn't hear from him about scheduling the next session, they called Norm, who said he wasn't sure what to do. Gordon was in the hospital.

He wished he'd done it earlier. He should have forced the issue when Joe was around, because Joe could steer *The Take One* as if he'd been born for it. In a lifetime short on woulda-couldas, this was the flashing exception. Cost to the wind, he should've forked out whatever he had to for a carpenter to custom-build him a fiberglass hydroplane board with a plastic chair bracketed on top. One of those crowded Fourth of Julys at Balboa, when the bay restaurants string up patriotic streamers across their patios—that's when he should have let her rip. The guys would have buckled him into the seat, attached the ski rope to the armrest and waited for him to holler what he always had imagined: "HIT IT!" Gordon dreamed the whole experience several times. *HIT IT.* The ski rope snapped taut, and he skimmed behind at 25 mph for a golden hour. Walter, Ivan: look at him now. Women and children in the other boats, as you'd expect, were stunned at his audacity because no one confused him with Evil Knievel. So, he made sure in his dream to give every one of them a puckish wink.

In reality, he committed a blandly responsible act. He phoned his life insurance agent to find out about his coverage in case of a recreational accident. The agent said water-skiing or similar physical exertion was an "uncovered risk" for a quadriplegic. Check the fine print. The claims department would refuse to honor his policy should he die behind a boat he had no business being behind. If that happened, the agent explained, Judy would lose the $100,000 payout without a chance for appeal. During one restless night, he thought about it and determined he couldn't cheat her of that money. Even chancing it for a minute outweighed any glory it'd buy him.

It was sort of late for hydroplaning, anyway. He'd had to sell his boat some months earlier to retire a debt. And now he had a more urgent problem. Cancer. The doctor said it was definitively cancer. Man, he should have water skied in '67.

CHAPTER THIRTY
Forgotten

In Hollywood, where the camera is king, your face is your business card. In the quadriplegic's world, monitoring body parts the camera never sees keeps you alive. For my uncle, it was what he was sitting on that spelled trouble. A bedsore on his right butt cheek tipped it off.

Gordon, as do most quads, had weathered a hundred of them. Until they became infected, none of the pressure sores—deep-tissue breakdowns caused by lack of movement—had made him suffer much. You can't hurt from what you can't feel. This one, however, was a nasty bugger. It had become severely inflamed and antibiotics were ineffective in stopping hot pus from spreading. Judy fretted something was really wrong.

She scheduled an appointment for him at St. John's Hospital in Santa Monica. After examining my uncle, the doctor said he would have to amputate dead tissue around the sore and patch it with a skin graft. Gordon agreed to undergo the operation only if it were a quickie. He still hoped to make it to Sydney, Australia to see clients before year's end. Several film projects also orbited. Director Claudio Guzman, who'd directed *I Dream Of Jeannie*, was hot to yank him down to South America.

He awoke in the recovery room on May 22 with Judy bedside. Dr. Wagner, a white-haired, seen-it-all-type, knocked on the door, somber. "It's not good, Mr. Zahler," he said. While scalloping tissue, he found sinister, granulated masses infiltrating Gordon's rectum all the way into his lower colon. "No bullshit, doc," Gordon asked. "How serious are we talking about?" Serious enough to schedule immediate exploratory surgery, the doctor said. They wouldn't know anything definitive until then.

They removed a slice of him a few days later for a tissue biopsy. The sample confirmed the doctor's hunch. The cancer had appeared at the skin-tissue level, metastasized without him being any the wiser and now there were black nodules colonizing much of his belly. The third surgery in seventeen days was arranged for early June. They would have to snip considerably more this time.

Roles were skewed during the wait. He was in the oncology ward. Judy's face was the puffy ruin. He acted as if he was facing an appendectomy. Her freckled hands shook feeding him water. Out in the hallway she smoked neurotically. Inside his room she set up house. Judy hadn't envisioned this. She never expected she'd be widowed so fast, because Gordon's anatomy was like one of those inflatable clowns that always bounced back no matter the shock of the blow. As a kid, he'd outlasted every fatal prognosis. As an adult, he'd been a compulsive risk-taker. Judy just wasn't prepared for this.

Odd thing about my aunt: she was a serial giver, a social creature, too, and often the most emotionally un-thawed one in the room. Her hugs reinforced this. In celebratory situations, she was the first family member to wrap her arms around an honored guest, "Kudos, dear…" When she embraced you, however, she did so rigidly, daylight maintained between bodies. Until Gordon's cancer, I remember her hugs being downright robotic.

My uncle was worried how she'd fare without him. On June 3, 1975, a few days before his big operation, he summoned my dad and Jack Perry to his St. John's hospital room. Pull up a chair, he told them: this could take a while. Gordon said they were there to be briefed on his affairs, because what he'd accumulated was too valuable to auction away in a rash estate sale.

Everything was inventoried in his head. From it he detailed the tape player for tourists, the deteriorating situation with Project-7, the $40,000-a-year his music royalties would net Judy to live on and the crook in Haiti. It was a tedious accounting, especially for my dad. Smelling that hospital disinfectant was déjà vu for him. Twenty-eight years earlier, he was a newly married man when his terminal father-in-law asked him to deliver a Christmas greeting to Gordon. Now

Gordon was doing the requesting of a middle-aged businessman who had reconciled with his wife. "Mil," he said, "watch out for Judy." If he died, he expected his business rivals would try and make a meal out of her to get back at him.

He was semi-doped up with a vague visual sense of people in lime green-masks when he was rolled under the operating-table lights. His hearing was sharp as ever. The surgeon told the nurse they would knock him out with a general anesthetic and rest him on his left side to operate. *My left side? Is that what they said? Jesus,* he thought, *they can't. My On/Off valve. Could they be that incompetent? My breathing will stop, and I have cancer this time.* Gordon tried shouting at them to stop, tried saying this was important, but with the drugs in him he slurred every syllable like the neighborhood lush. He hadn't been scared until now, until he grasped how powerless he was to stick around. *Don't let me die because of a goof. God, make them check their notes.*

He woke up, stoned sideways on painkillers, so the surgeons must have remembered about his left side. They had. It was the right flank they placed him on before removing his rectum and other parts during the colostomy. His intestines had been permanently rerouted to empty his crap through a bag attached to his side. All the black rot they could reach had been expunged from him. Actually, for a guy with cancer and a colostomy bag he was feeling pretty upbeat a week after the operation. "Look at this wonderful bag they gave me," he told Norm when Norm visited him at St. John's. "I heard Fred Astaire dances with one."

By late July, having spent weeks in bed living on pills and soup, he'd recuperated enough that the doctors agreed he could return to the office. It's exactly what he wanted, or thought he wanted. When he arrived, the files were a disaster. The mail was a foot high. He missed Jimmy. His four or five remaining employees offered him hearty welcome-backs, but his gaunt appearance embedded phony smiles on their faces that he saw right through. "Not you, too," he said. "Just bring me up to speed on what's been happening around here, will ya?"

Maybe he should have skipped the mail. Creditors conveyed sympathy for his cancer in one paragraph and issued ultimatums in the next. The indignities of being a desperate man had arrived. As such, the word "illness" trickled into correspondence he sent, this after twenty-five-odd years of letters never hinting at any affliction.

An English licensee who termed Gordon's canned music stale suggested he, "come up with one of his normally brilliant ideas." Sure, he must have reckoned. He would tug out one from his secret, save-his-bacon file, *no problema*. He was so hard up he had Norm make copies of his entire sound-effects library to sell retail. The flier for it declared that the fifty-five-box set was "selected from the master vault of 25,000 effects created by top Hollywood technicians." Almost no one bought it. One of the few customers was The Free University of Iran, and it botched sending its $6,000 money-wire from Tehran.

Optioned out, he phoned Boet Troskie in South Africa to ask for help. He had already gotten a loan from him during the filming of *Beautiful People*. Next he spoke with my dad and received $3,000. But a month later, the Project-7 people sued him for $425,800 in Los Angeles Superior Court for defaulting on his agreement. Gordon must have wanted to shout "Bite me" from the roof of the Lantz building. Or jump off it.

My mother's epiphany broke over an eight-dollar hoagie that she could barely make a dent in. We were at an Italian café with a window seat of a vacant lanai. It was one of those searing August days in Pasadena where the russet air erases the San Gabriel Mountains and people move without dispatch. Not me: I was here with an agenda. The plastic checkerboard tablecloth in front of us was cluttered with plates, a basket of focaccia bread, a photo album I'd cobbled together and assorted papers damp with my iced tea drippings. I was interviewing my mom for a final time. I was hoping she would quit stonewalling me. From her demeanor so far, it was sheer status quo.

Although pursuing this story had brought us closer, my mom's refusal to delve into the most sensitive areas of her past remained our cold spot. The blank glow of my laptop illustrated the bind I was in. Either I would fill the screen with my mom's forthright answers about her family or I would have to seriously weigh ditching the book and skulking back to the *Daily News*. None of the film archives I'd tapped, none of the old men I'd interviewed over pots of gourmet coffee, could provide the context that her recollections held.

Paychecks, the action; increasingly it was as though I'd junked my reporter's life to be the family archaeologist too incompetent to dig deep enough. *Let her come through*, I told myself. *There has to be a reason I'm here*. I reminded her of the news stories I had gathered about the murder of her grandfather in El Paso. She rebutted quietly, so as not to attract attention, that "none of that mattered to Gordon." I broached the subject of Judy's pregnancy from the slant of medical oddities. It crinkled her brow.

"That was a deep, dark secret, okay," she said. "I'm sorry I told you."

"Then why did you get me started on any of this?"

"Because I never imagined you were going to dredge all these other things up."

"You mean what really happened? Stuff that happened fifty years ago? Why are you so caught up with what other people will think?"

"Because I am. That's good enough."

"Nobody in your bridge group is going to care that Gordon wasn't an angel, or that the family had skeletons. You're that insecure?"

I should've censored that one out. My mom thrust out her jaw like the space creature in *Alien* and scowled. I tried an old reporter's trick and diverted her off the subject, planning to circle back later, by asking her about their discovery of Peter's retardation. It was a distraction, that's all. I didn't expect more than five minutes of homogenized family history I already had down pat.

She spoke for half an hour.

When she was finished, I'd learned about my retarded brother's permanent uprooting from the household on a few hours notice. I discovered that if my parents had heeded the doctors' stern warning about conceiving again, I'd never have been born. Was she telling me this to sidestep other topics?

I handed her the worst picture of Gordon in my collection. It had been taken at General Music about two months before he passed away. This was the dying uncle I remembered from St. John's, the same reptilian-gray complexion. In the photo, he is sitting in front of his Amega tape-synchronization deck in the equipment room, and the overwhelming impression is that the machine is running him. He looked awful, forty-nine going on sixty-four. My mom's posture stiffened when she studied it. "Shocking," she said. "It's not how I remember him. He always seemed to be, well, smiling."

I asked her if she ever contemplated how her life might have evolved had Gordon cleared the pommel horse at Marshall that day. Whether she might have buckled down about acting, or music or relocated to another city as a cultured college graduate instead of marrying the brainy engineer so young? "Of course I thought about it," she replied. Not exactly the rainbow amplification I needed.

Inside, I guess, I was rooting for her to stomp on her maudlin feelings and denounce her brother. She certainly had the ammunition. His wheelchair exploits couldn't undo the damage his acrobatics had hung on the family. His resurrection never replaced the twenty years swiped from his father when he died of heartbreak. It failed to reward Mama Rose with the lavender dotage she had earned. Going deeper, his accomplishments never compensated his sister for the loss of her most valuable commodity: her own potential. How he treated me was irrelevant. I wanted my mom to acknowledge the vastness of what he'd stolen from her instead of being a Pollyanna apologist for him. I wanted her to remember her fury when she screamed at him in the parking lot the night Mama Rose died.

Her stubbornness prevented her, and there was nowhere else to go, nothing else to reconcile except my own theory about the Zahler undertow. She'd refused to hear a single word on the subject when I'd raised it before.

"Well," I said, "don't you think what that stupid coach did after Gordon was hurt meant this was fate—that he was supposed to be paralyzed?"

"What nonsense are you're talking about now?" she said.

"About the gym coach. About how he hurt Gordon. You're not going to deny that, too, are you?"

"No, because I have no idea what you talking about."

"C'mon. The whole family must have known. Joe von Stroheim can't be the only one Gordon told. Think."

"I said I don't remember. Why are you pushing me?"

"Because it's important."

"To you it is."

"Do you want to hear it or not?"

She took her time before she nodded yes. Her face bunched the way Mama Rose's used to.

"Since this is going nowhere, I'll give you the short version. Gordon still had feeling below his neck after he landed on the gym pads. That's what he told Joe. He was dazed from hitting his head, but he remembered a tingly sensation in his hands and feet."

"So you're saying this happened in the gym. With everybody around?"

"Yeah. He'd feel his limbs for a second and then he couldn't feel anything. He was trying to explain that to the coach when the coach decided to lift him up on his feet. He probably wanted to get Gordon's blood circulating. But the coach shouldn't have done that. You never move somebody with a spinal injury until their neck is immobilized. Maybe they didn't know that in 1940."

"Go on," she said curtly.

"Well, when Turner stood him up, Gordon said he remembered hearing a snap, like a bone snapping. After that, everything below his shoulders went numb. He told Joe it was like a light being turned off. Years later he supposedly asked Dr. Risser about it and Risser said that might've been what made his paralysis permanent. Something about crushing the nerve instead of bruising it. Who knows? Risser said Gordon might've walked if Turner hadn't moved him. Sort of tragic, don't you think? He might've recovered."

"And you are sure about this?" my mom asked.

"Positive. Gordon told Joe he'd never forget that cracking sound."

Just then our waitress, an L.A. Valley-girl with pink, oversized gums, approached our table to see if we needed anything. My mom glared at our intruder. "No," she said authoritatively. "We don't need anything. Okay?" The waitress acted afraid to return after that. We wouldn't have noticed if she had.

Hearing about the secret of the Marshall gym, something deep in my mother broke free of an ancient grip. She sipped her ice coffee, thinking. In the silence between us her body language relaxed. Her brow lines smoothed out. Her jaw wasn't thrust, either. Studying her angled cheekbones, under the pleated skin, I could understand why an old boyfriend had crowned her "the belle of Sierra Madre" in a 1940s letter.

She asked to see the photo album, the one with the newspaper clips containing the murders, and nagged me to finish my coleslaw. You could tell she wanted a cigarette. We each took a few more bites of our food and she pushed her plate aside. Said she'd reached a decision: she would tell me anything I wanted. "Ask what you need. Let's get on with it."

I couldn't believe the change. It was as if my mother, the woman convinced Charles Darwin was a fraud, had started believing in the evolution of fate. From the killings to Gordon's oppression of Mama Rose, she described everything.

"All of what you have been raising is so painful I probably repressed it or made myself forget," she said in summation. "Gordon's accident cut me off from…from developing. I couldn't go to college. I didn't press it because I knew there was no money. But that changed my life."

I'd been focusing so hard on breaking her silence for the good of the book I hadn't contemplated what really mattered if I prevailed. Gordon's saga had zigzagged through the mists, down Sierra Madre

Avenue, unintentionally to the story of her. She was the silent victim when he pile-drove his urchin neck into the gym pads. His crash acted as a voodoo powder that caked my future mom in withering invisibility. As he was pitied, as he recovered, he was the star. All these years Muriel Bernice just needed illumination. Somebody needed to tell her, "Gordon wrecked what should've been the best time in your life. It wasn't fair." In my stumblebum, selfish fashion, I led her toward that. It was best present I ever gave her.

Two hours of Q and A later my mom wrapped up her sandwich and I drove her home.

My mother's acknowledgement of her stolen adolescence wouldn't just furnish her solace. It handed me answers I hadn't even consciously considered about the architecture of tragedy. The awareness came in drips and drabs, but come it did. Finally, the curtains pulled back over why my mom had donned the persona she had worn as the Zahler's "other child." This was why, even decades removed from Gordon's hospital days and family poverty, she fiendishly clutched social airs over salad forks and first impressions. Why she had wrapped herself in expensive clothing stores with groveling clerks. Why she had never done more with her own artistic talents, in effect letting them slip away into the bright blue cornfield of what might have been. It's what the wounded do. They adapt. They seek the control they can. They hunt for easier guises, pain-free ones.

I also hadn't known until her restaurant confession how much I'd lived with these wounds myself. That there were moments in my own boyhood when her yelling at me was her really yelling at the Marshall Junior High gym. She had been restless and hurting for so long that we all accepted that was who she was, not what events made her. Such peace came to me from my understanding, such lightness at knowing I was not the root cause of her sadness, that we have never slid back into our old quarreling ways.

CHAPTER THIRTY-ONE
Secrets of Hollywood

Gordon's knack for willing his body to defeat any scourge finally met an adversary more tenacious than willpower. Woozy headed, he dictated letters about frontloading music tapes to 3M that rambled nonsensically. He phoned Danny O'Brien in London and instead of percolating with deal points he forgot why he'd called. "Gordon," Danny asked over the transatlantic line. "Are you okay?" "Yeah," Gordon exhaled, "I'm still here." His mind had fooled him into attempting a nine-to-five routine when he never should have checked out of St. John's. One of the few tasks he managed to complete was having Norm donate 893 *Gentle Ben* albums to the only institution interested in receiving them: The Crippled Children's Society of Los Angeles.

By September the cancer reappeared in his belly. It hadn't spread elsewhere, a fact Judy offered everyone around. He underwent a battery of tests at St. John's, and Dr. Wagner said the "last course" for him was radiation treatment. He would have to submit to nine weeks of painless zapping with low-dose radiation beams administered by a three-headed machine. The gizmo looked like it'd been borrowed from one of Hugo's sci-fi movies. The objective was to cripple the cancer-cell DNA and hope. Gordon said he'd consider it.

My father came for another visit, alone this time. Though Gordon had needled my dad over the years for a controlling disposition he reckoned could have used a good goosing, Gordon respected my father's intellect. And he really needed it, he said, for his "big decision." As he lay in his hospital bed with the cancer he was sensationally unemotional about, Gordon told my father he was calculating. He was doing a hardheaded analysis of whether to submit to x-ray therapy or pack it in. "Mil" he said, "I haven't quite figured out what I'm going to do about this cancer. On one side…So, what do *you* think?"

Radiation it was. Judy and the aide drove him to St. John's for his early-morning laying on the table. There was no heat from the radiation gun, just whirling noise and waiting around. The first two weeks the side effects were so mild that Judy was dubious the machine was plugged in. The next four weeks they were devastating. Food pelted through him. He had no energy, some mornings barely able to open his mouth to ask for water. The oncologist adjusted the x-rays to his shrunken, seventy-three-pound body and that quelled his nausea. When his one good kidney acted up, his mood spiraled into ugly, where it resided as if it had been his true color all along.

The Gordon of fall 1975 was a caustic troll of a man who tongue-lashed his wife because she was near. More than that, the spunky spirit that had engrossed movie stars, tycoons, songwriters and classmates, the spirit that proved feet were over-rated, was gone. It was a cripple's rage now. He was mad. Mad about dying and madder still about how he was dying. Wasting away in the hopes of a medical miracle to bring him back until the cancer returned again was the antithesis of what he envisioned for himself. Didn't logging thirty-five years in a wheelchair buy him an exit juicier than mundane disease? It should. Bring him a lion attack on safari. Give him a malfunctioning jetpack freefalling to earth. If nothing else, persuade him that his whole circumstance was less pathetic than it seemed, because he felt as though he was wilting into the mattress coils.

One morning at Blue Jay Way, Judy asked him if he could handle some breakfast. She sat on a chair next to his contour bed.

"I already told you I'm not hungry. Get that through your thick skull."

"Gordon, I know you're feeling lousy but there's no need to be snide."

"Do me a favor and shut up, will ya?"

"Take your medicine with a little orange juice and toast before Lloyd comes and I won't say another word. I promise."

"You take the damn pills."

"But we're going to be late for your treatment. I thought it'd be easier if you…"

"Leave me alone."

"Lloyd's going to be here any minute."

"Bitch, you're not hearing me."

Sniffing hard, Gordon turned his head toward her. Before Judy knew it, he hawked a thick, yellow lewgie that tagged her squarely on the cheek. Judy tamped it with her hand and rose from the chair. She didn't speak for a minute, unsure whether to slap him or get away from him.

"You can be a monster, you know that?" she said. "I used to think you were brave."

Judy made Lloyd take him to St. John's alone that day.

Bob Glenn had switched coasts, a Hollywooder no more. He had relocated his family to Florida to work for an inventive curmudgeon named Arthur Jones, who was developing what would be the Nautilus fitness machine. Out in L.A. on business, Bob heard about my uncle, who he still regarded as one of his best friends, and volunteered to drive him to St. John's for a radiation treatment. After the zapping, Bob dressed him and steered him into the sparkling hospital corridor.

"Take care. See you next week, Mr. Zahler," a peppy young nurse said. She waved.

Gordon grinned at her twenty feet away. Under his breath he said: "Oh no you won't, sweetie. You won't see me because I ain't coming back."

It was done. The analysis he'd conducted while he'd shriveled into an intolerable little tyrant was complete. His choice actually turned out to be more rudimentary than it first appeared. He'd deduced there was no use in torturing himself any longer when the cancer had him. Let the creditors pulverize each other for what was left of his money, because Judy's share was protected. What mattered was his choice—his and only his. In deciding to call it a life, he'd abdicated on his own terms. In deciding to die, he'd grabbed back control over his life, which he hadn't appreciated until then was the truest, greatest thing of them all. It was the golden statuette that he could walk up and accept. While too weak to sit up much, Gordon's old twinkle seemed recharged by his choice. Bob noticed that.

In early December, he was in a private room at St. John's being treated for kidney failure and terminal-stage cancer. Sometime between then and December twentieth, my mother strong-armed me into a visit. During it my mom forced me to kiss him on his unshaved cheek. It was then Gordon stopped me from retreating from his bed so I might remember he cared. In no particular order he quizzed me about school, the Ali fight, how the Trojans would do in their bowl game and what kind of stereo I was asking for at Christmas. I said Sony. "That's great, kiddo," he said. "Sony's good." An hour later my mother bribed me for visiting him with a cheeseburger.

Judy conferred with Dr. Wagner on December twenty-first after Gordon had an awful night. "To be honest, Mrs. Zahler," he said, "we're all floored he's made it this long." Judy understood.

By primetime that evening, Room No. 215 rollicked with guests. Someone brought a tape player and was blasting old Glen Miller songs like a modern disco king. Cigarette smoke wafted over the "No Smoking" sign. Walter Lantz and Ivan Tors strode in together. Abe and Jack arrived not long afterwards in dour business suits with their wives in tow. A secretary came. Hank and George Gale, who Gordon had met through Ivan, loitered around his bed, as did Nathan Jones and a few other stragglers. Joe was the most conspicuously missing. Like others, he expected Gordon would outfox the cancer the way he had outfoxed everything else with the bead on him. All together, there might have been a dozen people there. The guest of honor acted hardly overwhelmed.

"Judy," Gordon said mid-point, "Run down to the gift shop

and get everyone some ice cream." Abe, ever the gentleman, volunteered to go in her place, but Gordon was adamant. "Nah, Judy will do it."

A girlfriend named Edie Novak went with her. In the elevator, Edie remarked, "I see he still pushes you around."

"Well," Judy said, "I understand better now."

The elevator stopped on another floor while a couple orderlies galumphed in. They noticed how deconstructed Judy looked—the smudged mascara, the caved shoulders—and she didn't care what they thought. She lowered her voice and described how Gordon had ramped up his background music sales so she would have money to live on. How he'd forgone the water-skiing was too intimate to disclose. "It was the most romantic thing anyone has ever done for me," Judy murmured. "And the last."

Edie's eyes were liquid orbs when the cab doors parted.

Back in the room, Judy went directly to Gordon's ear. She said she had overheard the nurses gossiping while she was signing papers. "You know what they said—that you must be somebody important to get all this attention. They'd had famous actors in here but nobody who ever had a party for him like this."

Gordon smiled, doubting her a little, and yet for once he let it rest. Around 9:30, the head nurse with the cleanup hitter's forearms came in and announced visiting hours were over.

Judy, as usual, spent the night in Gordon's room on a folding cot that was a foot too short for her. Gordon woke up around eleven, saying he felt exhausted. "Mind if I go back to sleep?" No, she said, rest. When he opened his eyes around three p.m., they were jaundiced slits.

"Judy," he said faintly.

"Yes, sweetheart."

"Thank you."

"Oh, for last night? Wild horses wouldn't keep them out."

Gordon shook his head.

"Then for what?"

"For retrieving that beach ball." A minute later he let out a loud grunt. "Jesus, it hurts. Like somebody's got a wrench on my neck."

"Hey!" she said. "You want me to call for a pain shot? I'll buzz the nurse."

"No," he wheezed, "I want you to call Muriel."

My mom, normally a put-put driver, arrived in Santa Monica from Pasadena in thirty minutes, record time. Gordon was breathing erratically when she reached his bed.

"He's been waiting," Judy said. Her face was red and she made no effort to cuff her tears. It was 4:09 in the afternoon.

"Gordy, I'm here. I'm here." My mom held his gnarled hand, which he hadn't felt since he was fourteen. "Is there anything I can do?"

"I. I…"

"What?" she said. "I didn't hear you."

All he could manage was a wink and smile. Then he let out an unimaginable groan, as much Tarzan yell as a death rattle, and was away into the ether on fresh legs.

EPILOGUE
The Ghost and the Guest

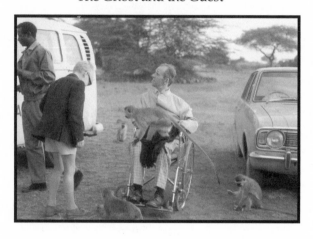

Behind his smirk, Gordon's unifying principle sat there all along. Will, he proved, is stronger than doctors. It is mightier than guilt and more enduring than wealth. Team it up with ingenuity and watch the confetti rain down. Only death can knock off raw determination, and even that is debatable if legacies stick. Gordon, I suspect, understood about anatomy what most doctors never could. While the body can be broken in countless places, the heart can never be paralyzed.

The downside is that the brand of will Gordon harnessed to build his Big Life enslaved the people he loved most. My grandma, with her twenty uninterrupted years of service to him, was the ultimate captive. He destroyed her household, refashioned a new one, validated her faith in his talent and then replaced her with a newer, sleeker woman when one came along. At least Judy saw the world on his dime. Both she and my grandma sacrificed bundles of themselves they never got back. Both of them kept alive the most fragile of beings, and that nourishment sustained their own care giving hungers. You want to know the recipe to survive a broken neck? Love, hope and duty. Judy and Rose cooked up buffets of the stuff.

In many ways, I am indebted to Gordon for breaking his neck because it propelled me backwards. Through it I met my grandfather and could embrace Mama Rose again. I discovered a Hungarian whiz kid foiled in America and a father and son murdered in their primes. By acknowledging them, I exposed versions of myself I'd tried to run away from, only to find I'd run in place. Now I can measure my problems against theirs. My whole family can. It was wrongheaded to have concealed the old tragedies and mistakes, even if the motivation was to protect us. Doing that relegated Joseph, Maurice, Nat and Dearie, my grandparents too, into fuddy-duddy, scrapbook people remembered for how they died, not the lessons in survival they bequeathed. If there is a moral here, it's that light really is antiseptic for families scars. Generations intersect, traits forward on, so be careful about burying the past or no complaining if it buries you.

As I've come to appreciate, yours truly was as gullible about his subject as my distant relatives Maurice and Nat were with their fateful moves. My enthrallment with the man I'd wanted to forget most of my life snatched me temporarily from the thing I did best: journalism. The journey chaperoned me from stability to isolation to depression to reconciliation. Was it ever worth it. From my quest to know him flowered so many blessings, so much self discovery, that I owe a king's ransom to this curiosity and, even more, my mom's persuasion campaign to nudge me into it.

Another shocker twined around my own sentiments toward my uncle himself. I could never have imagined when I began all this that my emotions would've hopped allegiances from loathsome memories of putdowns and ogre hands to unstitched love and vibrant pride towards him. But they have. I could not have anticipated treasuring the picture I keep of his inimitable face on my desk. But I do.

Strange just about covers it.

In fact, once my research was completed, I made it a point to drive by St. Rita's, his old Sierra Madre elementary school, to watch the children pour out the doors at the school's closing bell. In my mind, it was 1939 again, and Gordon was the lead scamp, unhurt, dynamite in dark britches Mama Rose liked him in. My God, these kids are babies, free spirited, bounding every which way, lucky not to get smacked by a car heading up Baldwin Ave. What would Gordon, my unlikeliest hero, say to the rowdiest of the bunch? Hopefully, "make your jumps non-lethal!"

Certainly, there were times on this quest when I wanted to leap off something myself. Family anguish over my snooping. Money struggles. Feelings of irrelevancy. Writhing as newspaper contemporaries won prizes and promotions while I bunked on Gordon's cold trail. The years took their time teaching me. Gordon's life wasn't a cautionary parable about what happens to naughty boys who don't obey their teachers. His wild, gallivanting spirit was more of a siren to sink your teeth into blessed opportunity, and that guts and determination didn't just spill out of a Hallmark card. They are born from real-life people whose names you'll probably never hear. If a dreamer with more head than body mass can make it through County General and Hollywood, what can shackle your own audacious ideas and dreams? Gordon would tell you to start scheming! He'd tell it to me.

Maybe, like everyone, I needed to suffer to get what was due me. Maybe on this earth we can't really grow until we bleed a bit.

Somewhere between his courage and his abandon, Gordon and his cast also furnished me with another philosophical nugget: character resides in rugged quirkiness. It lives in those who dream of hydroplanes and multiplexers and in grandfathers who compose songs on their steering wheel. It flickers in wave-jumpers and cunning bed-wetters, men who swim with lions and those who refuse to say "motherfucker."

Madison Avenue instructs us that normalcy is the key to a fulfilling life, but I say that is a lie of homogenization. It is a security blanket for people afraid to reveal who they are for fear of being abandoned. Don't worry. You won't be. Gordon, in surviving those stares, in going into the bush in that absurd body, licensed me to live blissfully abnormal with my odd name and retarded brother, with my impulsive zest and newfound love of gruff heroes. Gordon showed me that if you remember what counts, you'll parade your differences, the ones inside, and know the most pitiful freaks are those who cling to convention.

I've tried living this way as well as preaching it. When I take Peter out to dinner, I no longer worry about other customers whispering about "the weirdo" in my booth. Happy we're not like everybody, I use another approach. I try to get him to burp the special of the day, loud and proud.

Gordon's six-paragraph obituary appeared in *Daily Variety* the morning after he died. Five days later, his funeral was held at Forest Lawn Mortuary in Glendale. John Richards, a protégé of Mr. Burnell, conducted the service. But it was Nathan Jones who emceed the eulogy with an hour-long, improvised speech about Gordon's life that had the 250 or so mourners alternately rolling in the aisles or clutching tissues. Nathan, who disappeared after this ceremony, told everybody that Gordon had handpicked the closing song. People who knew him well chortled when the organist pressed the chords to *The Battle Hymn of the Republic*, because Gordon had no use for anthems. It was his parting gag.

The only memory I have from the affair was acting as a kid pallbearer next to my dad, Norm and three other men in black suits. I didn't understand why I was selected, other than being one of his nephews. Gordon's body was being interred on the slope of a steep, grassy mound whose surface was slick from the previous night's rain. Mourners' heads bowed solemnly at the gravesite as we hoisted the casket from the hearse toward them. In their bowing, most missed our Keystone Cops impression. It happened when the man in front of me slipped halfway to the gravesite. The casket lurch down, and all of us bobbled our grip and slipped on wet loafers before steadying the load. For a second, it seemed, Gordon's last joyride was going to be sliding down the knoll toward the cemetery's gate in his maple wood coffin with the six of us giving chase. In a way, I wished it had happened.

Judy tried to make a go of General Music during the next couple years. She flopped, which isn't to suggest she didn't live well. The music Gordon trafficked in paid her fat royalties. His interest in Lantz Music Co. stock alone would net her $250,000. All together, including the appreciated value she received from the sale of the Blue Jay Way house, my uncle's estate was valued at close to half a million dollars.

On the rebound, Judy dated a widowed businessman with no physical limitations or Gordon's *joie de vivre*. They fell in love. She moved in with him. They were planning their wedding when the man slumped over in his car one day, struck down with a fatal coronary. Judy's interest in conventional romance went with him; she'd never had much success there. Afterwards, she drew close to her niece Karen and my mom, volunteered for charities, became a devotee to the Instruction and eventually moved to a Pasadena condo. In 1990 the Benson and Hedges she smoked all those years repaid her with her lung cancer. She passed away that March at Huntington Memorial.

Three of Gordon's main associates weren't far behind him in dying. Old age took retired cartoon-magnate Walter Lantz, who really hadn't known what to do with himself since Gracie's death. Ivan Tors died of a heart attack in the Brazilian jungle in 1983 while scouting locations for an animal show. Nicholas Deak's passing was the showstopper by comparison. In 1985, a woman previously escorted from Deak-Perrera's office after claiming it had defrauded her walked nonchalantly into the company's executive suite in downtown Manhattan, shot the receptionist in the head with a .38-caliber pistol and then came for Nicholas. Though his murder stirred calls for gun control, Nicholas died with his pride already wounded. Two of his subsidiaries had filed for bankruptcy after a federal organized-crime report alleged their involvement in laundering more than $100 million for South American cocaine lords. The company refuted the charges.

Jamie Uys, the liberal Afrikaner, would become the celebrity from Gordon's bunch. In 1980 he released *The Gods Must Be Crazy*, the story of an African bushman who traveled to the edge of the world to destroy a Coca-Cola bottle that disrupted his tribe. The movie shattered the existing South African box office records and grossed in excess of $200 million in the U.S. A few years later Prime Minister John Vorster became a newsmaker of a different sort. He was forced to resign from office under pressure when his role in a giant government slush fund was exposed. Some of the rands he misappropriated were used to buy pro-apartheid media outlets. Both he and Uys are deceased now. In the new South Africa, where the black majority rules, there is TV for everyone.

A while back, my daughter Samantha sat with me as we watched Gordon's old travel slides. One showed him in his wheelchair with Mount Kenya in the background and a couple of yammering monkeys on his shoulder. He was smiling that crooked smile that telegraphed, "I ain't getting cheated."

Samantha, then six, giggled when she saw this. "Dada," she said, "Uncle Gordon was the greatest uncle you ever had, wasn't he?"

That was it: Gordon's ghost was reborn. It'd taught me you don't need legs to get to your dreams, just belief. "Honey," I told her, "you may be right."